Turkish Awakening

*Behind the Scenes of
Modern Turkey*

ALEV SCOTT

FABER & FABER

First published in 2014
by Faber and Faber Ltd
Bloomsbury House
74–77 Great Russell Street
London WC1B 3DA
This paperback edition published in 2015

Typeset by Faber & Faber Ltd
Printed and bound by CPI Group (UK) Ltd, Croydon, CRO 4YY

A CIP record for this book
is available from the British Library

ISBN 978–0–571–29658–3

FSC
www.fsc.org
MIX
Paper from
responsible sources
FSC® C013604

4 6 8 10 9 7 5 3

Anneciğime

Contents

Introduction

I had nearly finished writing this book when the Gezi Park protests broke out in Istanbul at the end of May 2013. Most of the book is an unwitting scene-setter for the protest movement that blossomed out of Gezi, a snapshot of Turkish society and some of the issues that precipitated and prolonged the movement. No one expected the protests, but they have shown the world, and Turks themselves, that the country is far more complicated than it looks from polling data. Voices of dissent are too often taken solely as a negative sign; the protests revealed many of the best qualities of a society that is varied, disparate and yet defined by a self-protective instinct of solidarity. It is a society that is patriotic but not quite blind to its faults; a society that wants to preserve the best of itself, but demands more than the government is perhaps willing to give.

I started writing this book with simple aims: to understand the Turkish people and the direction the country is going in. It is not an intentionally political book; I wrote it mainly for personal reasons, because I am half-Turkish, but grew up in England. My mother, like all Turks, is fiercely patriotic and I had absorbed from her a pride in a country that I did not know. This country is still in many ways a mystery to me, but my pride is now more informed, and balanced by an awareness of Turkey's demons. It is also strengthened by the extraordinary courage and determination shown by the many Turks who have woken up to what they really want out of a democracy.

As the once promising Arab Spring morphed into confusion, Turkey stood tall as a self-proclaimed 'moderate Islamic democracy', a shining example to the entire Middle East of how to do things. The West was looking to Turkey as an experimental marriage between democracy and Islam; many were hopeful, others cynical. Until the protests, things seemed to be going exceptionally well: foreign investors, politicians and tourists were dazzled by a flourishing economy in the midst of global recession, a strong, popular leader, significantly improved public services and diplomatic progress in the south-east with the long-standing Kurdish problem. These achievements partially masked a huge backlog of problems stemming from Turkey's awkward adolescence as a new republic. Not yet a century on from its creation in 1923, there were many serious tensions which the breezy confidence of the ruling AKP (Justice and Development Party) government was not enough to dispel. Those tensions were simmering beneath the surface until the protests in Taksim Square brought them dramatically into the public eye.

I had always been aware that Turkey reacted strongly to criticism both from abroad and at home; 'insulting Turkishness' in a public forum is illegal, and Turkey has the highest number of journalists in prison in the world, largely due to laws like this. When the Gezi Park protests gained momentum and the government sought to paint protesters as foreign agitators, terrorists and other 'dark forces', I realised just how insecure Turkey still is, how unwilling to listen to criticism from anyone, even well-intentioned fellow citizens. The way many Turks talk about their country sounds to an outside ear like religious fervour – Turkey is more than a country, it is a religion, and that is why 'anti-Turkish' sentiments are equivalent to blasphemy.

The protest movement of 2013 was a kind of tardy enlightenment, an expression of awareness that Turkey is not the blemish-free utopia that it insists it is. At the same time, it was a brilliant demonstration of what is wonderful about Turkey: the passion, courage and humanity of its people. Those who took to the streets were given an unexpected chance to make their voices heard, and they seized it. They are the future, and hugely significant for Turkey. But they faced condemnation not only from the government but also from many Turks who saw them as traitors.

People took to the streets in solidarity with the Gezi protests in almost every Turkish city, but the demonstrations were biggest in liberal cities in the west of Turkey: in greater Istanbul, in Ankara, Izmir, Eskişehir and Antalya. In these cities, there is a flux of people, a relatively free exchange of ideas, and society is far more open than in other areas in Turkey. A Turk living in the depths of Anatolia does not move in such circles, and is not so open to change. He may not follow politics closely, but he is aware of important facts: the lira is strong, Prime Minister Erdoğan is strong and the army is strong. Therefore Turkey is strong. He is the kind of man who would have been confused and threatened by the protests, rather than seeing them as the potential for improvement. He reflects a confidence in Turkey and in the government that is shared by many people across the country, a confidence that goes beyond patriotism and appears to be almost unshakeable.

When I first arrived, I sensed this pride and was curious to work it out, to decide whether it was justified, and whether I could claim it too – was I a disinterested, English observer, or a Turk coming back to join the party? What was the basis of this boundless patriotism, and would it be strengthened or weakened by nationwide protest?

When I arrived in Turkey, I could not speak Turkish, I did not know anyone and I certainly did not know what it meant to be a Turk. Two and a half years later, I am living in the wake of an extraordinary protest movement, deciphering political graffiti on the walls near my house and discussing the future of the country with my Turkish friends. I could not have chosen a better time to discover my roots, a time of change, when Turks themselves are working out what they want from the present and more importantly the future. This book is about a personal awakening but most of all it celebrates the awakening of the Turkish people.

1

Conversations with Taxi Drivers

The Naïve Newcomer to Turkey is best represented as a passenger in a yellow taxi cab, lost in the chaos of Istanbul. In the first months after my arrival, I fitted this tableau perfectly. Picture the scene: I am engaged in a highly animated, imperfectly understood exchange with a moustachioed man driving at speed through winding back streets. My attention is divided between the passing cityscape, a partially obscured meter and the rapid stream of Turkish coming from a man who expresses his emotions on the accelerator and brake pedals. My fear of death by dangerous driving has long since been anaesthetised: we are deep in a discussion about whether the extortionate price of petrol in this country is the result of secret machinations between Israel and France. Dull scepticism is rejected out of hand, so I suggest Iran as a third contender in the conspiracy and have the satisfaction of commanding his immediate attention.

Ever since I got my Turkish good enough for a basic conversation, I have made an effort to talk to taxi drivers. Most have been extremely friendly, a few suspicious of an inexplicably talkative girl. I have conversed with frustrated poets, acute sociopolitical commentators and gifted comedians. Many have just been homesick family men from some distant part of Turkey – often the Black Sea. People are drawn to

Istanbul from all over the country, so it is the best possible place to meet the gamut of national stereotypes. If you get a genuine Istanbullu taxi driver (which is relatively rare), he is guaranteed to lecture you about the good old days before country folk swamped the city with their religious nonsense and bad driving.

From an initially dispiriting level of miscommunication in the Turkish language, I gained confidence as the kilometres racked up and emerged as a kind of reverse Eliza Doolittle, using accented slang that has profoundly shocked my Turkish mother. 'My God, you sound like a taxi driver!'

Talking to taxi drivers taught me as much about Turkish modes of behaviour as it did language skills. Lesson number one was that Turks can be extremely open, with friends and strangers alike, leading to some rather uncomfortable situations for the uninitiated, uptight English passenger. I have only just graduated from this state. Once, I hailed a taxi outside the Bosphorus University where I had been teaching all day. I slumped in the back, exhausted, and gave the driver brief directions.

'Urgh, have you been eating garlic?' came the unexpected response.

I admitted I had, for lunch, some hours earlier.

'Well, you really stink. Don't take it personally, I happen to like garlic, but you might want to avoid confined spaces for a while.' The driver was being so spectacularly rude that I assumed I had not understood his thick Anatolian accent correctly. To dispel my doubts, he wound down all the windows despite the December chill and kindly handed me a stick of chewing gum as a refreshing reminder of Turkish frankness.

An upside of this disconcerting national trait is that people don't beat about the bush, which saves time and can be extremely helpful. The taxi driver with refined nasal sensibilities might not have had the most polished of manners, but he was not being unkind. I love the down-to-earth attitude of Turks, and have consistently been impressed by their spontaneous kindness – little gifts and offers of help, which by British standards seem almost sinister. It is a quality found in many Middle Eastern countries, although sadly sometimes a difference in sex limits meaningful encounters. I often feel short-changed in this respect. In the local food bazaar, the religious cheese-seller is all smiles with my boyfriend, chatting away, but he won't even look me in the eye, let alone speak to me. My involvement in the conversation is confined to eavesdropping and looking meek. Once the cheery cheese man gave my boyfriend a piece of halva, a sesame-based sweet, to try; my piece was carefully placed on the counter in front of me, as though for a passing bird. I do not resent the man – he is clearly generous and warm – and in fact, he is being as respectful as he knows how by not looking at me, the 'property' of another man. It is how he has been brought up. My quarrel is not with him but with the kind of Islamic fundamentalism that prevents and perverts well-meaning human connection. It is a shame – it would be nice to share my own jokes with the cheese man rather than living vicariously through my boyfriend, but I know it will never happen. Apparently, he rather sweetly asks after my health when I am not there.

Far more than elsewhere, I find that the way I am perceived by others in Turkey depends on how I am dressed, who I am with and where I am. In the most glamorous areas of Istanbul, like Nişantaşı, Bebek or Etiler, I am noticeably shabby, un-coiffed, probably taken to be a student hippy or worse. In downtown Istanbul, in poor neighbourhoods full of mi-grants, like Çatma Mescit (full of families from Sivas, central Anatolia) or Kadın Pazarı (Kurds from Van and Diyarbakır), the buses are packed, taxis empty and I am definitely a 'White Turk' (or what in Regency England would have been called 'Quality'). On a recent trip there, I started to chat with my driver, who seemed pleased to share his views on the world. Suddenly, a car swerved in front of him to switch lanes.

'*Kürt!* [Kurd!]' he yelled, shaking a fist.

From then on, every instance of bad driving was accredited to Kurdish origin. In the midst of my shock, I was interested to know whether the driver was using the insult jokingly or unthinkingly, as one might say 'bastard', or whether he actu-ally had a thing about Kurds. It turned out he did – he pro-ceeded to relate a recent news story about a Kurd who had married an English lady, started a property development pro-ject with her somewhere in Antalya, and then made off with several thousand euros. The possibility of a Turk, American or Samoan doing exactly the same thing had clearly not oc-curred to this particularly irascible taxi driver. The force of his prejudice was such that I despaired at the thought of try-ing to reason with him, and what really disturbed me was the realisation that he had judged me to be someone who was likely to share his views, being fairly well off and clearly not a Kurd.

The status and perception of Kurds among Turks is a very complicated issue, which I address later, but I brought up this example to demonstrate the fearlessness with which (male)

Turks share controversial views. In England, anyone with a private prejudice against some ethnic group will probably think twice before voicing it among strangers. There is a notion that expressing such views is not really the done thing, even if they are strongly held. I have often felt in Turkey that I have unfettered access to people's thoughts, which has been very educational.

Taking taxis in Istanbul is a form of instructive entertainment; I cannot count the number of contradictory conspiracy theories I have heard so far. I once had a driver who held forth on the subject of the disgraceful number of covered women in Istanbul – this man was a dyed-in-the-wool secularist, that much was obvious. I listened with half an ear until he asked me a direct question: 'Do you know what they do?'

Who?

'These covered women. All shut up at home together, all day. Do you have any idea what they're up to?'

No.

'*Grup seks!*'

Yes, group sex. Lesbian orgies, that was the vision this man had of secret goings-on in the most religious districts of Istanbul. Even in my wildest dreams I could not have envisaged, say, a paranoid BNP supporter in the depths of the Midlands making such a bold and imaginative Islamophobic accusation, but here was a Turk calmly stating what he regarded as the plain truth. Battling to keep a straight face, I suggested that this was the reason their birth rate was so high. Nodding gravely, he was about to continue his polemic when the intricacies of human biology filtered through the fog, and he shot me a frown as if to say: 'Be serious!'

The taxi business is a very good example of the lingering Byzantine practices still going strong in Turkey. Behind the ostensibly upright system in place, favours are bestowed, scores are settled, and nothing is straightforward. Driving a taxi in Istanbul, in particular, seems to me to be a great test of character, for the following reasons: Istanbul taxi licences are sold at supposedly public auctions, but these are widely reputed to be controlled by a mafia who make sure the right people get the licences, and then sell them on at profit. Subsequently, taxi owners pay (or likely borrow) around seven hundred thousand lira (£250,000) just for their unfairly expensive licence, which is a lot of money by Istanbul standards. Most owners then rent out their taxis for a hundred lira (£35) per half day. This is where the test of character comes in – some drivers choose to earn this money back honestly, with the meter and the shortest route. In the heart of tourist land, however, you will find specialist taxi drivers who quadruple the distance actually needed to drive from, say, a hotel near the Blue Mosque to Taksim Square, often neglecting to put the meter on, and sometimes even crossing over to the Asian side and back again.

I have little sympathy for these vultures, but I can understand the mentality of those who resent the system as it stands and try to buck it in an illegal but relatively honest way: unlicensed taxis. I must first make clear that all this information was taken from the horse's mouth, from both licensed and unlicensed taxi drivers – it is virtually impossible to get any official data on the taxi market, which in itself confirms the story that is widely supported among the community of drivers about mafia-controlled licence auctions. To protect the end value of licences, yellow cabs are the only legal taxis in Istanbul – there are no registered minicab company equivalents. Unlicensed 'pirate' taxi drivers are called *korsanlar* and are always extremely wary of getting caught by the police, because the penalties are huge. I once witnessed the arrest of a *korsan* driver, and it made a great impression on me.

One summer evening, I was eating on the terrace of a restaurant on the historic Rue de Pera in the European heart of Istanbul. Right next door was the aged Grand London Hotel, which is one of my favourite places in the city. Magnificently outdated and kitsch, it is a dusty testament to 1930s third-rate grandeur, full of florid porcelain, incongruous brass gas stoves and several miserable-looking, mangy macaws imprisoned among the potted plants. Outside this hotel is what purports to be the official taxi stop for a famous nightclub called 360 across the road – it is, in fact, manned by a couple of opportunistic guys who have taken the aegis of 360 to advertise their own private enterprise. As I was eating, a car pulled up and immediately all the passengers piled out, shouting. A man and a woman hurried off as fast as they could, leaving a worried-looking young man and the furious, walrus-like driver to have it out. After a great deal of bewilderment, I worked out that this was a *korsan* taxi driver, his passengers flown, and the worried young man was an undercover policeman who was beginning to realise that he had bitten off more than he could chew.

I will never forget that *korsan* driver. Middle-aged, beefy, his moustache bristling with rage, he railed against this poor policeman like some kind of supercharged King Lear, swearing his own moral superiority and denouncing the character of the trembling young man before him with biblical fervour. After a few minutes, the policeman called for backup, and a slightly more robust-looking man turned up to take on the driver. He was very quickly reduced to the same state of intimidation, as King Korsan bellowed and fumed amid a steadily growing crowd of onlookers. The climax came when the *korsan* realised that the policemen had locked his car and pocketed the key; in a burst of inspiration he grabbed a chair from outside the Grand London Hotel and lifted it threateningly above the windscreen of his own car. The second policeman hurriedly pulled out his radio and within a few minutes a siren announced the arrival of a van full of riot police, plus fifteen outriders. Surrounded by police, sensing imminent defeat, the *korsan* was by now like a mighty, wounded stag, awesome in his rage, pitiful in his capture. For a while I could still hear his cries and see gesticulating arms through the throng of uniforms. Then, in an eye-watering finale, he staggered towards the original undercover policeman, threw his arms over him like a father, and wept.

The disproportionate police response to an unlicensed minicab and the risible presence of the undercover officer aside, I like to think of this episode more as a spectacular lesson in the guts of the Turkish Underdog. In most countries in the West, if you're caught breaking the law, you come quietly, avoiding the stares of passers-by. In this case, our hero seemed to be positively fuelled by a gathering crowd, pacing the pavement like a majestic baritone on the Royal Opera House stage. The law was nothing to him – convinced of his own moral integrity, he refused to give in, until literally surrounded by police with batons. I admired him enormously, and

I saw a lot more of his kind of spirit during the Gezi Park protests which swept Turkey in 2013. Riot police made liberal use of batons, tear gas, rubber bullets and water cannon, but the crowds just kept returning, yelling for more gas.

For those who want a quiet life there are, of course, non-criminal substitutes for the licensed taxi. The best is the *dolmuş*, a shared taxi in the form of a yellow minivan with patchy seats and a marbled plastic dashboard. It is a wonderfully bohemian mode of transport, allowing you to travel for a few lira all the way across town with constantly changing travel companions, and a driver whose mission it is to hurtle along, stopping only to hoover up and spit out passengers in swift, profit-making succession. It is hectic but fun, much cheaper than a taxi, better than a bus, and a great showcase of Turkish chumminess. I love the atmosphere of a *dolmuş*, where you pass your money forward to the driver through the hands of several strangers, receive your change similarly, shout out when you want to get out, and are cheerily sent on your way by six new friends. There is a kind of comfort and trust among people here which I really don't see in Europe – it is absolutely typical of Turks that they are happy to throw themselves into a confined space with people they don't know, and treat them like family.

Dolmuş literally means 'stuffed', and that's exactly what they are. Once, I was squashed next to the door of a very stuffed *dolmuş* when, characteristically, the driver stopped to pick up two more passengers – a woman and her child. There were literally no seats left so the mother stooped awkwardly by the door and lifted her kid onto my lap.

'That's it – sit on your sister's lap. Good girl!'

I loved the fact that this lady automatically assumed that I would be happy with this situation, and that the words 'health and safety' did not cross the mind of a single person present. It is such a typical scenario in this country, and there is no paranoia about potential paedophiles lurking around every corner. I find it difficult to imagine an equivalent situation in London – a mother parking her child on your lap in an overcrowded minibus, everyone else smiling over at the pair of you, not a seatbelt in sight.

Turks love children. Nowhere else in the world have I seen not only women but men go soft at the sight of a small child, almost without exception. My favourite instance to date was the male security guard at Atatürk airport who was lifted from the depths of catatonic boredom to joyous raptures by an unruly toddler, placed in his care by a mother struggling with the X-ray machine. This uniformed young man chortled and gambolled with the child as the other guards gathered round him in an admiring group, subsequent passengers ignored as they passed through the detector.

This child-friendly attitude undoubtedly has a lot to do with the great importance of family, and close-knit households, in this country, but there is a most fundamental, human connection among people here that I have noticed in various guises. For instance, Turks are so much more relaxed when it comes to protocol, although there is undoubtedly a lot of annoying bureaucracy and paperwork on an institutional level. However, I have found that when there is an opportunity to use personal discretion, employees generally go for it, particularly if there is some appealing human interest.

When I arrived for my appointment to obtain a residence

permit at the intimidating governmental compound in Istanbul, I realised to my dismay that I had forgotten to get a formal reference for my residential address and had not even filled in the part of the form stating my reasons for staying in the country – a disaster. Luckily, my canny boyfriend was there too, and when the surly-looking bureaucrat asked the official reason for my stay in the country, he was treated to the script of a Hollywood romance: how we two had met, how I stayed against my better judgement, how we couldn't be parted, etc., etc. The official lifted dull eyes from the registration form, surveyed us with the ghost of a smile and uttered the immortal words: 'Love, then,' before stamping the seal of approval on my half-empty form and shouting out the next name in the queue. Clearly, his attention had wandered as he listened to the love story and computerised my form: to this day, my father's name is listed as 'London, UK'.

However unapproachable official Turks may appear, you can be sure that a human heart beats somewhere beneath the uniformed exterior. They can make your life hell, and I have heard many horror stories from my expat friends who have tried to get permits or merely an appointment for a permit and failed for no discernible reason. Sometimes palms must be crossed with silver. Sometimes a ridiculous love story must be narrated. Turks are capricious and therefore human, preferable by far to an anonymous computer system or the chillingly anodyne officials in the US or Britain. The more sinister side of the coin is that, quite often, there is no official accountability for the actions of state employees. Police, in particular, are notorious for asking for bribes from traffic offenders and beating up people in detention with no fear of recrimination. This is more a fault of the system than anything else. When human beings know they are not accountable for their actions, they can act in horrible ways.

If you sit by any road in Turkey and watch the traffic go by, you will notice that every so often a car, or more likely a *dolmuş* or lorry, will pass with brightly coloured block capitals painted across the top of its windscreen or back window. This will usually be the beginning of the standard Arabic prayer, shortened for practical purposes, or simply *Allah korusun* ('God protect us'), and will act as a kind of talisman to protect the car and its passengers on the sometimes treacherous roads of this country. In Britain and the US, people use 'Baby on board!' signs or messages of that nature to warn off other drivers. Turks bypass the human element of traffic accidents and address themselves directly to the powers that be: praying always helps, and a permanently scripted prayer on your car serves as excellent insurance. The Turks use the image of a blue eye – the *nazar* – to ward off the evil eye. This universal image is painted on the car or swings in the form of a glass amulet from the dashboard in place of furry dice, as standard policy.

Turks have a complicated relationship with religion, which I discuss more fully in later chapters, but the interesting element that I discovered at the beginning of my stay in Turkey is the extent of superstition, across the board. Even secular, highly educated Turks who have no time for organised religion and especially not for their devout Turkish neighbours use superstitious expressions unthinkingly, even when these expressions contain religious language. I include myself in this – in fact, while for the most part I saw expressions and gestures used by my mother and grandmother widely mirrored in Turkey, there were a few I grew up with that I think were old-fashioned even by Turkish standards.

If you keep an ear open on any street corner in Turkey, within a couple of minutes you will have heard *Inşallah* ('God willing'), *Allah korusun* and *Maşallah* ('Thanks to God'). The last is equivalent to the universal 'touch wood' and is indeed often accompanied by this action. All these phrases flow through Turkish conversation as naturally as taking breath. If you happen to be eavesdropping on a particularly traditional group of Turks, you might hear *Tövbe*, which is a fearful reaction to someone expressing a potential calamity, no matter how improbable. For example, 'If you leave I'll pine away and die' might be countered with a *Tövbe* – 'May God guard against such a thing!' It is equivalent to using a cancel button and sounds rather comical to a non-Middle Eastern ear but someone like my grandmother would not have felt comfortable without saying it, just in case. In fact, she would have also bitten the end of her little finger as a double precaution – she once told me this was to remind her of the pain that would otherwise result from these reckless words. As a child, I accepted this as a very sensible-sounding practice and adopted it myself. I was always aware that it was not normal, however, and would hide it from my friends by murmuring the *Tövbe* under my breath and pretending to bite my fingernail.

When I arrived in Turkey I realised that *Tövbe* was pretty superstitious even on home ground; when I first used it aloud, at last, in company, there was general amusement. I was told that it was a very provincial thing to say, and it was at that point that I began to work out the kind of life my grandmother must have had in her homeland. In London, she was resolutely true to her Turkish roots. She had a method of warding off the evil eye, a kind of extreme precautionary measure: if someone had said something particularly nice about one of the family, she would set light to the tips of a few dried olive leaves, which she kept in a little jar especially for the purpose, and wave them dramatically in a circular motion around the victim's head to ward off the jealous spirits, muttering a prayer as she did so. The smoking leaves left a delicious smell which I would sniff greedily while trying to look pious.

When I ask Turks about this practice they look as perplexed as a British person would, and I wonder whether this particular example of damage limitation is peculiar to the distant lands of Northern Cyprus or whether it is just outdated, as my wonderful grandmother was, several decades removed from her homeland. Was she an example of the expat's singular adherence to customs and mores which, in the forsaken country, have morphed and developed quite considerably in the intervening time? As this kind of practice is only really performed in the privacy of the home, among family, it is difficult to tell. The more conventional method of protecting someone from the evil eye is to pour molten lead into cold water over their head, a service often performed by coffee-cup readers and other gifted practitioners of the supernatural.

As with the Western 'Thank God' or 'God forbid', the religious element of these expressions is hardly ever acknowledged, at least consciously. Most people use them more or less unthinkingly, and they have become equivalent to 'That's a good thing' or 'That's a bad thing' or 'I hope so' (*İnşallah*). I'm sure religious people do invest more in their original meanings, especially for expressions like 'God forbid!' because fear is a powerful catalyst for belief. This goes for everyone, however, and I still hold that these phrases are basically manifestations of the kind of superstition you find all over the world.

One absolutely unparalleled branch of mumbo jumbo, held in high esteem by many otherwise sane Turks, is astrology. I am still surprised by the number of closet irrationals among my friends and colleagues, who regularly check their horoscopes, anxiously anticipate lunar eclipses and even employ fortune tellers to check the stellar alignment potential of new romantic partners. Obviously an interest in astrology is not a specifically Turkish thing, but it is surprisingly popular here. Superstition in general is a deeply ingrained part of Turkish culture, and most Turks grow up with grandmothers reading their coffee dregs and interpreting 'signs'. These grandmothers are in turn adhering to a feature of their youth, just as I still feel compelled to touch wood, having done so in my formative years.

What fascinates me is the lack of respect that secular yet superstitious Turks have for their religious counterparts. Religion is a hugely problematic subject in Turkey, for many reasons, but since the founding of the republic it has been regarded in 'progressive' circles as the bane of modern life, when expressed publicly. This is due to the legacy of Mustafa Kemal Atatürk's reinvention of Turkey as a secular country in the 1920s, and the considerable efforts he made to stamp out the stuffy, superstitious elements of traditional Ottoman society and the close-minded conservatism which is still referred to as the 'village mentality' of Anatolia.

After the First World War, Atatürk brought Turkey back from the brink of collapse. The country was shaken by defeat in the war, under a crumbling Ottoman excuse for a government. After the precarious victory in the war of independence which followed, Atatürk decided that Turkey needed a healthy dose of radical, modern secularism to present a progressive face to Western challengers. Many people equate Atatürk's push to modernise with a specifically anti-Islamic agenda, but this is not true. He was anti-backwardness, be that the result of religious practice or the broader traditional mores which included superstition, antiquated hierarchies, unbending social etiquette and a general distrust of outsiders and their ways. His reforms were not targeted mainly against religion per se but against the stagnant conservatism that regarded things like scientific education and industrialisation with the utmost suspicion. It is easy to see why Atatürk felt that efforts to nurture a gradual, cultural change might prove too uncertain and lengthy to risk at such a formative time, and that radical steps were necessary; he masterminded a kind of Emergency Enlightenment, which was basically imposed on the Turkish population. While his intentions were admirable, it is also easy to see why such an abrupt departure was too artificial to remain ingrained in a Muslim nation forever. The strength with which Kemalists cling to Atatürk's ideals is testament to the force of his vision, but it is also seriously outdated and over-rigid. Law 5816 exists to punish 'crimes committed against Atatürk', some eighty years after his death. This is not just a symbolic law: people have been imprisoned for insulting Atatürk or indeed the ideology of Kemalism. Professor Atilla Yayla, an academic from Ankara University, was suspended from his post, tried and sentenced to fifteen months in 2008 for suggesting that the early Turkish republic was less progressive than it is often portrayed in undergraduate textbooks. Overt or covert, criticism of Ataturk is seen as nothing less than blasphemy.

From a certain point of view a religious analogy is completely inappropriate here, but actually it is striking how similar the Kemalists are to evangelicals, following the inspiration of a quasi-prophet – the only difference being that the gospel of Secularism is preached. Kemalists are as devoted to Atatürk and his doctrine as religious fanatics are to their idols, and his life story, teachings and speeches are taught extensively and emotionally from kindergarten up to university. When a man is a demigod and the country of his making an ideological utopia, laws which punish those who insult him are not so surprising. In addition to Law 5816, there is another law which has put scores of journalists and academics behind bars: Article 301, which punishes those who insult Turkishness. Two notable Turks who have been prosecuted under this law are Hrant Dink, the Turkish-Armenian journalist whose murder in 2007 is now being reinvestigated under suspicion that it was the product of a major criminal conspiracy, and Nobel Laureate Orhan Pamuk, who is no longer welcome in this country after he called upon Turkey to accept responsibility for an Armenian genocide.

Kemalism and Turkish patriotism are not synonymous, but it is easier to understand the strength of Turks' feelings towards Turkey when you can understand the strength of

Atatürk's legacy. Kemalism has many of the characteristics of a cult – albeit one forged with the best of intentions, for the protection and indeed survival of a nation on the brink of destruction. For a country still insecure about its status, still haunted by the crisis that galvanised the new republic into being from the wreckage of the (Islamic) Ottoman Empire, institutional secularism is seen by many Turks as the defining and protective quality of the nation, to be preserved at all cost. That is not to say that they deny their religion – almost all Turks regard themselves as Muslim, even if they do not practise. It is written on virtually any Turkish ID card you care to examine, because it is the standard entry which must be actively changed if you are of a different religion or do not want any religion recorded at all. Despite this assumption of Muslim identity, what might be called, in distasteful tones perhaps, 'overt' displays of Islam – burqas, religious schools, even the use of the Arabic greeting *salaam* – are deemed to insult the idea of 'Turkishness' which Atatürk wanted to make the primary element of a person's identity, replacing religion. This definition of 'Turkishness' is cherished and jealously guarded by the considerable Kemalist demographic, which includes a significant proportion of academic and artistic circles, although this is slowly changing.

Friends in England often ask me whether Turks are gradually getting more religious, or whether the government is imposing religion on them. Neither is true. The AKP is a religious political party and it reaches out to the considerable religious demographic of Turkey. Despite Turkey's fame as a secular state, there has always been a traditionally conservative majority in the population. Until recently, these people have been sidelined by nationalist governments and military juntas, but the AKP not only respects religious Turks, it courts them. During the holy month of Ramadan, for example, large posters featuring a smiling Prime Minister Recep Tayyip Erdoğan wish passers-by a happy Ramadan in an elegant, calligraphic script. He promises his supporters more mosques and religious schools. Religious Turks feel personally cared for, and secular Turks feel threatened. The AKP are secure in the knowledge that they have the unquestioning support of a huge swathe of the population, and they are not interested in pacifying the rest.

Erdoğan's ability to polarise the population is impressive – roughly half of Turkey's 75 million hate him, half love him. That, at least, was the case at the 2011 election; in the light of the protests, the scale has probably tipped against him, although his most ardent followers admire him more than ever for taking a strong line. For many, he is a new Atatürk – a strong, fearless, charismatic leader who has a bold idea of where he wants to take the country, and who also understands his religious base. Erdoğan appeals to ordinary Turks because he comes from a modest background, has a covered wife and worked his way up from nothing. He nearly made it as a professional footballer (giving him automatic kudos), and worked as a bus driver before getting involved in politics. It's almost as if someone has made up his CV specifically to appeal to the large portion of ordinary working Turks who had previously been ignored by relatively privileged politicians who made them feel guilty for practising their religion, for example by banning headscarves in public institutions.

Republican Turkey's respect for strong, charismatic leaders

stems from the extraordinary hero worship of Mustafa Kemal Atatürk. Every Turkish leader since Atatürk has struggled in the shadow of the great man, and many people suspect that for Erdoğan he is a particular nemesis. Erdoğan represents many of the religious values Atatürk tried to eradicate, and on a few occasions has nearly slipped up by showing his true feelings towards the national hero – once he obliquely referred to the notoriously raki-loving Atatürk as a 'drunkard'. Erdoğan has also surreptitiously reduced Atatürk's legacy by curbing military celebrations on Republic Day, and by urging his supporters to carry Turkish flags 'not bearing any other symbols' (many Turkish flags traditionally incorporate a portrait of Atatürk). Still, Erdoğan has usually been careful not to make his feelings too obvious because he risks alienating the religious nationalist Turks who might otherwise vote for him.

I have worked this out only gradually, and when I first arrived in Turkey I was completely bewildered by the complexity of its politics. I had no idea how to unpick the various threads of religion and nationalism, and Atatürk's legacy confused me. I needed basics. I would ask myself: what is it that connects Turks, above and beyond their abstract sense of patriotism? What creates a sense of belonging to something called 'Turkey'? What is concrete?

Sometimes I look at a Turk in the street and think, 'That woman has rolled thousands of *dolma* [stuffed vine leaves] in her life,' or 'That man has consumed hundreds of *döner* kebabs.' Food is something all Turks share, alongside a myriad of other experiences like the modulations of the muezzin's call to prayer, the smell of rosewater cologne, the melodies of songs everyone knows from childhood. These things connect people more strongly, more tangibly than convictions of national identity. They are the day-to-day make-up of what it is to be a Turk.

Turks are fundamentally happy to be Turkish, taking delight in shared experiences as well as pride in the concept of Turkey as the best motherland in the world. Alongside the ubiquitous portraits, busts and flags of Atatürk in this country, you will often find his most famous quotation: *Ne mutlu Türküm diyene*, which translates as 'How happy is the one who can say "I'm a Turk."' It is their equivalent of 'God Save the Queen', but more individualistic and thus more powerful. It is inscribed over the entrances to army bases and is part of the student oath that every Turkish child has traditionally had to utter, every week. This oath also includes a vow of Turkey-serving ideals and the promise: *Varlığım Türk varlığına armağan olsun*, 'My existence shall be dedicated to the Turkish existence.'

I once had a discussion with a Turkish friend, Bülent, about the intensity of Turks' feelings of attachment toward their country, and why this often prevents them from living abroad. Bülent asked me: 'Do you worry about England when you are away? No. England will prevail, it is not vulnerable like Turkey.' By contrast, many Turks feel that Turkey is being ruined both materially, for example through excessive construction (as was the catalyst for the protests at Gezi Park), and ideologically, for example by the repression of free speech, reflected in the huge number of imprisoned journalists and the self-censorship of domestic media. Turks who tend towards conspiracy theories are always worried that

Turkey is under attack from foreign powers, as Erdoğan claimed in the midst of the Gezi protests.

Bülent, a twenty-seven-year-old, incurably romantic leftist liberal, is nostalgic for a country he has never really experienced – the Turkey portrayed in leftist songs and poetry – but he still feels strongly that he belongs to this country, and he has the protective attachment of a father towards his wayward child. This is obviously a strange overturning of the normal child–parent relationship of citizen to motherland, especially in a nationalistic country like Turkey, but it somehow works both ways. That is why my mother still, after forty years of living in England, reacts very defensively to any criticism of Turkey. She left it, quite aware of its problems, but she cannot brook any foreign attack on the country that instilled such an indelible sense of owning and being owned.

I have come to realise that the question of Turkey's identity crisis is a very Western formulation. Westerners assume that Turks are confused about their identity because Turkey is a country torn by contradictions and impossible to pigeon-hole. The Western view of Turkey is heavy with clichés, the general line being 'a nation torn between East and West, treading the line between Religion and Democracy' (note the Western assumption that the two are a priori mutually exclusive). The clichés have a point, of course, and lead to the legitimate question: in a country so filled with people of widely varied descent, where ethnic minorities are in fact the majority, surely it must be natural for people to question their national identity? The answer is that the racial melting pot of Turkey is, if anything, the *reason* why Turks are so sure about being Turkish. They have to be – it is what welds them all together in the utopian national dream that Atatürk created, which has been perpetuated for nearly a century through the sheer force of his vision. This is not to say that all Turks agree about the political direction Turkey is going in; that was dramatically demonstrated by the Gezi protests. While they may disagree on politics, I have never met a Turk who is not proud of being Turkish on a fundamental level.

America is a nation of assorted immigrants, a genetically disparate country just as Turkey is, and patriotic in the same way – though not to quite the same extent, because it is not as young and insecure as Turkey is. Every American is proud to call herself an American just as every Turk is proud to call herself a Turk. This sense of belonging is an incredibly important part of their personal identity, but it does not preclude an interest in their particular family heritage. It is precisely because the sense of national identity is so strong in these two countries that people can explore and celebrate their roots.

Every American who has an Irish background will unfailingly tell me all about his potato-digging, freedom-fighting ancestors, and every Turk with Georgian blood will tell me about how her great-great-grandparents left everything to travel to the Black Sea coast of Turkey in the nineteenth century. This heritage is chronologically remote but closely treasured, and the Turkish and American fascination with previous generations is a totally human vanity. Everyone wants to feel connected to their particular past even if they have never visited the country of their forefathers and none of their surviving family has even a hint of the accent. The rapidly developing market in DNA tracing is evidence of people's desire to explore themselves, to create an individual backstory which makes them unique.

However, it is only in relative security that people can do this. Ultimately, a Turk is a Turk. Their Arab or Greek or Azeri ancestry is a pleasing flourish to their persona, but not integral to their being. Being Turkish is the fundamental thing, and they feel part of an important whole when they take the oath of allegiance or put a portrait of Atatürk up on their wall, and Americans are similar. It is when people feel uneasy, fearing that perhaps they do not belong, that they try desperately to fit in by obscuring their ancestry. The Turk with Georgian roots boasts of his great-great-grandparents because they have no impact whatever on his Turkishness. He is secure, quite possibly a member of a nationalist political party, as ideologically Turkish as it is possible to be.

Coming to Turkey as a half-Turk was far more complicated than I had expected. My name, for a start, caused just as much bewilderment as it has always done. In England, it was an embarrassment in the state school yard of my childhood, but then became a point of interest in London's politically correct social circles. In Turkey, the unexpected reaction of people I had just met was scepticism. Inevitably, I would be interrogated: *'Türk müsün?'* ('Are you a Turk?') On ambiguous visual evidence and indisputable aural evidence, I was clearly a foreigner of some description, a *yabancı*, so what was I doing masquerading with a Turkish name? I am a peculiar fraud in Turkey – mislabelled foreign matter.

Foreigners are much more of a scarcity in Turkey than in the UK, which is why their otherness is more significant; why would these people accept me as a Turk when I was much more unusual and interesting as a Brit? A Turkish name became something to be justified, rather than exhibited. I soon realised I couldn't even pronounce my own name properly; I started practising the way others said it. It was when this happened that I realised I had a lot to learn and change about my self-perception if I wanted to be more than a product of my British upbringing with a quirky name attached. In other words, I had to understand what it means to be Turkish.

As I taxied my way around Istanbul in the first few months of arriving in the country, all these existential musings were yet to come. What struck me initially was the bewildering visual variety of Istanbul, and then further afield, as I explored other areas of Turkey. To understand the social complexities of the country, I first had to get the lie of the land.

Istanbul was a formidable starting point. I caught glimpses of the city in all its uptown, downtown, chic and shabby guises; a kind of complementary slideshow to accompany the running commentary of freely expressed Turkish opinion provided by my driver. This city is both the beauty and the beast of cosmopolitan aesthetic, full of historical treasures, soulless apartment blocks, great sweeps of coastline and miles of urban motorway. Its very variety is overwhelming. En route to work, I would pass by manicured residential *sites* (gated compounds, pronounced as the French *cité*), ancient cobbled alleyways, bustling farmers' markets and gargantuan shopping malls, ending up in the skyscraping sprawl of Levent – the City. Further afield, on the Asian side of town, a new financial heart is growing on the outskirts of the sleepy suburbs of the city – Ümraniye, so grim and remote as to be a rival Slough. Back in fashionable districts on the European side, you could be forgiven for thinking you had wandered into Mayfair on the streets of Nişantaşı, which is characterised by Louis Vuitton and Prada stores, a few independent designer *atölye*s and bejewelled ladies swilling large glasses of rosé outside smart Italian restaurants. Ten minutes south, a very different picture awaits you in the grey underbelly of Dolapdere, where local *bakkal*s (corner shops) provide the only splashes of colour with their crated fruit on pavements patrolled by stray dogs and glue sniffers.

Istanbul is set apart from other patchy metropolises by its trump card: the most spectacular setting in the world. Threaded by the Bosphorus and the Golden Horn, dotted with scattered hills and the nearby Prince's Islands, this city is unrivalled in the majesty of its geography. The most dramatic and uplifting ride in Istanbul is the crossing of the Bosphorus bridge from Asia to Europe – a gradually unfolding view of Ottoman palaces, Byzantine churches, fishing ports and a glittering sea beneath you is quite literally breathtaking and reduces even seasoned Istanbullus to wondering silence. It is during these crossings that I remember why I put up with the frenetic chaos of this city. Living in Istanbul is like dealing with an opera diva: you accept the tardiness and the tantrums because you cannot resist the beauty of her art, a gift which silences the mediocrity of all rivals.

2

Urban Empires

Stepping out of the yellow taxi cab, you are immediately reminded that Istanbul is a city of noise and mayhem. Car horns, endless construction work, artificially magnified calls to prayer and the responding barking of dogs form an unrelenting soundtrack as soon as you open a window or step out of the door. I felt extremely English on arrival, dropped into a bubbling pot of public emotion – angry lovers, bawling street sellers and operatic tramps assailed me on a daily basis. The city teems with approximately 16 million people, and an ever-increasing number of arrivals from rural communities and Western tourists mix with disgruntled indigenous residents, resulting in an inevitable clash of different behaviours. Tensions simmer in traditionally conservative areas which have become newly hip, attracting liberal, often Western crowds who are not always welcomed by the existing residents.

Once of my dearest friends is Andrew Boord, who has been living in Istanbul for twenty-five years and is actually now a Turkish citizen (the name on his Turkish passport is 'Enver Borlu', the result of a bizarre interview with a senior official who was trying to approximate 'Andrew Boord' during the application process). He rents out his flat in Galata, a beautiful, historic part of town which is now popular with musicians and Western journos in particular. Andrew can command a sizeable rent for his flat from short-term visitors, but the only problem is the crazed xenophobe who lives in the opposite building. This maniac can be relied on to shout abuse at whoever happens to be staying in Andrew's flat, accusing one French couple of 'fornicating in broad daylight' in view of this man's window. 'Take no notice,' said Andrew. 'He always says that.' The next day the couple were awoken by a loud thud and went out onto their balcony to discover a large plastic bottle filled with what could only be urine, crumpled and leaking with the force of impact among the flowerpots.

There is nothing Andrew can really do about this man – the police are totally uninterested and luckily the short-term nature of the let means Andrew can juggle tenants without too much trouble. Longer-term residents are less lucky. Amanda and Taylor, two American friends of mine, live in an expensively converted apartment in a run-down part of town, and they like entertaining. Most of their neighbours are religious Turks and are very suspicious of the stream of expat friends who visit the building. One Monday evening I attended a dinner party there; quite early on, someone downstairs complained but no one took any notice. At about 11 p.m., when a few guests remained, Taylor began coughing in what we thought was a theatrically exaggerated manner. Soon, however, everyone in his vicinity was spluttering, with streaming eyes; cries of 'Tear gas!' were heard over the mêlée as we fled to a bedroom at the opposite end of the flat. Ridiculous as it seemed, it was undoubtedly tear gas we had inhaled – I knew the tell-tale rasping of the throat – and the most plausible explanation was that a neighbour had left a canister near the front door to put an end to festivities. The hysteria of the situation somehow took a comic turn and, to spite the party poopers, we remained in the flat, red-eyed but jolly, taking it in turns to gasp at the open window while we polished off the wine. We have since found out from the friendly newsagent that the local branch of the Muslim Association is across the street from this flat, and has a great deal of influence among the neighbours. Amanda and Taylor are considered to be bad influences on their children, in particular. The last tenants of the flat, also foreigners, were beaten up by their irate neighbours and ended up in hospital; Amanda and Taylor are flat-hunting again.

The urine-flingers and tear gas wielders are fairly extreme examples of guerrilla neighbourhood watch tactics, which I cite only to show how strongly some residents feel about what must be an alarmingly swift invasion of people with very different values from their own. I've known some London neighbours to get nearly as angry over an unkempt hedge or stolen parking spot. Most of the time my neighbours have been almost overwhelmingly hospitable, taking particular care to welcome me in the same way they would a guest, seeing themselves as surrogate family to a displaced waif with no apparent family of her own. The extremes of neighbourly behaviour – kindly matron versus aggressive, religious zealot – are almost irreconcilable but demonstrate the gamut of Turkish behaviour and ideals.

Less worrying are the squabbles between like and like – for example, the bored and frustrated gangs of Turkish youths who have no real quarrel, but who feel the need to guard their territories over-zealously. I used to go to school in Stanmore, in north London, and these Turkish gangs remind me of the Ali G types in the rather boring suburbs of London who strut around with oversized hoodies and talk of knives, but who are really grade A students making regular visits to their grannies and taking care to avoid parking tickets. In a similar vein, I have seen puffed-up Turkish youths circling each other and trading insults in Tophane, only to be broken up by their scolding mothers telling them that dinner is on the table and how dare they be late – some of these mother hens don't even bother to emerge from the kitchen, but scream out of windows on high. The 'gangs' disperse immediately, with a few feeble parting shots, and no doubt the same sequence repeats the next day.

Since the 1970s, there has been an extensive migration from rural to urban areas in Turkey, and the greatest example of that is Istanbul. In many ways, this enormous city is a microcosm of the country, containing pockets of quite distinct communities from, say, Urfa, Kayseri, Diyarbakır or Rize, as well as the traditionally 'Western' areas of Bebek, Beyoğlu and Moda, which can look like London or New York. In Fatih, a residential, conservative community near the historical area of Sultan Ahmet, the proliferation of burqas and beards has led to its nickname of Little Afghanistan (though the residents are eastern Turks, not Afghans). If I want to visit the area, I wear trousers or a long skirt and top. I do not feel under any kind of moral pressure, as such, but one instinctively does not want to be the oddity, the cultural alien. It is bizarre that a mere five-minute taxi ride from here brings you to Beyoğlu, where you could be forgiven for thinking you were in the West End of London, short skirts and public smooching aplenty.

Whenever female friends come to visit me in Turkey, they generally ask the same question pre-arrival: 'Can I wear what I like, or . . . ?' There is always a little note of apology and hesitation, which comes I think from a combination of not wanting to appear ignorant of Turkey's current state, and not wanting to offend me by thinking my country religious and, by association, backward. The truth is that it is a fair question. The country is a wonderful mix of people and this means that you have to adapt, chameleon-like, to various communities, testing the waters as you go. This is as true of Istanbul as it is for areas in the east, the south and in the depths of the Anatolian Plateau.

Funnily enough, I feel more comfortable in traditionally conservative parts of the country – Gaziantep, Urfa and Kayseri, for example – than in some parts of Istanbul. I think this is due to the relatively relaxed attitude of people in central and south-east Anatolia doing things as they have always done them, rather than in the metropolis, where they are trying to establish themselves as rightful residents, battling against the forces of ugly, secular modernity. There is a kind of belligerent attitude displayed by some religious Istanbul residents which must be a reaction to the proximity of people who are fundamentally different from them – people like me, for example – whom they see as a threat, and who make them keen to protect their pious identity in an 'us against them' kind of way. By contrast, traditionally religious communities in the east have the security of majority and are benignly curious about foreign visitors, for the most part.

Until last summer, the annual One Love music festival was held with great success on Bilgi university campus in the district of Eyüp in Istanbul. It was sponsored by the Turkish beer company Efes Pilsen, and resembled an average British festival in terms of over-eighteens drinking and dancing to various B-list acts. In July 2012, supposedly under municipal pressure, Efes was forced to withdraw its name from the festival and the sale of alcohol was banned, effectively finishing the event. Why? Some people argued that, because Eyüp is an area famous for its mosque, it was not appropriate that an event involving alcohol should take place there. Actually, it had nothing to do with that. An announcement from Prime Minister Erdoğan himself cleared up the confusion: 'They want all our youth to be alcoholics,' he was quoted as saying in domestic and international media. 'For God's sake, how can this happen? How can anyone allow alcohol to be sold on a school campus? Will the student go there to get drunk on alcohol, or find knowledge?' Strong words, from a strong leader, and widely applauded despite the secular voices of dissent. The prime minister said he had personally called the school's administration over the matter: 'I said, "What on earth is this?" And I told them we were upset over this.'

Not only was alcohol banned at the upcoming festival, it is now not allowed at Bilgi at all. Previously popular alcohol-serving restaurants on campus are no longer in business. The once thriving student community – a patchwork of gallery spaces, restaurants and student common rooms – has gone quiet, as have the campuses of other universities.

Aside from sweeping laws governing the sale and consumption of alcohol, there have been a number of specifically anti-alcohol decrees during the AKP's rule, which remain one of the primary sources of unease among secular Turks about the direction the government is taking. The decrees usually affect the most bohemian and fun-loving area of Istanbul, the European district of Beyoğlu, and often occur during Ramadan, when Muslims do not drink.

Beyoğlu is a huge area in Istanbul, encompassing traditional neighbourhoods like Kasımpaşa, where Erdoğan grew up, as well as the tourist-beloved bar districts like Asmalı Mescit, Cihangir and Galata. This means there is an unfortunate clash between the jurisdiction of its AKP mayor and the pockets of decidedly secular entertainment. There is an even more unfortunate clash when the prime minister gets involved, which does not happen as often as might be expected, because he has very little reason to go to Beyoğlu. When he does, as happened during Ramadan in July 2011, he does not usually like what he sees.

Ramadan is always very difficult when it falls in summer months, because the days are longer (meaning more time without food or drink for those fasting) and the heat makes it tougher to go without water. Even worse, secular people like to eat outside, which is demoralising for the fasters. In fact, there is an unspoken code in largely Muslim countries that you do not eat or drink on the street during Ramadan, out of respect for others. The areas I mentioned in Beyoğlu – and in particular Asmalı Mescit, legendary place of revelry – are different, being almost exclusively patronised by cosmopolitan, secular Turks and tourists, and indeed composed entirely of bars and restaurants.

In July 2011 Prime Minister Erdoğan was exasperated when outdoor restaurant tables held up his motorcade en route to a whirling dervish ceremony in Galata. Worse, he

was enraged when one of the al fresco drinkers raised an ironic and highly offensive glass to him, or so the bar owners said.
A week later, police removed all outdoor tables and chairs
from the areas of Galata and Asmalı Mescit, leaving behind
a puritanical ghost town in the busiest tourist month of the
year.

Despite the local council's loyal protestations that the
tables were removed because the restaurants were transgress-
ing the legal quota for the area, which had indeed been a
long-standing dispute, it is too much of a coincidence that
the blow fell so soon after Erdoğan's visit. For one thing, the
restaurants all paid a hefty rent to the municipality for each
table they used, meaning that those in charge did not have
much motive to ban them, and had never done so before.
I talked to a restaurant owner in Galata, whose tables were
on a pedestrian square and thus completely exempt from the
charge of blocking pavement traffic, and he showed me the
Beyoğlu Belediye (council) contract he had signed only a
month before for the renewal of his table rent. It is difficult
to believe that the municipality would suddenly take the decision of its own accord to remove tables without a word of
warning. Two years later, the tables are still gone, casting further doubt on the council's claims; if the requisite fines had
been paid, why not put the tables back? Ironically, during the
Gezi protests, when police were concentrated up by Taksim
Square, many restaurant owners took advantage of the absence of police further downtown to bring their tables out
again, and diners could enjoy eating outside once more. This
arrangement worked perfectly until tear gas wafting down
from Taksim Square forced everyone inside again.

As was evident during the One Love festival incident, Erdoğan makes no secret of his opposition to alcohol and his direct involvement in curtailing its sale and consumption. While the reasons given by the government for the restrictions on alcohol are often health-related, Erdoğan has a way of turning the whole debate into a moral crusade which involves protecting Turkish youth from a tragic descent into alcoholism. There have been many instances in the past decade where he has offered life coaching advice to the Turkish public at large, for example the catchy one-liner: 'Eat grapes, don't drink wine.' He has also declared that the national drink is no longer raki (alcoholic) but *ayran*, a non-alcoholic drink made of yoghurt.

The law of May 2013 restricting alcohol was particularly inflammatory. Among many other things, it dramatically limited the sale and advertisement of alcohol, dictated that bottles of alcohol must carry graphic health warnings, like cigarette packets, and all films or programmes on television must have images of alcoholic drinks blanked out (as on Iranian television), so actors look like they are drinking pixelated blurs. Egemen Bağış, the Turkish minister for EU affairs, defended the law to other EU ministers on the grounds that some parts of it had been approved by the World Health Organisation, such as the ban on selling alcohol from 10 p.m. to 6 a.m. Bağış pointed out that it was unfair to accuse the AKP of Islamic authoritarianism when countries like Sweden implemented the same rules.

This would be a fair point, if it were not belied by more sinister elements, for example the rule that no licences will be given to shops or restaurants within a hundred metres of either a school or a mosque. In urban areas, everywhere is within a hundred metres of either a school or a mosque. No new licences will be given, and there is widespread concern among shops, bars and restaurant owners who already hold licences that these will not be renewed when the time comes. The censoring of alcohol on television is the most distasteful part of the law for many secularists because it seems more like moral censorship than anything else, depicting the drinking of alcohol as a failing from which the public must be carefully shielded. Many Turks resent not so much the practical restrictions brought in by the government but the lecturing tone with which they are presented. The official attitude is that 'we know better than you', and Turks hate being patronised.

As a result of the table ban in Asmalı Mescit, which cut the revenues of restaurants by about seventy-five per cent (according to the owners I talked to), thousands of local residents, bar and restaurant owners and secular Istanbullus from elsewhere in the city came to protest, carrying chairs and banners, down the main shopping street of the city – İstiklal Caddesi. As with almost all demonstrations in this country (until the explosion of the Gezi Park protests), it had no effect whatsoever. The year following the table ban, police cordoned off the base of Galata Tower in Beyoğlu, where young people used to gather on summer nights to watch gypsy bands perform and have a beer. The beer element was crucial: the square was turned into a crime scene, taped off and out of bounds. Ousted revellers made a point of sitting on the street and drinking en masse, just outside the taped-off area, while a brace of bored policemen sat in a car within it, watching them. As with the outdoor table ban, there was a nominal excuse for the decision which was not alcohol-related – in this case, the 'noise' caused by those drinking in Galata Square. Again, protests achieved nothing.

Turkish police are probably the most over-deployed police force in the world, certainly when it comes to mass presence at generally peaceful gatherings. They attend the umpteen protests that begin in central Taksim Square in droves, quite often outnumbering protesters, and impressively arrayed with riot gear, batons and water cannon. They pour out of trucks whatever the nature of the protest – colourful pro-LGBT marches, rallies against the PKK (the Kurdistan Workers' Party, a militant Kurdish rights organisation), nationalists, religious anti-Kemalists, anarchic socialists, out-of-work teachers, theatre directors – you name it, the police have duly attended in their requisite riot gear. Sometimes they arrest people for simply being present at a protest, if it is deemed too politically threatening. They are a reminder both of Turkey's violent past and of the lingering unease in the relationship between government and the Turkish people. Most of all, they show institutionalised paranoia.

In 2012, Taksim Square in central Istanbul, the traditional site for democratic public protest like Trafalgar Square or Parliament Square in London, was closed for massive 're-development plans' which included a shopping mall and a replica Ottoman barracks. Every May Day, the square has been the venue for generally peaceful marches, where workers' unions, opposition supporters and any disgruntled members of the public gather, sing and wave flags. In the past, there have been violent clashes with police but the years leading up to 2013 passed without incident; I attended the demonstrations on May Day 2012, and the atmosphere in Taksim was not only peaceful but positively festive as people sang songs about Kurdish freedom in the morning sun. The planned construction of the mall served as an excuse to ban people from the square on 1 May 2013, and when they tried to gather in nearby Şişli, they were blasted with tear gas and water cannon by twenty-seven thousand police specially mobilised for the event. Public transport was suspended and the bridges over the Golden Horn were closed for the first time since the national state of emergency in 1978. The city reacted with horror to the crackdown, little knowing that this would be a pattern repeated again and again just a month later.

Police are more wisely deployed in Turkish football stadiums, especially when any of the big teams from the *Süper Lig* are playing – Galatasaray, Beşiktaş or Fenerbahçe. A month after my arrival in Istanbul I was taken, innocent as a lamb, to the now destroyed İnönü Stadium, home of Beşiktaş, to watch a 'friendly' between them and Karabükspor. How nice, I thought. I had never been to a football match before. On entering the stadium, I was extremely glad to have borrowed a black and white scarf from my friend, thus mixing in with the sea of frighteningly impassioned Beşiktaş fans massing for attack well before the match began. I was also glad to have a seat in their ninety per cent of the stadium, as opposed to being in the tiny wedge of seating reserved for brave-hearted Karabükspor supporters, who were surrounded by a protective net. At the end of the game, the net proved its worth: the Beşiktaş fans, rendered fuming, incoherent beasts of war by a 2–2 draw with an inferior team, started tearing the plastic seats from under themselves and hurling them down onto the pitch, onto the heads of players (now surrounded, suitably for once, by riot police) and most particularly the referee. Anyone near the incarcerated Karabükspor fans was hurling whatever came to hand at the provident netting, a hail of chair shards and other missiles, as red flares flew through the smoke-filled air. It was a truly apocalyptic scene, on an otherwise quiet Saturday afternoon.

I had never seen so many people acting as one, like a force of nature, with an elemental wall of sound to match, and I did not see it again until the Gezi protests. What was truly remarkable, however, was what these fans were actually shouting. My friend helped me decipher the lyrics of the Beşiktaş chant: 'Eagle [Beşiktaş's symbol], you are my life! Black and white blood runs through my veins . . . I would die for you, my only love!' This powerful love elegy was being chanted lustily by thousands of sturdy, moustachioed men with fire in their bellies, as well as a few cans of Efes and an unquenchable thirst for the destruction of the unfortunate Karabükspor players. Their cries read like the love poetry of a lesser nation, yet they were delivered in hoarse unison to men paid monstrous amounts of money to retain a reasonable place in the league, or merely to entertain, as in the case of this far from friendly match. Plastered onto huge posters around the stadium were slogans like: 'I would give up my mother and father for you, I swear to God.'

It was at that point that I understood that, for secular Turks, football is a religion – a cause, something to fight for, to worship – a bit like Turkey itself. United in their love for the game, fans are divided by which particular team they support, like sects of the same religion backing rival caliphs. Beşiktaş represent the working man, Fenerbahçe 'everyman' and Galatasaray the educated man. It is imperative, when someone asks which of the big three you support, that you base your answer on a split-second assessment of the man asking the question. Fenerbahçe is the safest. Alternatively, giving the name of an obscure British team is accepted without demur as a foreigner's privilege.

The participation of major football team supporters in the Gezi protests was crucial, especially the members of Çarşı, the main Beşiktaş fan club, whose slogan is *Herşeye karşı!* – 'Against everything!' Çarşı fans are notoriously anarchic troublemakers, no strangers to clashes with riot police in the aftermath of Beşiktaş games. During the first week of the protests, Çarşı members assumed natural leadership of the resistance down by the Beşiktaş stadium. One memorable night, they commandeered a bulldozer from somewhere and charged straight at enemy lines, scattering riot police everywhere. After that, they managed to steal one of the police's water-cannon tanks. This was probably the glittering apex of their anarchic careers.

The peaceful counterpart to the football stadium is the even more male domain of the *berber* (barber) or *erkek kuaför* (men's hairdresser). I get a peculiar thrill from accompanying male friends here. There is an unspoken rule that, as a woman, I have no place within these hallowed walls, and I must admit to deriving satisfaction from watching foam-covered beards bristling in outrage as I cross the threshold, scandalised looks multiplied in mirrors on all sides. It feels as though

I have travelled back in time to a gentlemen's club in Edwardian London and poked my head into a drawing room full of placid old men discussing cricket and decrying the latest antics of the Suffragettes. In fact, a more plebeian but barely updated form of this drawing-room scene can be found in any backgammon café or rather sweetly named 'social club', anywhere in Turkey. Smoky and drab, filled with the clunks of dice and the rasping commentary of sport on the telly, these are the sole preserve of wizened old men with much time on their hands and weighty issues to discuss. I have only glimpsed this anti-harem from the street; I would dearly love to go in one day and join in the topic at hand but I can predict the appalled silence that would fall like a guillotine and, frankly, I don't have the nerve.

The *berber* is different; a place of work, it is bustling with men in white overcoats wielding trimmers and combs, customers pinioned beneath towels and the impending razor. Often I come with visitors from London for whom I have to translate, although I cannot resist abusing this power and instructing the barber to leave a modest goatee. By far the most dramatic part of the shave is the finale, when the barber jabs a stick of flaming cotton wool into his victim's face to burn off fine cheek hairs, swiping mercilessly into ears and nostrils, and leaving a delicate whiff of hair *brûlé*. By the time a rough head massage and the dousing of hair in copious amounts of lavender cologne have been performed, the previously gung-ho English traveller is a perfectly coiffed shell of his former self.

The barber is yet another example of an old-fashioned tradition which is still very much going strong, regardless of the invention of Gillette disposable razors and 8 a.m. office starts. Of course, not every Turkish man visits the *berber* every day, but there are a huge number of them about, and I have never seen one empty. Most are packed. Why?

The *berber* is basically a social club in another guise; for most regular customers, it is not so much the shave they go for but the camaraderie. It is a time-honoured, gently macho ritual: Turkish men like to groom themselves, but they like to do so in the company of other men: tea is consumed, politics discussed, wives complained about. It is another example of the wonderful Turkish appetite for sharing life with peers, a kind of unassuming assertion of the right to be sociable, a quiet stand against the individualism of our times.

Much of what is now, to the Western eye, old-fashioned, is for a Turk timeless, because it is rooted in a sense of community that is here to stay in the teeth of encroaching modernisation. Neighbourhoods in the middle of Istanbul still have a village-like feel; I remember being woken by the hoarse cry of a street seller on my first morning in Istanbul: '*Sarımsakçı geldi, sarımsakçı geeeldiiii!*' ('The garlic seller has arrived!') I had no idea what was being said at the time. A young man was slowly pushing a hand cart through the street, full of garlic as advertised, and interested old biddies were poking their heads out of windows above. Regular customers started lowering coins in baskets from fourth storeys, while the more sceptical waddled down in their brightly coloured *şalvar* (baggy trousers) to examine the cloves at closer range. A similar scene greets the arrival of the cucumber seller or the *hurdacı* (rag-and-bone man), who gathers unwanted old knick-knacks from anyone decluttering their home.

Some hawkers have hijacked technology in disturbing ways. I was alarmed one day to hear what I thought must be the police addressing someone – potential terrorists? – through one of those megaphones that, to a Londoner at least, mean serious trouble. Looking anxiously through my window, I saw in the street below a beaten-up van, decrepit megaphone perched precariously on its roof, colourful blankets piled in the back and inside a very portly old codger speaking incoherently through the handset: 'Blankets fifteen lira only, yes sisters, fifteen lira, don't miss them!' Another unexpected arrival was that of the *deterjancı* (detergent seller), his truck piled high with unmarked bottles of Cif and Domestos decanted cheaply from wholesale containers.

Supermarkets are a relatively recent craze in Turkey, challenging a very strong culture of specialised something-sellers in the street, or the regular, ubiquitous farmers' markets. For the average Turk, there is no suspicion or stigma associated with buying from an unlicensed, rickety cart, as there would probably be in London. For me, the change from Tesco Metro cashier to bellowing garlic farmer in the middle of the city was a glorious introduction to a more free-spirited, and indeed free-marketed, way of life. The culture of street selling encourages an atmosphere of community beyond anything else. The supermarket is synonymous with anonymity – packaged goods bagged by a bored, callow youth with no interest in who you are or whether you will come again. The garlic seller's livelihood depends on his product and enthusiasm and repartee. He comes to you. He comes to the neighbourhood like the Pied Piper and unites Turkish housewives in the constant chore and joy that is preparing food for a large family.

Turkey is a wonderful mixture of opportunism and trust. One of my favourite domestic sights is heavily laden washing lines stretched from the windows of one house to those of its counterpart across the street – neighbours sharing and airing their laundry with not a blush on either side, an admirable arrangement of mutual convenience. There is a very blurred line between a Turkish family homestead and its surroundings; emotions, raised voices and curiosity spill over from beyond its walls in a way that you just do not experience in England or other chilly European societies. One's home is decidedly not a private space but a box at the opera of suburbia, both viewing point and exhibit. It is an open door. Some expats find the lack of privacy here irritating, but it is an indelible instinct of the Turkish psyche to share, and in place of solitude you receive untiring kindness, (unsolicited) advice and the support of as many burly matriarchs as you could wish for. That this goes for the middle of Istanbul or Ankara as much as it does for a rural town speaks for itself.

Social differences definitely exist here, and snobbery is neither politically incorrect nor outdated, but at crucial moments it simply melts away. This, too, is part of a shared humanity which is hard to express but so obvious in action. A friend of mine moved here from America and for the first months of her residency took care to avoid the alarming-looking tramp who passed his time swigging beer outside her door and occasionally asking for a lira. One day, Gill arrived outside her house with an antiques dealer who had carried an Ottoman sideboard home for her. He asked for his tip, and had no change for the hundred-lira note which was the only money she had on her. Gill was starting to panic when Musa the tramp piped up from his recumbent position on the step below them. 'Don't worry, lady – here's a tenner. Pay me back whenever.' Gill was understandably both touched and a little embarrassed by this, and from thenceforth exchanged pleasantries and further lira with Musa the tramp, who referred to himself as *kapıcı* (doorman) of her building, and was indeed quite effective at keeping everyone at bay.

There are surprisingly few tramps in Turkey. I think this is because of the very strong ethos of family support, and in the absence of family, the Islamic culture of charity, which means that the local mosque often takes care of struggling members of the community. This does not happen when the problem is drink or drugs, hence the presence of tramps swilling beer. My favourite local personalities are the crazy buskers with no talent, for example the dancing Michael Jackson impersonator with the permanent streak of paint in his hair and a gaping hole in his trouser seat, moonwalking in everyone's way on the busiest Beyoğlu streets. More respectable is the man who looks quite smart from afar, in a shabby suit and slicked-back hair, who sings in the distinctively warbling style of Ferdi Tayfur, Turkey's moustachioed answer to Tom Jones in his seventies heyday. This gentleman politely but relentlessly serenades couples dining outside restaurants until he is paid to go away either by his intended audience or the desperate restaurant manager.

A much more cohesive and significant presence in the margins of Turkish society is the *çingene* (gypsy) population. There are more than two million Roma here, which is not counting the gypsies from Dom and Lom backgrounds in the Middle East and the Caucasus who have wandered over to Turkey. To me and, I think, to most people, they are something of a mystery – classed sometimes as an ethnicity, sometimes as a marginal social group, they are maligned and misunderstood as a stereotype. Where do they come from, why are they so attached to their nomadic lifestyles, and why is it primarily the women who work (at least in the Middle East)? In Turkey as in most Middle-Eastern countries, gypsies beg. But in Turkey, they also have a commercial integration into the community, even if they have no political voice. The first thing most visitors see in the centre of Istanbul is Taksim Square, which is bordered on two sides by flower stalls run by gypsy ladies wearing bright scarves and baggy *şalvar* trousers. In some neighbourhoods they sit on street corners peeling figs or shelling walnuts, and in others they do odd jobs like cleaning the copper pots most traditional Turkish households still use in their kitchens. They very rarely work for an employer, even off the books – they are their own bosses. One gypsy man I talked to had accumulated enough money through the odd jobs of his family that he could afford to buy a car, in which they all slept every night, and in which, crucially, they could travel. It would seem that, even with the potential to buy into a middle-class lifestyle, gypsies prize their autonomy and independence of movement above anything else.

I understood a lot about Turkish compassion by observing the street life of Istanbul. One of the things that struck me most forcibly was the absolutely natural and welcome presence of stray dogs and cats in the street. When it comes to sheer number and collective charisma, the hordes of dogs and cats win hands down. A constantly shifting but permanent diaspora, they constitute perhaps the one minority population which has survived and even flourished through the political upheavals of Istanbul's past. They tend to keep to a particular district like loyal residents, and are considerably more treasured than their human counterparts.

It is one of the most charming paradoxes of Turkey that a nation of Muslims who are told from an early age that animals are dirty and to be avoided are real pushovers for a cute or diseased stray in the street. Essentially, it is a testament to the natural warmth and kindness of the people that animals here are constantly cared for, fed, watered and even vaccinated courtesy of locals and indeed state vets. Having a pet is still a fairly new concept, strictly for the emerging middle and upper classes. Most Turks would not dream of keeping a filthy dog in the house but will go out of their way to drop off a bit of meat to the aged Alsatian on the corner, provide him with a bowl of clean water and generally keep an eye on him. One of my favourite photographs from the height of the Gezi protests was a weeping Labrador being tended to by protesters in gas masks who were tenderly spraying alkaline solutions into the dog's eyes to neutralise the effects of tear gas. At the medical tent that was set up in Gezi Park, a young veterinary student treated stray dogs and cats while her medical student colleagues treated their human owners.

Some locals devote themselves entirely to caring for the city's legions of flea-bitten waifs. Once, when leaving my house, I was startled by the sight of an elderly gentleman in a tattered overcoat standing motionless in the middle of the road, arms outstretched like an urban scarecrow. With no obvious cause, it looked like he was holding up the traffic in a personal protest of some kind until I noticed, below most on-lookers' eyeline, a small kitten cavorting under the wheels of the nearest car. The aged cat lover did not budge until this animal was safely on the pavement, by which time several irate taxi drivers were leaning out of their windows and shouting at him. Unmoved, he settled down with the kitten and a bag of food he removed from an inside coat pocket, and I realised that this extraordinary person was the mysterious local Cat Man who left bowls of food and water and well-fed kittens in his wake. A few months later I saw him asleep on the steps of a local mosque, surrounded by his dependants. Considering the price of vet-bought dry food, I wonder how this man affords his mission of mercy. I wouldn't be at all surprised if the vet gave him knockdown rates, knowing the destination of these bags of food. That is one of the wonderful aspects of the Turkish community – ruthless in business, they band together for a common cause like cat charity.

Strays create unnecessary fuss in Istanbul considering how happily integrated they are. The municipalities want to round them up, rather as they did in 1910, when all the strays were deported to an island off the mainland of Istanbul and ended up eating each other. Animal rights enthusiasts want to round them up and put them in care homes. In fact, the status quo is just fine – they are independent, self-respecting agents of the streets who are fed and cared for: an ideal arrangement. They belong to everyone, and no one.

The care of strays is one of the instances in Turkish society where collective instinct is directly at odds with official practice. If any of the ministers voting for the bill to round up strays were to encounter a capering puppy on the street, I bet fifty lira he would give it a pat on the head or at least a kind word. But he would go ahead and vote to evict strays anyway, because policy is policy. *Burası Turkiye* – 'This is Turkey.'

3

Social Growing Pains

'This is Turkey': I have heard this so many times as an explanation for inexplicable Turkish norms. It takes some time to get used to the way things are done here, partly because traditional customs have an unexpected way of cropping up in a society which is modernising with lopsided enthusiasm. Turkey is still a very young country making its way in the world. The struggles it is going through at the moment bring to mind the predicaments of an adolescent who is simultaneously self-confident and insecure. Turkey is coming of age.

Mass migration, urbanisation and a growing awareness of human rights in the past fifty years have changed the social, economic and physical landscapes of Turkey, but it is the social landscape that is the most difficult to navigate. For a fairly relaxed Brit, Turkish etiquette has been intimidating because it is so complex, so imbued with history, and cannot really be taught; instead, it must be second-guessed like an erratic maiden aunt. I only realised this after I learned enough of the language to notice the subtleties of the ways people interact. I wince to think of the mistakes I must have made early on, the teas I should have accepted, the praise I should have lavished: clumsy blunderings through the pitfalls of Turkish convention. Paradoxically, underneath the filigree of social niceties is a steel core of uncomplicated good will and warmth. Turks have a humble and humbling generosity, especially towards guests, which cuts through the elaborate tradition with which they often cage their interaction.

The idiosyncrasies of Turkish conversation are endless: specific modes of address, the polite use of passive and impersonal verbs, phrases for everyday interactions – what you say to someone working, someone eating, someone whose food you have just consumed, someone ill, someone with a family member newly deceased or betrothed. 'Congratulations' will not suffice for good news, nor 'Sorry to hear that' for bad. You must tailor your words to the occasion, in age-old format, or risk causing grave offence. You must also be wise to traditional practices. I once offered to pay for a freshly fried doughnut (*lokma*) handed to me by a kind man on a street corner in Selçuk, noticing too late the surrounding mill of people and remembering that the public distribution of this particular sweet is traditional on the part of a recently bereaved Turkish family. The money in my hand seemed suddenly sordid as I fumbled for the correct words of condolence for this grieving man.

Turkey has retained a sense of community in which everyone is involved in everyone else's affairs, their good news and their bad, and this is formalised in language – people communicate, on all levels. The village-like interdependency of Turkish society has remained despite the huge urbanisation of the last few decades, and has thrived with technology like mobile phones and Skype. The average Turk speaks to their family several times a day and will know the details of their ex-neighbour's second divorce settlement or a distant cousin's circumcision ceremony via an impressive network of gossip intelligence. I soon noticed that Turks communicate not only with their closest circles but also with complete strangers much more readily than Europeans, at least in informal situations.

In Turkey, if you have even a brief exchange with someone working – at a desk, hauling concrete, cooking – you wish him or her well as you leave: *Kolay gelsin*, which literally means 'May it come easily.' I have become so used to saying this that when I visit England I have to stop my impulse to translate the phrase into English. Approximations are always clumsy: 'Take it easy' sounds American and slightly patronising to an English ear. 'Good luck' is portentous and uncalled for. In fact, the expression itself is uncalled for in England because there is no expectation that a stranger will take any interest in your activities, or vice versa. In Turkey, recognition of others is natural, even if it is just in the form of an offhand, oft-repeated expression. *Kolay gelsin* is a simple sign of solidarity which transcends social class, promising nothing while radiating good will. Turks have a lovely way of saying goodbye to someone: *Güle güle*, which literally means '[Go] laughing'.

There are plenty of other phrases like this: *Geçmiş olsun* – 'May it pass' – is what you say to someone who is ill or generally having a tough time. 'Get well soon' is the less frequently repeated and more specifically medical equivalent in English, but it doesn't cover the pan-sympathetic sense of the Turkish, which can refer to someone's financial troubles or just a bad hair day. It is such a simple phrase, little more than a voiced smile, but equally cheering.

I am certainly not saying that Turkey is a socialist country, or particularly socially progressive, but it does have this indelible, shared humanity which persists despite – or perhaps because of – the upheavals of its troubled past and present. I can sense a similar atmosphere in descriptions of Britain during the world wars, when people united in fear and unaccustomed hardship. That was temporary. In the relatively emergency-free society of today's Britain, everyone minds their own business, even if this is belied by the cowardly anonymity of a Facebook profile.

The downside of the importance Turks place on social expression is the huge capacity to get it wrong and cause offence. Turks are notoriously sensitive. If the offender is a bumbling foreigner on uncertain ground, he or she is benignly forgiven, but less fortunate are offenders in the international political arena. In August 2012 the Turkish media and main opposition party responded with hysteria to a photograph published by the White House of President Obama holding a baseball bat while talking on the phone to Prime Minister Erdoğan about the Syrian crisis. The photo was deemed highly offensive, the baseball bat simultaneously incomprehensible and aggressive. The White House press secretary's excuses of the importance of baseball season fell on sceptical ears and the power balance between Obama and Erdoğan was construed as darkly as possible.

If Turks are easily offended, so too are newcomers to Turkey who are unused to the particular rhythm and nuances of Turkish conversation. There are several characteristic expressions and signs that, if one is not informed, range from the bewildering to the downright offensive. For a start, in place of 'No', there is a dismissive lift of the head or eyebrows, often accompanied by a sharp click of the tongue. This indescribably rude-looking and -sounding gesture seems to imply complete disdain, as though the person in question cannot even be bothered to open their mouth to answer you. It is almost as common as actually saying 'No' and not in fact rude at all. Nestled amongst various Italian-style hand wavings, emphatic pinched fingers and so on, my absolute favourite Turkish gesture is the deliberate, double, palm-to-palm hand wipe, to denote something complete or finished. For example, 'I never saw him again,' or 'She spent *all* his money!' would be accompanied by this gesture to add gravitas and irrevocability.

Having only ever been spoken to in Turkish by my grandmother in early childhood, I was amazed to discover the usage of epithets and modes of address in a context outside the home. *Canım*, for example, literally means 'my soul' and was, I thought, extremely affectionate. So it is, but I quickly discovered that one applies it to anyone who isn't actually your boss or father-in-law – to customers in a taxi, friends, strangers in the street, lovers or animals. I have decided that it is equivalent to 'my dear', although it still, somehow, retains its heightened significance for loved ones. That is one of the beauties of Turkish: the freedom you are granted to invest as much as you want into a language that is, fundamentally, laced with passion and affection.

Having addressed my big sister as *abla* throughout my life, I understood it to mean 'big sister'. And so it does – but you can also apply it to any female, about the same age or older than yourself, whom you happen to encounter in an informal setting. I am *abla* to anonymous strangers, or the rather confusing *ablacığım* (pronounced 'abla-jum') – literally 'my little big sister', used affectionately. To friends I am Alevciğim ('darling Alev'), and in a formal setting I am 'Alev *hanım*' which cannot be satisfactorily translated into English but is equivalent to individualising 'madam' – 'Madam Alev', which is quite nice, if one doesn't think of brothel owners. Alev, or any first name used by itself sounds rather bare and blank. Turks like to create a kind of relationship, whether formal or informal, with everyone they meet, and they do this initially through tokens of language before an established, mutual understanding is reached. Adding either an affectionate suffix or a respectful title to someone's name shows the speaker's good intentions, come what may, and establishes a vague power balance within which Turks feel more secure.

When I started travelling around Turkey, I discovered that, while Istanbul is a glorious mix of Turks from all over the place, there is a kind of cohesive, relaxed vernacular here which one does not always find elsewhere, especially not in more traditional or rural communities. For example, in Kayseri, a very conservative city in the middle of the Anatolian plain, I was no longer *abla* and my boyfriend was no longer *abi* ('big brother', or 'mate'). Instead, he became *hocam* ('my teacher' – traditionally a teacher of the Koran) and I was *yenge* (literally 'wife of my brother'). The latter conveyed respect to me – it would be politely assumed that we were married – while suggesting a brotherly camaraderie between the taxi driver and my boyfriend, although not as relaxed as *abi*. *Hocam*, likewise, is more a term of respect than a literal form of address. It is, significantly, not really applied to women, and the only time I have been addressed as *hoca* was when I was actually a teacher at the Bosphorus University. In Ankara, the capital city, *hoca* is often used, not because people are necessarily conservative but because it is a student town. Students ironically call each other *hoca*, 'teacher', and it has spread and mingled with the traditional, Anatolian use of the term.

Turkish is the linguistic equivalent of a crazy fruit salad, with Turkic roots, a great deal of Arabic vocabulary both 'Turkified' and lifted directly, many Persian words and quite a considerable body of French. These French words were transliterated to suit the Latinised form of Turkish that was introduced by Atatürk in 1928, in place of the Arabic-Persian script. Over the past century, certain words and modes of expression have come in and out of currency, reflecting shifts in Turkish society. Aside from my taxi driver impersonations, my mother was also shocked by the amount of Arabic vocabulary I use, words like *maalesef* ('unfortunately') or *selam* (a standard Arabic greeting). *Sağ ol* ('thank you') is not an Arabic phrase but it is a good example of an old-fashioned expression now very much in vogue. Its direct French-Turkish counterpart – *mersi* – is now fairly rare, and only really used by people above the age of thirty or so, and of a relatively privileged background. My mother, her vocabulary frozen in time from when she left Turkey in the seventies, uses *mersi* not because it was particularly chic to do so, but because it was normal; only peasants said *sağ ol* at that time, she says. This expression, meaning literally 'be healthy', was associated, at least in my mother's circles, with backward, rural Anatolians who had more in common with their Middle Eastern neighbours than the more Western-facing, self-styled 'progressive' Turks. The latter sprinkled their speech with the French that retained kudos as the former language of the late Ottoman noblesse and the formal language of banking and bureaucracy. Thus, a formerly civilised, urbane word has become slightly passé and pretentious, while Arabic equivalents are both populist and popular. This has a lot to do with the huge rural migration to cities that has been taking place over the last thirty years in particular, meaning that the divide between snooty city types and the rustic masses has largely been worn away, and the latter's parlance has prevailed.

The mass migration of the last few decades has had important social consequences in Turkey. There are many more young people in cities competing for jobs and spouses, more office-centred jobs as people move away from agricultural employment, and interesting clashes between the inherent machismo of Turkish society and attempts at sexual equality in the workplace as women struggle up through the viscous grime of ingrained patriarchy. There is also a big patchwork of people displaced by choice, as it were: about half a million people move to Istanbul alone every year, and many of them have come from the East or Black Sea regions.

Turks are always interested in origins. Most big-city dwellers these days are originally from elsewhere, so people are always curious to place each other. The question which comes even before 'What's your name?' is *Memleketiniz neresi?* – 'Where is your hometown?' While Turks are very patriotic on a pan-Turkish scale, they are also deeply devoted to the particular area where they were born, or where either parent was born. Finding out that a stranger comes from anywhere in a hundred-mile radius of one's own hometown is a cause for huge celebration on first meeting. Any geographical connection, no matter how arbitrary, is something of a triumph in this enormous, scrambled country, and the 'neighbour' is seized on almost like a long-lost relative – probably a sign that Turks feel fundamentally more comfortable in a smaller community than the modern super-communities in urban areas today.

Although migration is now the norm, Turkish language reflects a time when people stuck with the community into which they were born. The word *yabancı* is derived from *yaban* (wilderness) and means both 'stranger' and 'foreigner'/ 'non-local'. It reflects a village-like sense of community in which only immediate friends and relations were familiar, and anyone new to the area was big news (this is still the case in many rural parts of Turkey). Other terms like *yurt dışında* also reflect this – the phrase literally translates as 'outside the area of the tent', so would have originally been used to mean anywhere outside the immediate family homestead in the Turkic nomadic regions. Now it means, simply, 'abroad' – anywhere from Greece to the Gambia. Originally, *yabancı* was most frequently used in the 'non-local' sense, but it increasingly applies to people from distant countries as more and more tourists come to Turkey. As not only a non-local, but indeed a Genuine Foreigner living in Turkey, I normally provoke a Turkish Inquisition on first meeting. There are several questions that I expect to be asked: How old are you? Are you married? Where do you live – but where *exactly*? What do you do? Is that well paid?

Coming from England, the irrepressible and slightly possessive curiosity of Turks towards outsiders and their tendency to ask what the English would stiffly call 'personal' questions seems impertinent, vulgar and unnecessary. The Turks, if they stopped to consider it, would probably consider their own behaviour friendly, and moreover honest. In England, we ask these questions silently, sizing a new acquaintance up, but Turks just go ahead and ask the questions they want to ask, bypassing unnecessary preambles about the weather, dispensing with artifice.

Is this really sinister or judgemental? Turks take an interest in you, particularly if you are foreign; they want to place you, to work you out, and yes, the questions are superficial, but they are a start. When I first arrived, I was offended by the questions and thought: 'Why does it matter how old I am or where I live? Don't they want to know Who I Am?' Then I realised that that was a vain hope, in both senses of the word. It is impossible to discover someone's true personality initially, so you might as well get the basics. The real cause of offence, if one is honest, is their interest in how rich you are – money just isn't taboo here in the way it is in England.

A great deal of Turkish interaction must be taken within context – without this mantra, a foreigner can feel beset by intrusive interrogation or unwelcome opinion. The extension of the Turks' interest in other people's affairs is their tendency to pass comment, without invitation or encouragement, regardless of their relationship with their interlocutor. Comments on other people's appearance, in particular, are perfectly acceptable. If you have lost a little weight, this will be pointed out in graphic terms: 'My God, you're wasting away, you're like a pencil! What's happened?' Or the reverse: 'You know, you've put on weight, you must be very content, *maşallah.*' In fact, once your Turkish friends are passing comment on you like this, it is a sign that you are part of the fold, so taking offence makes no sense at all.

When I worked briefly in a media office in Istanbul, I was perplexed by the contradiction of hierarchies. On one level, employees were extremely deferential to their superiors – *hanım* ('madam') and *bey* ('sir') were used even after many years of working together, and people took care not to challenge anyone in a higher position at the company. This led to a rather staid atmosphere, with orders issued majestically from on high and dutifully followed by underlings, but at the same time, the social undercurrents in the office did not quite match this professional hierarchy. The receptionist, a voluptuous lady called, to my private amusement, Fatma, was the lowest-ranking employee apart from the tea lady. With very little to do other than observe the goings-on of the office, she took great interest in her co-workers, especially their consumption of food. Once, our rather formidable editor hurried into the office eating a sandwich as she juggled BlackBerrys and stacks of files, drawing instant criticism from Fatma: '*Bihter hanım*, every time I see you, you're eating! You really must think of your figure.' Commenting on someone else's weight in Britain, even among friends, is so taboo that I couldn't quite believe that fat Fatma was chastising her own boss, while addressing her as 'madam'. It perfectly summed up the singular balance between respect and closeness here, the complete opposite of the British brand of stiff informality, which involves calling someone by their first name while keeping an awkward distance from them, both socially and physically.

In so many ways, Turkish interaction is the opposite of English interaction, and the easiest way to summarise the difference is that Turks are more heartfelt in their dealings one to one. Yes, there are many intricacies of Turkish etiquette and tradition, but fundamentally Turks are incredibly warm and display a wonderful kind of generosity, particularly to individuals. As a visitor to any but the most touristic of areas, you have a kind of exalted social position as a guest. Turks will give you not only all the food in their house, but everything at their disposal – including their house, if you need accommodation. They will spend hours of their time helping you, expecting nothing in return. You will pay for nothing. As a guest, you have to be careful to temper your admiration of anything they own, because if you are too effusive they will immediately present it to you as a gift. Their generosity is overwhelming, especially at the beginning.

And yet, sometimes, Turks' lack of civic spirit is astounding. They seem to have very little regard for other people in the public sense – they will ignore red lights, queue-jump, or build a hideous building on a prominent hill, spoiling the view for everyone else (the view from their house will be great). It is one of the most puzzling contradictions about Turks: they can be totally selfless with individuals and totally selfish in a public domain. It's almost as if they do not recognise a nameless public as composed of people; they only really acknowledge a face, a name and a personality standing in front of them. It is the same thing with prejudice towards minorities – a Turk might tell you that they hate Kurds, for example, but if a Kurd knocked on their door they would be welcomed in and treated with the same boundless generosity all guests are shown. Traversing Istanbul traffic, one must be careful not to be mown down, because Turkish drivers spare no thought for other drivers or pedestrians – we are all obstacles in their way. Yet I will never forget the time I fell over on a steep hill in Istanbul, grazing my foot – within a few seconds I was surrounded by a crowd of concerned faces, outstretched hands offering me handkerchiefs and worried voices debating the whereabouts of the nearest pharmacy. I had been suddenly transformed into an individual in trouble, the focus of everyone's attention and offers of help.

It is almost the opposite in England. The English are instilled with a strong sense of civic responsibility, binning rubbish, queuing and driving in an orderly manner, well-behaved parts in the well-oiled machine of public life. When it comes to one-to-one interaction, however, it all gets rather embarrassing, and no one looks anyone else in the eye unless absolutely necessary. Knock on a door in your street and the likelihood is that a suspicious voice will ask your business through the intercom, notwithstanding the 'Welcome' mat underneath your feet.

In both countries, there is of course a big difference between the friendliness of people in big cities and in smaller communities, the latter being much warmer. Nevertheless, Londoners and Istanbullus live in comparable environments, and Istanbullus, while considered terribly stuck-up and cold by other Turks, are considerably warmer than Londoners. Having lived in both cities, I find myself making an effort to keep up with my Istanbul neighbours in little ways, like trying to have food stocked for unexpected guests. I didn't give that a second thought in London.

The downside of city life here is the 'survival of the fittest' code on roads and public transport. One-way streets exist only in name, pedestrian crossings are apparently invisible, red lights optional. There is little respect for any 'system', police are seen to be corrupt (lazy and bribable), so anything goes – it is all about taking your chances and cutting across another car before he cuts across you. Brits are appalled when they try to so much as cross a road here because in Britain, traffic laws are not only upheld but valued, and the sense of order this gives public life extends to things like bus queues. No one will arrest you for jumping a British queue, but you will incur universal disapproval because it is simply *not* the done thing. Turkey is in many ways lawless, but it is more human, more vital.

During the occupation of Gezi, the Turkish norms I had got used to were blown completely out of the water by the most powerful displays of civic responsibility I have ever seen, in Turkey or anywhere else. Something important was at stake, and Turkish citizens rose magnificently to the challenge. They not only queued, they formed human chains to carry crates of food and water from donation points to distribution tents. The survival of the fittest mentality was transformed into co-operation and solidarity, as people organised themselves to cope with the flood of donations that were received throughout the day and the injured people who needed treatment at the makeshift medical centre in Gezi Park. All the warmth and generosity usually reserved for individuals was poured into a crowd of people in a way that was quite humbling to watch.

Coming from the stiff, rather impersonal civility of England, the intensity and intricacy of Turkish interaction was initially disconcerting. Early on, I decided that the general maxim of 'take within context' was key to coping with the unexpected challenges of living here. The area to which I have most struggled to apply this is sexual politics. Turkey has an undeniably macho culture, both in business and within social circles, and working out the choreography of gender role-play can be exhausting. For all the efforts made by Atatürk to raise the social position and importance of women, his legal reforms were not matched by change in underlying social attitudes to any great degree. Lingering old-fashioned expectations of male and female behaviour mar the supposed equality of the sexes with hidden and pernicious traps for the uninitiated. In many ways Turkish society is Middle Eastern and no matter how theoretically liberal the family, how independent-minded the woman or broad-minded the man, there are certain expectations that must be met.

The serious side of this affects women's rights, education and autonomy; I address these in the next chapter. What I have found both amusing and exasperating is that, even in the cosmopolitan, liberal circles of Istanbul, Izmir and Ankara, where women are apparently as independent as men and old-fashioned stereotypes are looked upon with scorn, there are so many ways in which archaic mores cling on far less obviously but more tenaciously than a headscarf. Relationships follow strict rules. Both men and women must behave in a certain way, at least in public. There is, of course, an element of this in every society – I am not claiming that anywhere is sexually apolitical. But I have found it much more formulated in Turkey than in the UK.

Sometimes the stereotypes are right under your nose. Mandatory identity cards in Turkey are issued at birth and are blue for male citizens and pinky-orange for female – a relatively harmless but aggravating instance of thoughtless gender typecasting, putting the Turkish authorities on a par with the designers of Mothercare products. No doubt it was decided by some bureaucrat that it would be a cute differentiation, and books for Turkish children are colour-coded similarly by equally thoughtful publishers.

The most troubling thing for me has been the way Turkish women seem to accept this stereotyping without demur. The quintessential middle-class, urban Turkish woman has a depressingly uniform brand of femininity. Her ladylike conduct is – to the best of her ability – above reproach, as is her groomed exterior, which usually involves immaculate hair and shiny high heels. She is polite and strangely anodyne, rarely expressing controversial views – it is almost as though she is nervous of showing any personality, lest that spoil her perfect feminine veneer. She must also know, consciously or subconsciously, that most Turkish men prefer to go unchallenged. She tends to adopt a little girl's voice, especially in male company. A Turkish friend of mine from London is fluent in both English and Turkish, and when she speaks the latter her voice is noticeably higher, as though she has inhaled from a small helium balloon. I was very struck by this the first time I heard her speaking Turkish, thinking how odd it was that she sounded more natural in English than in her mother tongue. Somehow, rightly or wrongly, Turkish women have decided that men like them to act like little girls, and they are playing that part as best they can. The result, unfortunately, is a brigade of infantile Stepford Wives who have been, ironically, stripped of their femininity in the very act of trying to out-feminise each other.

Interestingly, the older Turkish ladies I have met have been really fun. They are considerably more opinionated and, frankly, engaging than the women my age. They are usually elegant but not over-groomed, more likely to make bold jokes or outrageous statements, and are generally more relaxed. I think this must be because the pressure of competing to attract men has passed, and they can be themselves. There is a tiny elderly lady who lives in the apartment below me. She is terribly sweet, like a frail sparrow, but on Saturday and Sunday evenings, without fail, there will be a single empty beer bottle outside her door, a cheering sign that she allows herself a naughty treat in her old age. Young Turkish ladies of the type I have been describing never drink beer.

It might be that young, unmarried Turkish women are just less relaxed than their older counterparts, but it might also be a sign of the times. In today's Turkey, as in China and Japan, there has been a huge surge of professional women in cities, who aspire to marrying successful, wealthy men of the same or higher social status. There are simply not enough of these men, so competition is fierce. They have Western aspirations to have a career and find a worthy match, but Turks are fundamentally conservative and Turkish women are expected to get married and have children without too much hanging around after university. They are pulled both ways and are, I think, unhappy in their new, undefined roles.

By contrast, women from rural areas are decidedly more gutsy than the city girls I have described above, usually because they are married off in their teens and are already managing a family by their early twenties, as well as working outdoors. In doing all this, they develop tough personalities, and I was particularly struck by the directness of the women in the Black Sea area. Perhaps it is precisely to differentiate themselves from these kinds of women that the middle-class city girls take such pains to cultivate their princess act – they are emphasising the fact that they must be cherished and polished, not put to work in the fields.

Never have I felt more like a tomboy than in Istanbul. Confusingly, I am also, by virtue of my Britishness, rather exotic. I do not act like a Turkish woman of my equivalent socio-economic bracket, so Turkish women are often suspicious of me. They are equally suspicious of any Turkish women who do not behave like them.

My ex-flatmate Selin is, to all intents and purposes, a European woman, and more cosmopolitan than most. She is a single thirty-something entrepreneur who dates whoever takes her fancy, travels extensively all over the world and lives in the flat she bought by herself a few years ago in downtown Istanbul. Being a Turk born and bred, she also knows how to cook traditional dishes, how to modify her register and personal news when speaking to elderly family members, how to bargain with a tailor for best results, and more or less how to avoid becoming the subject of gossip. The last is particularly difficult. However much the qualities of independence are supposedly cherished by the 'progressive' classes in Turkey, I have found that women like Selin are generally treated with suspicion, especially by other, less free-spirited women. The gender gap is wider than most people care to admit, and Selin-types are thought to fall disconcertingly somewhere in the middle, with their decidedly masculine quality of self-sufficiency. Selin is perfectly aware of this and I know she sometimes feels torn between her background and her inclinations, however exuberantly carefree her lifestyle demonstrates her to be.

This sounds like a very bleak picture, but it is changing. It was only about ten years ago that people started living separately from their parents before marriage, for example – and very few do, even now. The restrictions of living with one's parents have obvious ramifications on the kind of independent adulthood young people can experience before settling into marriage, setting people like Selin apart. I am not considered a Turk in this respect and seem to be exempt from the same kind of judgement, which is mainly a relief, although it can be disconcerting to feel I am operating outside the realms of local social mores.

Nihal is another atypical friend of mine, whom I do not count as fully Turkish. She is half French, grew up in Paris and moved to Istanbul when she was twenty-two. We agree that it is difficult to have Turkish female friends, and she recently confided to me that, apart from me, all her female friends in Istanbul are lesbians. Two of them are, moreover, transsexuals. 'I have a freak show of friends,' she jokes. Apparently, one of the transsexuals likes Nihal because she treats her like a proper girl, not a sexually confused man. Of course, these are quite unusual examples, but it is telling that socially marginalised people feel much more comfortable with someone who is basically French than with a Turkish girl.

Far more entertaining than the middle-class Turkish female stereotype is the male equivalent: Macho Man. While being, of course, extremely manly, he is highly strung, dependent on his mother and vain. He will readily tell you that he is on a diet or considering a new tattoo. In Turkey there are generally fewer stigmas surrounding the subject of personal presentation, and men are not afraid of vanity. This strikes me as an offshoot of the Middle Eastern propensity towards open displays of prosperity, wealth and, by extension, good looks. In Europe, vulgarity and overt personal displays are considered unseemly, whereas in the Middle East there is a much more straightforward attitude to personal advertisement.

Furthermore, what is deemed 'manly' is totally different in these two regions – European men like to differentiate themselves from women when it comes to personal care. Less is more, and Franz or Fred won't necessarily feel comfortable advertising the amount of time or money they spend on their appearance. Turkish men, by contrast, do not consider it unmasculine to care about their looks; their masculine identity is secure if they are earning money and successful with women. If a Turkish man can spend money on a new suit, or a personal trainer, or an expensive scent, it means he has money to burn and that is the ultimate proof of success. He is the epitome of the L'Oréal slogan: 'Because I'm worth it!'

Gender stereotypes are one thing in Turkey, but the general attitudes to sex – or the potential for sex – are more unsettling. For example, it is culturally accepted that men cheat, and that women do not. If one suggests to a Turkish philanderer or *kelebek* (butterfly) that his wife might be doing exactly the same thing as him, he is offended and incredulous. This is not an attitude unique to Turkey, but it goes noticeably unchallenged here.

The L'Oréal poster boys are jealously guarded. Unmarried women are a threat, especially foreign women. When introduced to a couple, you have to take particular care to court the female contingent for a decent amount of time to show your good intentions, effectively ignoring the male until such time as you are deemed to be safe. It is tantamount to flirting with this woman as her partner looks on, because what you are doing is exaggerating your friendliness to the woman to make up for any attention subsequently paid to the man: a bizarre trial period of unbalanced, sexually tense diplomacy, which is not a promising start, I think, to any friendship. The whole exercise is very tiring and I tend to avoid the hassle by making friends with single men, thereby adding to my wanton foreign persona.

The rules of love in this country are intricate and stressful both for courter and courtee. Men will not give up and women will play all the games in the book. It is exhausting for all concerned. When a relationship is finally achieved, it has the qualities of a legal document drawn up by the senior partners of Slaughter and May. Unrelenting jealousy is taken as read; in fact, most Turks would probably be seriously affronted by an unconcerned partner, and immediately suspect foul play. If the couple are not together at the same social gathering, modern technology comes to their aid: constant messages from '*Aşkım*' ('My Love') pop up on the BlackBerry, the real name of the sender lost in the mists of sentimentality of their interminable courtship. When they are together, silence and boredom reign. It is almost as if the girlfriend or boyfriend is a possession, something which must be safeguarded like a hard-won Hermès handbag, but not enjoyed once gained.

I was once in a club at an advanced hour of the night, music raging and dancers raving. It was a small, crowded space, and I soon noticed a boy and a girl sitting on the sidelines. They were watching the dancing in bored silence, like on-lookers at an awkward school prom. I realised that they were a couple but didn't want to dance with each other for some reason. She could not dance with anyone else because he would get jealous, and he could not dance for the reciprocal reason. It was deadlock. Uncharitable though it sounds, sometimes it seems as though the only thing Turkish couples have in common is jealousy.

The world over, powerful women in business have the reputation of being uncommonly ferocious, having fought their way to the top of a male-heavy world. In Turkey, this is particularly true because not only are they fighting the statistics of a predominantly male workforce but also a much more inherently macho environment than their Western equivalents. Just as we are appalled watching *Mad Men*, or other television programmes which capture the atmosphere of dated, sexist working environments, so am I when observing Turkish office politics.

When I worked as an English coach for bankers in Istanbul, I was astonished by the difference between the men and women with whom I worked. While their levels of English were more or less the same, the men chattered blithely away, grammatical errors aplenty, while the women sat in silence and had to be invited by me to speak. This of course meant that the men got more practice and spoke more fluently, even if their errors continued (they rarely listened to corrections). The women spoke haltingly, using impressive vocabulary but seldom. It was obvious that they were not nearly as confident or as used to voicing their opinions as their male colleagues, which irritated me no end and provoked me into unceremoniously silencing the men on a regular basis.

There is, as far as I know, no gender gap in salaries for equivalent jobs in Turkey, and many businesses are making an effort to promote female employees to counteract the current discrepancy between the sexes in top positions. This is an important example of the improvements being made in Turkey at the moment. Unfortunately, there is an apparently immovable dinosaur of a problem in the form of old-fashioned sexual dynamics. Women seem very happy to conform to their unthreatening, meek stereotype, and do very little to quash the expectations that they would rather go off and have a family instead of fighting the competition for their superior's job.

Out of the chrysalis of this unpromising situation come a few Thatcheresque dragonflies who simply flatten the opposition en route to top positions at big companies and even heads of region for internationals. A friend of mine working for McKinsey came from London to Istanbul to interview for a job at a Turkish computer gaming firm. Confidently expecting that her dazzling CV and precocious position at McKinsey would count for something, she was unpleasantly surprised by her interrogation at the hands of the female CEO of the Turkish computer company.

'What can you offer us? You can't even speak Turkish. Do you understand the Turkish market? Explain yourself.'

As my friend related this, I had in my mind's eye an image of a cross between the Queen of Hearts in *Alice in Wonderland* and Miss Trunchbull from *Matilda*. This lady does, in fact, have a reputation for being unpleasant, but I can think of at least a couple of other Turkish she-dragons in top jobs who have the same aggressive manner. Whether or not she was such a bully in the playground, she has either developed this personality over time to cope with the pressure of out-performing male competition, or her natural aggression has made it possible for her to succeed on what is otherwise too brutal a playing field. It is probably a mixture of both.

The upshot of it was that my friend was intimidated and put off by this CEO and went back to London with a new appreciation for the working environment she had previously taken for granted. If she had been interviewed by a male CEO, she would most likely be working in Istanbul today, but she might also have felt isolated from a clique of female colleagues. When office politics become harder to negotiate than the job itself, you know there is a problem.

4

Women Undercover

Visitors to Turkey are often confused by seeing covered and uncovered women socialising together. They ask questions like: 'Don't they despise each other?' 'Isn't it awkward?' 'Doesn't the headscarf-wearing woman look at the bare-headed girl and think: you're going to hell?' 'Surely the uncovered girl thinks the covered one is backward?'

If this were the case, they wouldn't be friends. There are definitely some religious women who wouldn't choose to associate with nonreligious women, and vice versa, but the happy reality is that friendships like this do exist. It says a lot about our Islamophobic preconceptions that we expect them not to; in London as in Istanbul, I can be friends with a Jew or a communist, and we can find something in common beyond religious or political beliefs. I take these visitors' incredulity as a sign that they see the headscarf as a kind of blinker, physically representing a mental blockage, an inability to recognise other people as worthy of trust or even interaction. Turks share a great deal beyond religion, if this is indeed a divisive subject: the ostensibly nonreligious Turkish woman might be a sincere believer who does not see the need to wear the headscarf; the headscarf-wearer might wear it from habit, but have private doubts or questions about Islam. Perhaps they are engaged in a passionate theological discussion, perhaps not.

Headscarves are a hugely emotionally charged subject, variously taken as symbols of repression, freedom, feminism and chauvinism depending on individual viewpoint. I particularly object to the use of headscarves as a political tool, or a vehicle for social pressure, on either side of the debate. My personal feelings on the subject were tested shortly after I moved to Turkey.

In the bitter January of my arrival, I was walking along a shopping street with my scarf pulled up over my head to keep warm – I have done this since my teen years in London, and it simply didn't occur to me to stop doing so in Istanbul. As I walked with my friend past the outdoor table of a café, one of those seated, a lady in a headscarf, looked and nodded at me in a subtle but unmistakable gesture of recognition and sisterhood. My Turkish companion, an uncovered girl, got no such look. I cannot quite explain why this was so unsettling – partly, of course, because it was unexpected and unmerited; this lady had totally mistaken me for someone religious and akin to herself in her beliefs. It was also that my friend was ignored in what otherwise might have been a straightforwardly friendly gesture that really bothered me. Most of all, the realisation hit home that, even in this most Western-seeming part of the country, a habit that I had formed for practical reasons in a secular country had suddenly taken on a religious and cultural significance. The lady's recognition had been a form of congratulation, an acceptance into some kind of club – I felt like a fraud while resenting her mislabelling. While I had been prepared to modify my dress to fit in with conservative expectations (covering up in religious areas, basically), I had not expected the opposite problem – that covering up for practical reasons would be automatically taken for religious intent. Hitting the covered nail on the head has turned out to be surprisingly difficult; for instance, when scrupulously dressing in my baggiest trousers and cardigans in the south-east of Turkey, where plenty of women wear fetchingly fitted outfits while keeping the mandatory headscarf, I stood out both as a *yabancı* and a terrible dresser.

One of the most ridiculous contradictions of the Middle East is the habit of pushing the limits of what is sartorially permissible for a woman, while keeping within the confines of superficial conservatism. I noticed this most in Lebanon, where women are often covered but at the same time exercise considerable freedom to show off both their body and a flashy fashion sense. I have seen many a young Arab girl dramatically made up and wearing an outfit that can only be described as provocative, despite the fact that she is also wearing a headscarf and no flesh is showing. The clingiest of long-sleeved nylon tops, cinched-in belt, spray-on jeans and tottering diamanté heels are – to a Western eye at least – at odds with a headscarf, though this is always colourful and usually matches either the clingy top or eye-shadow colour. The whole effect is bizarrely paradoxical and quite mesmerising.

Interestingly, I do not see this as often in Turkey, where covered girls seem to be conservative in both intention and dress, and do not seem to be fighting their covered state. I think this might be because there is a broader spectrum of Islamic expression in Turkey, in that many women who do not wear headscarves are still accepted as Muslim. In other Middle Eastern countries there is a stricter cultural code, where Islam is synonymous with certain rules (like keeping covered as a woman). In Turkey, you can be both an un- covered woman and a Muslim, and that is one of its great strengths. However, secular Turks increasingly worry that the country is headed towards a more Middle Eastern mindset in which everything is black and white: no headscarf, no Muslim credibility.

I have a great deal of sympathy for those Lebanese girls. They are young, hormonal, and want to show themselves off – why on earth not? The fact that they manage to do this despite the intended restrictions of their conservative code of dress is actually a victory, but it is patently ridiculous and the restrictions can only serve to exacerbate the girls' frustra- tion. You see this kind of small-scale rebellion at every level of conservatism. I have observed Arab tourists in full burqas in Istanbul shopping malls with only their eyes showing – but what eyes! All the effort that would have been put into an outfit is concentrated on the only tiny strip showing us who this person is – eyes so immaculately dressed in mascara and eyeliner, eyebrows shaped to perfection, that the difference between this and the shapeless black sack she is wearing is al- most, but not quite, comical. If, as in some cases, the eye area is covered by a mask or visor, you must look downward to the feet for some sign of personal identity or femininity – beau- tifully pedicured feet in exquisite Jimmy Choos or Manolos. I find these cases very sad, and quite different from the young girls who have managed to buck the system.

Significantly, there is a huge amount of money in the Islamic clothing industry, which is expanding fast in Turkey with the growth of the religiously conservative middle class.

Companies like Primo Moda advertise items for women such as the Hasema bathing suit, or 'burkini', which covers the body from top to toe, and long cotton sleeves for 'when you wish you could wear that three-quarter-length shirt if only it were long-sleeved'. These kinds of brands declare themselves the champions of the 'modest but fashionable woman', which is fair enough, but what I cannot reconcile is the paradox between the nature of the clothing on sale and the alluring pose of the model in the photographs, the same pose you see in mainstream fashion shots everywhere. Clothes look better worn by attractive women with hands on hips and arch expressions, which is why the companies advertise them this way, but this is directly at odds with the ethos of modesty which supposedly defines the brand. The female form is a battleground in this kind of situation – the line between glamour and dowdiness is stretched and blurred in the quest for the acceptable yet attractive marriage of modesty and femininity. It is total hypocrisy.

Burqas, like headscarves, are a highly emotive subject in Turkey. There are, of course, critics of conservative Islam everywhere, but in Turkey overt displays of religion are seen by many as a terrible betrayal of the principles of the secularist, modern republic as envisaged by Mustafa Kemal Atatürk. From 1923, he brought in a series of reforms to prohibit the wearing of traditional and religious clothing, starting with the fez (the famous 'Hat Law'), and including, most significantly, the law relating to 'Prohibited Garments' in 1934. These garments included the veil and turban, and Western-style dress was actively promoted in their stead.

Burqa'ed women can be seen as far afield as Harrods or

the Champs-Elysées, but their significance in Turkey is different. There is the recent surge in Arab tourists to Turkey to account for the presence of these particular ladies, but the burqa'ed form in general is a relatively new sight in Turkey, stemming from a religious demographic steadily growing in confidence since the mid-eighties, after the coup in 1980. The rules governing the wearing of headscarves and burqas in public institutions have a long and chequered history in Turkey. Women have been turned away from universities, civil service positions and indeed government posts for wearing a headscarf, but throughout various periods in the last thirty years the rule has been ignored, bent and reinforced. In February 2008, the AKP put forward a bill to revoke the headscarf ban in universities, demanding that everyone should have an equal right to education, but five months later, Turkey's Constitutional Court upheld the ban, arguing that secularism was an integral part of Turkey's constitution. In 2010, the Higher Education Board (YÖK) sent a circular to universities telling them to ease up on the 'no headscarf' rule. Many universities complied, but many others insisted on observing the ban and prevented headscarved students entering lectures and classes. The most recent call for headscarf acceptance came in the controversial 'Democratisation Package' put forward by the AKP in October 2013, further escalating the legal back-and-forth between defenders and critics of the ban.

The burqa is by no means ubiquitous but is not uncommon in some parts of the country, including some parts of Istanbul, as I discussed in the opening chapters. While I have many sympathies with the Kemalist point of view, and admit to finding burqas disturbing, I think headscarves are a different matter. I would not wear one out of choice myself, but I do think that a non-judgemental attitude is much healthier given the indisputable fact that the majority of the Turkish population is religious in practice as well as theory, and women from a religious background in many cases feel more comfortable and indeed more free to go about their business if they can wear a headscarf in public. I can even understand those who charge headscarf-banning authorities with the very crime of which they are accused; namely, repression. Reciprocally, I very much welcome not feeling judged for being uncovered in areas where most women wear a headscarf. It should work both ways; sometimes it does not.

My mother spent the weeks preceding my departure to Istanbul trying to convince me to leave all my summer clothes behind. She is scarred by her own experience of arriving in Ankara as a naïve, mini-skirted student in the sixties, fresh from provincial Northern Cyprus, excited to wear her fashionable new clothes in the capital city of Turkey. When she was walking down a busy street one day, a venerable old man called out to her. She stopped politely, waiting for him to approach, whereupon he slapped the back of her bare thigh so hard that she had a red handprint of shame to mark the rest of her journey. She does not want me to go through a similar experience, which is fair enough, but I have learned my own way.

A lot of the fear and hate that secular Turks feel for their religious counterparts is fuelled by the notion of rural Turkey, in particular the east, as a backward, fanatical society that drags the country back to the Dark Ages and stops it from fulfilling its potential as an advanced state on a par with (the rest of) Europe. Religion should not be confused with poverty, obviously, but one can see why it is easy to unconsciously equate these impoverished, devout communities with the problems that plague them.

In my mind, the problem is not religion but a very deep-seated patriarchy, which makes it difficult for girls to participate fully in either school or an independent career. This situation self-perpetuates from generation to generation, mainly due to the socially cancerous effects of a generally poor education system. It is hard to make the distinction between patriarchy and conservative religion, particularly when it comes to girls being excluded from school, and this is not the place to attempt it. I can merely report what I have heard and observed.

Despite nationwide rules applying to school attendance, the number of girls in high school is significantly lower than boys in every region of Turkey, and particularly in the east. This is often due to very large family sizes which call for everyone to chip in to the agricultural labour central to many households' livelihoods, and the care of the younger members of the family. The fact that girls (and in many cases boys too) attend just a couple of years of school and then drop out is obviously detrimental to their future prospects. Both in Antep and in Diyarbakır, I was struck by the sight of children climbing over the fences of school yards to play with their peers at break time, unnoticed by harassed teachers amid the mayhem. It was clearly a daily occurrence; a very sad token of what these kids were missing out on both in terms of camaraderie and formal education.

Beyond this root problem, there is a fundamental lack of autonomy that extends to these girls when they grow up. They are restricted in terms of financial independence, choice in marriage and opportunities to socialise. The ramifications of breaking free of these restrictions are occasionally reported in national media in the form of honour killings, for example. Again, this is widely viewed in the West as a phenomenon peculiar to Islam, but I think it is inextricably linked to the more archaic, regional mores of family identity and kinship, which are much harder for an outsider to understand and indeed to criticise. Either way, what is really needed is not criticism but an attempt to solve at least the basic problems.

The greatest beacon of hope I have seen in the east of Turkey is an organisation called the Turkish Grameen Microfinance Project (TGMP), which offers business loans to women all over the country, but most significantly to repressed women in the Kurdish and Arab communities in the southeast of Turkey. All across rural Turkey, from Antalya to the Black Sea, I have seen women working in fields, chopping wood, planting crops and hoeing. In cities, where the public eye is more present than in the countryside, women work in the home, raising huge families. Either way, Turkish women work just as hard as men, if not more so. The difference is that they do not get paid as men do, and that is why the TGMP is so revolutionary in that it gives them the chance to take financial responsibility and the potential to make a lot of profit from their own enterprise.

In May 2012 I visited the regional project headquarters in Diyarbakır, Urfa, Mardin and Gaziantep, where I interviewed many of the women and the people who run the project. It was founded in 2003 by Dr Muhammad Yunus, the Nobel Peace Prize-winning creator of the microcredit concept, and Aziz Akgül, a former Turkish MP with Kurdish origins, from Diyarbakır. After much initial scepticism, both from the Turkish government and rural women unexpectedly offered the chance to be self-employed, the scheme has had resounding success; so far more than $100 million has been given out in loans, there is currently a hundred per cent pay-back rate and around sixty thousand women are actively en-rolled in the scheme as I write. Groups of women from any particular area sign up to secure each other's loans in the event of someone being unable to repay, which simultan-eously gives the participants confidence while galvanising entrepreneurial energy – no one wants to let the side down. Moreover, the enormity and novelty of being entrusted with money means that these women are extremely cautious in-vestors. Those who fund TGMP do not expect huge returns, but there is easily enough interest generated to cover costs, consistently.

TGMP serves as a significant counter-example to Turkey's generally poor reputation in the areas both of gender equality and interaction with Kurdish and other minorities. These women, as former victims of religious suppression, terror and domestic violence, are at face value the least likely of success-ful business people. Yet here they are, proudly independent and quietly working away, while women's-rights NGOs, des-pite sterling efforts, achieve very little in the face of ingrained patriarchy.

Most of the TGMP loan holders I met were shy, unassuming ladies who looked nothing like entrepreneurial social pioneers, although that's exactly what they were. You got the sense that while they were ambitious for their children, particularly their daughters, they themselves were working because they had to, and the benefits of social and financial independence were secondary to supplementing the household coffers.

Occasionally, however, I came across some unabashed feminists. Safiye Hanım, whom I met in Diyarbakır with the local TGMP co-ordinators, was in her element as she showed us into the restaurant she bought six months ago, chattering all the while and sporadically shouting instructions to her all-male staff in the kitchen. She belongs to the flamboyantly covered class of ladies I mentioned earlier, more common to countries like Lebanon; her vivid purple eye shadow demanded notice, and her personality burned through the headscarf she wore as if it were an accessory of purely sartorial choice. Safiye sat us down and ordered *pide* (a kind of bread filled with cheese or meat), obliterating our protests with a dazzling hostess smile.

'Of course you must eat! Alev *hanım*, you are new to Diyarbakır? Welcome, eat, eat!'

Safiye, with impressive initiative, approached TGMP when her husband was laid off work as a *dolmuş* driver as the result of an accident. Most newcomers are referred to the programme by friends, or are gradually persuaded to join by TGMP employees who conduct a sort of conversion crusade, methodically targeting local homes. Safiye, however, approached the organisation herself, bullying the Diyarbakır office staff with relentless charisma into advancing an unprecedented amount of money, straight up, so that she could put down the deposit for the purchase of the restaurant. The TGMP girls accompanying me on this visit fell silent, intimidated, as Safiye turned to the subject of her monthly credit allowance with all the assurance of a seasoned City trader: 'Three thousand lira? What a joke! Girls, how can I run this lot on that? I need at least ten thousand. Tell Mehmet Bey [the chief of the Diyarbakır office] what I want, he won't refuse me. We understand business, Mehmet and I.' When I asked Safiye whether her male staff resented being subordinate to a woman, she laughed and yelled out to the kitchen: 'Ali! Serdar! Do you resent me? No? Back to work then!'

I spent my last day in Diyarbakır, a Monday, in the TGMP headquarters speaking to women who came in to collect their weekly allowance, plus the odd insurance payout. The first of them arrived at nine in the morning, and by eleven the offices were packed with seated and standing women, but it was oddly quiet save for the calling out of queue numbers and a low hum of conversation. It was like a very refined and sedentary market, wads of cash handed here and there, women waiting patiently in turn for the means to run their lives. A few of the women were pregnant and many had children with them. When I asked one lady why her son was not in school, she told me that state schooling is only provided from the age of seven; before that age parents have to pay for private schooling. This is a hindrance for mothers trying to work; in an attempt to solve the problem, some mothers choose to take their older children out of school to look after younger siblings, and, unsurprisingly, those chosen are generally girls. This was yet another example of the inadequacies of an archaic education system affecting the future chances of girls or the freedom of their mothers, and I had to temper my reaction in the presence of this quietly resigned lady, steadily answering my rather impertinent questions.

A further benefit of the TGMP programme is the social support which is not explicitly planned but comes about organically due to the clublike nature of the organisation, and is as valuable to the women involved as the monetary help. Because the programme is restricted to women, husbands of prospective members are relaxed about allowing their spouses to attend meetings and work with the other women involved. This is actually quite rare, considering that many women in these communities are not allowed to socialise out of the house alone. They are given the opportunity to discover solidarity in these group scenarios, they realise that they are not alone with their problems of marital disputes or violence, and it acts as a form of therapy.

On the flight back from Diyarbakır, I tried to work out what it was that had impressed me so much about TGMP, aside from the extraordinary cases and individuals I had met. Something was missing, but in a good way: an agenda. There is no rhetoric about gender empowerment or social change, or any political content to the programme whatsoever. It is completely direct and straightforward, giving money to the women running their own businesses, ensuring independence and self-respect through the very simple procedure of giving a manageable loan. Even better, the secondary effects of the project are beginning to be felt, and at the very least, sixty thousand women are successfully running businesses in some of the most patriarchal, impoverished and conservative areas of Turkey – something which I very much doubt any government could have achieved, even if they had the inclination.

Seeing these kinds of women makes me optimistic about social progress in the east; TGMP is of course a catalyst, but I have seen signs of change in other cases, which gives hope that, gradually, the idea of education and independence in women as a positive thing is catching on in the area. It is not something that can happen overnight; I hope it happens within my lifetime.

One evening in the old quarter of Mardin, my boyfriend and I were toiling up the hill to the castle and its unparalleled view of Mesopotamia. It was one of those occasions when both of us were rather tired and secretly would have happily given up to go and have some *çay* and narghile somewhere, but neither wanted to be the first to voice this. Occasionally we encountered a shepherd or villager coming down the hill, exchanged our *selam*s and eyed them enviously as they descended. Suddenly, happy voices hailed us from on high and we looked up to see a child and young woman in an almond tree by the side of the path, vigorously shaking the branches and scattering furry green almonds onto laughing family members assembled below. We were invited to share the almonds (surprisingly delicious when unripe) and to inspect their small garden and house.

Jumping down from the tree, the young woman, headscarved like every local woman I had seen in the area, cheerily held forth on the magnificent view of Mardin stretched out before us. It turned out she was about to leave her hometown and head off to Mersin University to take a degree in religious studies. Her family were very proud of her. I have to admit that when I heard the subject of her degree my heart sank a little, before I forced myself to consider her situation fairly. Here was a confident young woman, devout but unfazed by a foreign couple, so far showing herself to be more open-minded than I was. The attitude of a Kemalist, which I have undoubtedly absorbed to some extent, is always that of automatic suspicion and distaste when confronted with a mix of religion and education: it produces a sort of mental curdling akin to the mixing of yoghurt and lemon. Put in perspective, however, this young woman's prospects were very much preferable to the fates of girls who, for generations, have spent their formative years in fields rather than classrooms. This girl had been to school; she was making her own choice to go to university and will lead a relatively independent life, compared to her grandmother or even her mother.

The older generation, while not in a position to enjoy educational opportunities themselves, are also getting used to the gradually shifting lie of the land. On the bus from Urfa to Mardin, I chatted to an old lady who told me with great pride that her granddaughter was sitting exams for university entry, but she was prouder still that all her daughters were married and mothers themselves. This lady came from a generation whose foremost priority for their daughters was security, and in the east that still means marriage and cementing family life with children and more children (the average number per family in the eastern region comprising Mardin and Siirt was seven in 2011). Unfortunately, it does not look like the government is interested in reducing the poverty and strain caused by huge family sizes – in fact, quite the opposite. Erdoğan has repeatedly called for Turkish couples to have at least three children in order to ensure a booming economy. He explained it succinctly: 'One or two children mean bankruptcy. Three children mean we are not improving but not receding either. So, I repeat, at least three children are necessary in each family, because our population risks ageing.' During the Gezi protests in 2013, Erdoğan claimed that unspecified 'forces', jealous of Turkey's growing power, had tried to scupper the Turkish economy by encouraging birth control and abortion, but declared that he would not let this pernicious situation continue.

On 25 May 2012, Erdoğan announced at an AKP Women's Conference that 'abortion is murder', sparking a media frenzy. Over the next few days, a bill effectively banning abortion was discussed. Significantly, this issue was raised smack bang in the middle of another incredibly controversial subject, namely the furore over the Uludere air raid which had happened five months previously and had recently been brought back into the media, much to the government's detriment. Thirty-four Kurdish smugglers had been killed on the Iraqi border by Turkish soldiers, who had apparently mistaken them for PKK (Kurdistan Workers' Party) rebels on the basis of aerial images provided by US surveillance. Erdoğan has never apologised for the incident, and seized the occasion of a press conference to tell journalists that 'every abortion is an Uludere'. The extraordinary nature of the bill's announcement seemed to achieve what critics of the government saw as an attempt to distract attention from Uludere to something which would not, in the end, be put into practice, and which would in the meantime please the government's religious voting base.

The new legislation would change the present ten-week limit for termination to four weeks, at which point most women do not even realise they are pregnant. It sought to eliminate any feasible exceptions, including pregnancies resulting from rape. The Turkish government, we were assured, would magnanimously take into foster care the babies born of rape. As an addendum to the abortion bill, it was also proposed that Caesarean sections should become less easily available. This seemed more reasonable, since around fifty per cent of mothers in Turkey are given Caesareans as a matter of course, because in state hospitals it is more convenient for the doctors to be able to schedule births, and in private hospitals, more profitable. But Erdoğan's questionable claim that Caesareans limit mothers to two births immediately cast suspicion on his motives.

Of course, an outcry ensued, with protests all over the country, petitions, noted feminists writing impassioned articles like the Turkish novelist Elif Shafak's for the *Guardian*, and a great deal of foreign interest, especially from the EU, who immediately cautioned the Turkish government against restricting women's right to choose. Ironically, Turkey introduced the current abortion law nearly thirty years ago. It is hard not to view the current situation as a serious regression.

Bolstering theories that the bill was only proposed to draw attention from the Uludere raid, and to gratify the AKP's considerable devout following, nothing concrete was passed, but the subject has not been dropped. It has resurfaced sporadically since its sensational introduction, with the AKP trying to include clauses in the proposed new constitution relating to the 'healthy continuation of the human race', which, among other things, would prohibit sperm banks because 'every child has the right to know his father'. A tour company which foresaw a gap in the market and started advertising three-day 'abortion trips' to destinations such as London, Northern Cyprus and Bosnia had its licence revoked by the Ministry of Tourism.

You can be as cynical as you like about the AKP's political manoeuvring, the judicious timing and juggling of its contentious announcements, and claim that they are mainly for show, but there is an undeniable undercurrent of religious rhetoric that is, to my mind, disturbing. By all means, allow people to practise their religion, and to have an unexpected baby, or wear a headscarf, or fast during Ramadan. But it is when Mehmet Görmez, who as head of Turkey's Religious Affairs Directorate is both government official and high-ranking Muslim cleric, says that 'The mother is not the real owner of the foetus she carries [. . .] It is a gross injustice to handle this issue as a women's issue, as men have always held the greatest responsibility in this issue throughout history' that my blood really boils. It parboils on hearing this sentence uttered in a purely religious context, but what really angers me is the political voice this man has. Turkey needs to wake up to the real issues surrounding women's rights. In 2011, women's participation in the labour force fell to thirty-one per cent. In the same year, the name of the Ministry for Women and Family Affairs was changed to Family and Social Policies, at a time when women's rights desperately need addressing. The last thing anyone needed was a bill limiting abortion.

Being a woman with a firmly secularist outlook and a Muslim mother, I have a rational respect for religious Turks but am often surprised by my unexpectedly strong emotional reactions to being treated as an alien entity by certain Turkish men. I have already spoken of my sad, one-sided friendship with the Cheese Man – that I have become used to. But odd occasions catch me out; for instance, in Urfa my boyfriend and I were given a tour of the nearby Atatürk Dam by a friend of a friend called Burak (incidentally, the name of the Prophet Muhammad's horse). An otherwise lovely man, I noticed he never directly addressed me or really looked at me. When it came to our goodbyes, I thanked him profusely and held out my hand. He looked away and made no move to meet it, leaving me to lamely back away. In hindsight, it must have been quite a comical scene, and indeed my boyfriend joked about it as we walked off, but I was upset. At the risk of sounding melodramatic, I had felt like an Untouchable – which, of course, I was. In my hitherto sheltered state, I was convinced that some great outrage had taken place – an offence to my sex and my status, something that must surely be illegal in modern society. When I asked my more knowledgeable friends about this behaviour, it turned out that the man was probably a Shafi'i (a member of a certain school of religious law within Sunni Islam); if I had touched him (or, worse, the other way round), he would have had to wash and pray to cleanse himself.

Since then, I have grown more used to examples like this, and have learned, at least in part, not to take offence from individuals. Islam should not only be thought of in terms of crazy fundamentalist examples like this. Mehmet Bey, for example, was the model of gentlemanly behaviour, kind, patient, working for very little money with women on the

TGMP project, a typical AKP-supporting, moderately religious Muslim. How these two men could identify with each other is slightly beyond me.

There are plenty of liberal women like me in Turkey, but they are more equipped to deal with the gamut of social and religious etiquette, having grown up with it. In a way this makes life easier for them, but they are also judged unfavourably by the Turkish standard, which I am not. They are often in the slightly uncomfortable position of having Western aspirations fettered by the expectations of their family and social group, in some cases, or even just by their colleagues and acquaintances. Even if these expectations are not expressed, women like Selin, my ex-flatmate, are acutely aware of what is expected in Turkish society, and are either consciously or unconsciously shaped by that.

Recently I had an enlightening conversation with a Turkish gardener called Murat, who worked for a friend with whom I was staying in a village on the Aegean coast. He was enquiring about the other guests, and the conversation turned to who was sleeping in which room. It was clear that he was rather shocked that unmarried young couples were sharing rooms, and I took the plunge and asked him to explain why.

'These people are in love, but not married?'

Yes.

'And tomorrow they might love someone else?'

Maybe.

'In Turkey, we men like to know we are the first, we look for *kızlık* [literally, 'maidenhood']. In England, don't they look for that?'

I tried, hesitantly, to explain that people change, love fades and blossoms again, etc., but was aware of sounding rather lame and Bertie Woosteresque after Murat's unapologetic, hardline logic. I must point out that he was not condemning our lifestyle, and did not mention religion once – he had the slightly prudish outlook of many Turks, but I think he genuinely wanted to know why it didn't bother us that our partners had previously loved Another, or even Others.

Critics of traditional Turkey are cynical about this obsession with *kızlık* (virginity, basically), saying that Turkish men feel secure marrying virgins because there is no chance that they will be compared unfavourably, as a lover, to another man. Whether or not that is true of the majority of cases, I am not convinced that such a premeditated concern is at the root of it. It is not such a peculiar phenomenon, and while to an English ear it may sound rather Victorian, you just have to look at the Bible-bashing belt of the US today, or the Catholics of southern Italy, to see that it is far from being particular to Turkey or indeed Islam. I think it is rather a primeval instinct, and in the case of Turkey, at least, it has only a coincidental religious slant; in an archaic society, everything you do is part of your religion, because your religion is formed by what you do – relatively few people actually read the Koran, but many of its edicts are part and parcel of their communities, which have been formed over thousands of years. Mores like the prizing of virginity predate formal religion across much of the world. It must also be said that Turks are indescribably romantic – 'my one true love' is the sentiment that no doubt reinforces this particular tradition (to suppose that it created the tradition would be appropriately but misguidedly romantic in itself).

To return to Murat's attitude, which mirrors that of many Turks I have met, I would like to make clear that I was not, and very rarely am, made to feel judged for being different. Murat, for instance, was almost childlike in his quest to understand my attitude, and to explain his own, with not a hint of rebuke in his voice or expression. I had a long girly gossip with his wife the following afternoon, and when she expressed the hope that my boyfriend and I would get married it was in no way a holier-than-thou, 'lest you rot in hell' hope, but the genuine, generous impulse of one human being wishing happiness for another. I have often felt that, despite my supposedly open mind and liberal attitudes, I am much quicker to judge these people than they are to judge me.

Too often people in the West, and indeed some from the East, regard women in headscarves as fettered, unhappy, symbolic of some dark Islamic threat, as though the headscarf were as simple as a uniform of repression. In Turkey this is even more the case because Atatürk's anti-religious rulings emerged in conjunction with unambiguously progressive changes such as granting the vote to women; in the 1935 general election, eighteen female MPs joined the Turkish Parliament before women in many European countries even had the right to vote. Thus (anti-)religious reforms and social reforms have been mixed up in the Turkish psyche for a long time, leading to a deeper distrust of religion among some circles than seems reasonable. The current government is attempting to solve this, but it still remains to be seen if it will succeed. More to the point, I am not convinced that religious and political figureheads have done an awful lot to support women.

I wonder if Prime Minister Erdoğan ever thinks of Atatürk's stirring words in the early days of the republic: 'If, from now on, women do not share in the social life of the nation, we shall never attain our full development. We shall remain irremediably backward, incapable of treating on equal terms with the civilisations of the West.' Depressingly, things have regressed since then. In July 2010, at the International Women's Meeting in Istanbul, Turkey's current leader proclaimed: 'Men and women are not equal. They only complement each other.'

I find it even more frustrating when Turkish women merrily jump on the misogynistic bandwagon. In 2012 the head of Erzurum's Women Entrepreneurs, Zeynep Çomaklı, gave a speech in which she said: 'Woman should not be governors or district governors. You should make a sound when you slam your fist on the desk. Not every post is a post for a woman.' Çomakli may not be as public a figure as Erdoğan, but she is a woman, supposedly a role model for ambitious women in Turkey. The struggle to achieve sexual equality seems even bleaker when women are fighting themselves as well as male politicians and family members. With or without headscarves, sexual equality remains an important goal in Turkey and, unfortunately, it sometimes feels like a goal which is very distant.

5

Transvestites in Tarlabaşı

A male friend of mine who used to live in Syria once said to me: 'It's very easy to be gay in Syria. Men are so affectionate with each other that it goes unnoticed. Besides, homosexuality doesn't officially exist, so really . . . what's to notice?'

Striking though this revelation initially was, I realised that there is a similar situation in Turkey, definitely a Middle Eastern country in this respect. There is plenty of what in a Western country would be thought of as homosexual behaviour, but relatively few of the men having sexual relations with other men would consider themselves gay. They are probably married fathers of four, their sexuality not in question either to outsiders or to themselves. Turkey is relatively free of the strict classifications of sexual behaviour that are in place in Western societies, but it is equally free of the Western tolerance for men who openly profess a preference for men over women. In a country where many young men in conservative communities are either in arranged marriages or unmarried, without the option of casual relationships with women, a kind of homosexuality of convenience is not a surprising outcome. It is accepted as normal in practice (rather like old-fashioned English attitudes to boarding school and the navy), but not in theory – homosexuality 'by choice' is first ignored, then condemned, which is bad news for gay rights.

Physical affection between Turkish men does not have the same implications as it does between Western men, where it is unusual and therefore must be classified as gay. Turks in general are very affectionate, and what Americans call bromance is absolutely the norm. Men unselfconsciously link arms while walking down the street, kiss each other on the cheek, give a gentle squeeze to the shoulders of a seated friend. I have to admit it was odd for me at first, used as I was to the chilly timbre of most English interactions, but now it is perfectly normal, and I have got used to regarding affection between men in the same spirit as affection between women. When I am in England I miss the displays of public affection which are symptomatic of the warmth felt between men, women, friends, even the most casual of acquaintances in this hot-blooded country. This warmth does not equate to sexual interest, but sometimes they can overlap. What is refreshing is that there is not the same stigma attendant on male affection that still persists in, say, the UK, despite the politically correct attitudes that have been encouraged in the last few decades to remove it.

I live in Beyoğlu, which is the gay hub of Istanbul and full of areas which resemble very down-to-earth versions of Old Compton Street in Soho. A couple of years after I moved to Istanbul I met Ami Nouvel, a documentary maker based in Berlin who was making a film about Kurdish 'gay for pay' sex workers in Beyoğlu. I was intrigued by the project and joined him on set.

Ami's main focus was Aquarius, a gay brothel in Beyoğlu. It has a licence for a sauna but is in fact very well known on the grapevine (and indeed now in *Lonely Planet*) as a brothel. I was absolutely not allowed in by the owner, who threatened to call the police when he saw me, but I managed to sneak in a side door with Ami and his crew when the owner was welcoming two Japanese tourists in. We entered into a long, dingy hall filled with wet towels being dried by two industrial-sized fans at either end, and as we walked along, these swirled to reveal young men in tiny *hamam*-style towels wandering to and from clients in rooms off the hall.

We found out that the six employees of the sauna were all brothers of varying ages, from a big Kurdish family which had moved to Istanbul from the south-east around fifteen years ago when the father was jailed for having 'terrorist sympathies'. The second eldest brother runs the joint (but does not work there as his brothers do), and looks like a typically conservative, religious Kurd. At one point I was astonished to see him perform his prayers in a corner of the reception room as we chatted outside to his young brother who was offering his services to both Ami (who is gay) and me. What I soon realised was that these men did not consider themselves gay – they were merely doing a job, and getting paid very well by Istanbul standards. They were at pains to distance themselves from their professional persona when they talked to us, flirting outrageously with me to prove their heterosexuality, which was rather strange. The eldest of them, Sabri, confided to us that two of his brothers had never been with a woman and this was a source of great misery to them. They were clearly confused about their sexuality but wanted to class themselves as straight to outsiders, and I think a great part of this was because they were from a conservative family. They claimed to only ever act as the active partner, because they saw that as the more masculine of homosexual roles, but it is really impossible to know whether that was just an attempt to save their pride.

Sabri was wonderfully open with us, probably flattered to be treated as a person rather than a sex worker, and eager to discuss the peculiarities of his trade. He told us that twenty years ago there was much less competition in the sauna industry and the service provided was much more perfunctory. Competition is now fierce, and clients demand more – they want 'love', some semblance of affection and conversation, so that it has become about more than the act itself. Sabri's brother, Mustafa, had just come back from Singapore, where he had been taken by an overly attached client who now referred to him as his 'boyfriend', taking him on long holidays because he didn't want him working for anyone else. Mustafa had mixed feelings about this. He was unhappy because he saw himself as a straight man working for money, but this particular job overlapped into the realms of relationship. He was adamantly straight, but appreciated the money and the lifestyle – a tricky dilemma. One comfort, at least, was that he was the active partner in this particular sexual relationship.

Crucially, there is a big difference in Turkey between a man's possible roles in sex: the *aktif* ('active') participant is adamantly a Man – *Erkek*, executing his manly duty, notwithstanding who his sexual partner is. He might be rather embarrassed to be discovered with a man rather than a woman, but his (hetero)sexual identity would not be in question, as it would in the West. The *pasif* ('passive') participant is the 'unmanly' one, who might suffer prejudice. In Ancient Greece, a similar hierarchy existed in relation to the active and passive

roles of homosexual lovers: in brief, the former were respected and the latter were not. To illustrate the current attitude
in Turkey, one only has to look at Tarlabaşı Boulevard in Beyoğlu, which is liberally scattered with transvestite prostitutes
at all times of day. They quite regularly pick up customers,
who do not seem unduly worried about being spotted going off with a faux femme fatale. The transvestite is probably
cheaper than the female prostitute in a brothel nearby. That
is about as complicated as it gets, for the punter. Interestingly,
the gay brothers in Aquarius charged considerably more than
transvestite sex workers; the former charged 250 lira an hour,
whereas transvestite workers charge around thirty (pre-bar-
gaining). I learnt the latter by persuading a very embarrassed
male friend to ask one broad-shouldered lady her price late
one night in the street as we passed; I followed at a discreet
distance so as not to blow his cover.

I occasionally go and drink tea with a traditional Turkish
tailor called Selçuk, a small, bespectacled and very respectable elderly gentleman with a surprisingly naughty twinkle
in his eye, whose office is in Tarlabaşı. We chat of this and
that, and one day he related an anecdote that could only
have happened in Turkey. The previous evening he had left
work and was walking to the bus stop on Tarlabaşı Boulevard
when one of the transvestites on the street corner opposite
his office yelled out: 'Oi, four-eyes! Let's make a baby!'
Selçuk had seen the funny side of this, declined the offer and
trotted on his way, but I found it astonishing that a man who
prays five times a day did not have a more outraged reaction. When Selçuk was telling the story, he used the word *yu-
muşak* (soft) to describe the transvestite, in this case meaning

effeminate or camp. Selçuk's tone was amused rather than aggressive or disgusted, and about as far from the menace of 'faggot' as possible.

There is definitely homophobia in Turkey, but it usually takes the form of childish teasing of men who are openly camp and therefore deemed 'unmanly', as opposed to those who simply want to have sex regardless of with whom. When there is discrimination or hostility, it is reserved for those who make their homosexuality part of their public persona, and the most hardline reactions come from very conservative circles (Selçuk excluded), just like in the West. Strangely for a Westerner, men having sex with men per se is not such an issue. Here, men are defined fundamentally by their *erkeklik* 'manliness' and not (necessarily) by their sexual partners, while in the West it is often seen as an admirably modern virtue to be 'in touch with one's feminine side' and yet, technically, straight.

The attitudes of Turkish authorities on the subject are rather Victorian. For a start, homosexuality has never been outlawed in Turkey, as it was in, say, Britain. That is mainly because it has never been legally acknowledged, much like lesbianism in Britain. There is a popular legend that Queen Victoria, when asked to sign a bill outlawing all forms of homosexuality, struck out the references to women because she thought the concept of a lesbian was ridiculous, rather like that of a unicorn. How can you outlaw something that does not exist? In fact, references to female homosexuality were never included in that law in the first place. The same has been true in Turkey of male homosexuality, a concept historically disregarded or rather, unchallenged by authority. Lesbianism, of course, was also ignored. The lack of legal recognition means that homosexual couples have no representation, and their partnerships are not accepted in law, nor their right to adopt. There is also no legislation to prohibit discrimination on the grounds of sexual orientation. Interestingly, the army prohibits passive homosexuals from signing up – or, alternatively put, lets them get out of conscription – but active homosexuals and bisexuals have no such allowances made.

As there is no conscription for women in Turkey (although there are women serving as officers in the armed forces), it is difficult to know what the equivalent rules would be for lesbian conscripts. My guess is that there would be no such rules. The asymmetry between gay men and gay women the world over is fascinating, but it is particularly striking in Turkey. A Turkish friend of mine, Merve, has not come out as a lesbian to her parents because, she says, they would simply not comprehend what she was telling them. Lesbianism is an even more uncharted and unrecognised concept than male homosexuality in most parts of Turkey. Merve comes from a traditional working-class family from Mersin, in the east, but she has many lesbian friends from Istanbul and more open cosmopolitan areas who are in exactly the same predicament.

There are several elements to this non-recognition of lesbians: on a practical level, according to Merve, being a lesbian in its most stereotypical form simply goes unnoticed because lesbians are less alarming to a traditional Turkish eye. People seem more sensitive to and less forgiving of a man appearing effeminate than a woman appearing un-made up and butch – she is less obvious and, crucially, less offensive to the average Turkish observer than a higher-status person (man) pretending to be lower-status (woman). Among those who are aware of their existence, lesbians also have the reputation of being less exclusively gay than men, in that they tend to have relationships with people of both genders more often than men do. Whether this is socially circumstantial or a natural biological preference is open to debate, but either way it makes lesbianism seem more like a lifestyle choice, and therefore less threatening to a homophobic person, than a gay man exclusively having sex with men, who might be viewed as beyond redemption.

Because women in Turkey are simply less in the public eye than men, there is less discourse about their private sexual preferences and habits. Lesbianism is not much talked about, and perhaps this is cyclical: women are less willing to drop the bombshell that they are gay because it would be so unprecedented, therefore it is not discussed, and so the veil of ignorance is preserved.

In much of the Middle East, lesbians are simply not accepted in any sense, because women are not deemed to have the right to choose their own identity. A woman cannot declare herself a lesbian because that is not within her remit as a female who is de facto ruled by a man (be that her father, another male relative or her husband). The man in question makes all her decisions, so an identity-defining choice like declaring herself a lesbian is simply unheard of. Therefore, while a man declaring himself gay is worrying and certainly not welcomed, it is at least accepted as a choice. A woman does not have that luxury.

When a Moroccan acquaintance of mine (reluctantly) decided to come out to her parents, she was very apprehensive about their reaction, even booking herself a flight the following day so she could drop the bomb and escape immediately. As it turned out, they were relatively relaxed about the revelation, and her mother even teased her for being so melodramatic in announcing her sexual preference: 'Do you think you invented this? Your aunts were up to the same kind of thing, but they grew out of it. If you don't, that's OK.' This is another attitude towards lesbianism that must be both patronising and strangely liberating: the sense that sexual contact among females is simply a phase, not amounting to much, and definitely nothing to threaten the union of a man and a woman that is a Middle Eastern woman's duty and indeed destiny. The upside of this depressing dismissal is a freedom to indulge in what is seen as innocuous behaviour. Of course, this should not be the case but, currently, it is preferable to the hostility which would be shown if lesbianism was revealed as something to be taken seriously, a real preference for women to the exclusion of men.

The Turkish government occasionally gives its tuppence worth on homosexuality, and this is never encouraging. In March 2010 the Minister for Women and Family Affairs, Selma Aliye Kafav, declared that 'homosexuality is a biological disorder which can be treated'. The mayor of Ankara, Melih Gökçek, is a notorious instigator of smear campaigns, and one of his most infamous jibes was directed at the opposition deputy of Tunceli, Hüseyin Aygün. Gökçek asked Aygün on Twitter whether he was gay, on the grounds that he took part in the Gay Pride march in Istanbul during the Gezi protests, adding sarcastically that it was his constituents who really wanted to know.

Compared to other Middle Eastern countries, however, Turkey boasts an explicit and vocal gay community: there are equal rights protests conducted by LGBT activists, a thriving gay party and arts scene in Istanbul, the Pink Life Queer-Fest in Ankara, a similar event in Antalya and many dynamic university LGBT groups, particularly in big cities. During the Gezi Park occupation, LGBT activists had a prominent stand at the Taksim entrance to the park and were almost always well represented in protests, presumably feeling safe in the atmosphere of inclusive and distinctly leftist solidarity that so characterised the period.

There are also plenty of unofficial gay organisations, or venues, if one knows where to look. My friend Andrew, whose alter ego, Doris, has become an Istanbul legend, can wax lyrical on the many gay cinemas and parks he has visited in his twenty-five years in Turkey, the way he can tell if a taxi driver is amenable to an engagement ('Where to?' 'Wherever you want') and the lingo he uses to sound out potentially gay acquaintances. It is quite extraordinary, discovering through him a hidden community which one would never know about without someone on the inside. It is as though a secret Soho beats a steady and ardent pulse under the veneer of run-of-the-mill establishments and ordinary-looking Turkish men serving beers or negotiating traffic.

Sometimes the secret Soho is not so secret at all. The area in which I happened to settle in Istanbul is near Tarlabaşı – a shabby, brothel-riddled pocket of Beyoğlu, known for its proliferation of prostitutes of every kind – male, transvestite, transsexual and regular. Beyoğlu is the most chaotic, minority-filled metropolitan area I have ever encountered, traditionally home to people of all ethnicity, religion, profession and sexuality. Due to this eclectic and all-embracing reputation, it attracts homosexual and transsexual men from all corners of Turkey who could not be openly gay in, say, Diyarbakır in the south-east or Kayseri in central Anatolia. Beyoğlu is also where all the LGBT organisations of Istanbul are based.

Tarlabaşı, where specifically transvestite and transsexual sex workers now operate, used to be the home of the Greek and Armenian communities in Istanbul, and still reflects this in some of the beautiful, decaying neo-classical architecture of the buildings; sadly, these minorities were driven out in the fifties after the race riots. Despite its position just above the Golden Horn, near fashionable bits of town, it has never recovered from its history and is going through a ruthless process of forced gentrification. A private construction company (whose CEO is, incidentally, the son-in-law of the prime minister) has bought up most of it and is transforming the decrepit, beautiful houses into expensive apartments and shops. While the old Tarlabaşı was unseemly, the new one will be fake, and I think it is a great shame.

Prostitution – of either sex – is technically legal in Turkey, and far more widespread than most people let on. While some of the brothels are controlled by the government (lucratively, it might be added), many more are run by a mafia of pimps and brothel empire-owners, some of whom are extremely rich individuals. One of them, the Armenian Madame Manukyan, was the number one taxpayer in the whole of Turkey for five years in the 1990s before her death, receiving an award for her contributions from the tax office. Tarlabaşı in many ways resembles Amsterdam's red light district, without as many sex shops. Sultry voices invite passers-by to their less than sumptuous quarters from behind grilled windows, trying out all the major tourist languages until they get a response. Down the road in Galata, there is an extremely well-organised brothel that has all the hallmarks of government support – there is a security check at the entrance, complete with uniformed guard and metal detector, a sign prohibiting under-eighteens and a lengthy queue winding down the street outside, particularly on the weekends. The newsagents on the street seem to have bought up half the country's import of condoms, displayed in wicker baskets outside the shops.

There is one street in particular in Tarlabaşı, affectionately known among my expat friends as Tranny Alley, where sturdy-calved ladies with suspiciously narrow hips and enviable manes of hair loiter throughout the day. Early one afternoon, I counted five, all arrayed side by side in true sisterly fashion. There is clearly a hierarchy, those lucky enough to be fairly petite pulling off stiletto heels to lend elegance to an ensemble relying heavily on leopard print, miniskirts and zipped faux leather. Taller models make the most of a commanding presence and yet shorter skirts. Many is the time I have watched a man walk past one of these exotic ladies, walk slowly back, have a brief discussion that can only be about money, and either walk off for good or follow her to some nearby brothel. The meagre thirty lira (about £10) quoted to my friend is sadly indicative of the cut-price market for one of the lowest sectors of society, self-employed in the most unmonitored of service industries.

Retired prostitutes-turned-pimps hang around in the same

area, and are identifiable by their advanced age and air of undisguised dejection. Most of them have ceased to make any effort, and the one I generally notice, who seems to be something equivalent to the Godmother of Sin, sports a grubby tracksuit and hangs out in the shell of a gutted house. Pimps are more essential for transvestite and transsexual prostitutes than for most, because these workers are usually excluded from brothels – not by law, but by other, more conventional prostitutes. This means that they hang out on the street, where they are more visible, more instantly available – but also more at risk. Transsexual sex workers are often treated like freaks and are the subject of vicious attacks, which is why they are actually more likely than other sex workers to want to be part of a union. These compounding disadvantages might be the reason why transsexuals are actually more likely to want to be part of a union than other sex workers. They have everything to gain and nothing to lose, unlike the women who want to keep their heads down and who fear only the social repercussions of being employed in the sex trade. Transsexuals have their whole identity to fight for.

So, it seems the sisterhood is not as tolerant and all-embracing as one would hope. The exclusion of transsexuals by biologically female sex workers is worrying but not that surprising given the broad social prejudices already existing towards transsexual people. Furthermore, female prostitutes in such a well-known, saturated area probably resent any kind of competition and seize the chance to exclude openly gay and decidedly unmanly transvestites who have fallen into the way of prostitution. When I say 'fallen in', it is not actually a coincidence that male transvestites end up as prostitutes in Turkey. There is often not much else that these men can do if they want to be openly homosexual and moreover express their desire to dress like a woman. It makes sense, financially, to exploit what would be a crippling disadvantage in any other walk of life. And, crucially, there seems to be plentiful, public demand for their services – something that is not, I think (I cannot be sure), so widespread or at least blatant anywhere else in the world, with the exception of Bangkok.

Because transvestites are not regarded as men, and are not women either, in the eyes of most Turks (and, it must be said, many people the world over), they have practically no status at all, and are often prey to attacks by the police. It is legal to be gay, to wear women's clothes and to work as a prostitute, so police stop transvestites on grounds of blocking traffic or violating the law of 'exhibitionism', march them to the nearest police station and fine them about seventy lira (£25) a time – about their day's earnings. They often beat them up, with no fear of repercussions at all. Who would come to the aid of a prostitute of dubious gender, or seek justice on their behalf? This is the uglier side of the colourful gay scene in Istanbul.

Confusingly, and unfairly, there is bountiful affection for famous transvestites and even transsexuals all over Turkey – even, bizarrely, among conservative Muslims. There are several ostentatious transvestite pop stars, for example, adored by conservative and secular Turks alike. The trendsetter and original grande dame of popular music was Zeki Müren, who bore more than a passing resemblance to Julian Clary and was hugely popular from the 1960s onwards in Turkey, Iran, Greece and further afield. He pioneered heavy make-up and impressive bling and was obviously gay without making any statement about it. In an Islamic country, it is astonishing that he had what amounted to a state funeral on his death in 1996, and hundreds of thousands of visitors a year travel to his posthumous museum in Bodrum on the Aegean coast. Bülent Ersoy is a transsexual singer with similar kudos, who has been a more vocal advocate of gay and transgender rights since the 1980s.

These co-existing attitudes are paradoxical, but perhaps no more surprising than the contrasting responses to a heavily made up woman who happens to be a successful pop star on television, and one who is leaning out of a brothel window – the first is impossibly glamorous, the second a slut. Transvestites have to contend with more prejudice unless they follow in the stilettoed footsteps of Zeki Müren, and sadly, that is a very remote possibility.

Despite the depressing side of Tarlabaşı, there is joy to be found in the lurid wig shops, the hustle and bustle of honest competition, speculation on breast veracity, the largely non-judgemental co-existence of kebab sellers and their fantastically clad customers. It is a scene I have not witnessed anywhere else in the world, and least of all in an Islamic country. I am consistently amazed by how open the whole thing is – it is localised, and of course similar scenes do not abound throughout Turkey by any means, but it is still remarkable. I think it must be somehow linked to the Turkish trait of being totally matter of fact about anything to do with commerce. Sex is sex, and if someone is willing to pay for it, it's on offer. Just as Istanbul is characterised by whole streets or even districts devoted to one commodity or market – lamp shops, tailoring, musical instruments, blankets, kitchenware – so, too, there is an area devoted to sex, which is convenient for all concerned.

There is an interesting dynamic between the 'gay for pay' sauna workers and their transvestite/transsexual colleagues. When I interviewed the Kurdish boys at Aquarius I discovered that they lived next door to transvestites. The boys were very disparaging about their neighbours when they talked to Ami and me, but they were clearly good friends with them, spending much of their time together, chatting and sipping tea. However, the fact that some of them are transvestites and some of them are supposedly straight men creates a hierarchy, with the trans sex workers decidedly worse off. I am not sure where female prostitutes would fit into this hierarchy but my guess would be at the top, an intriguing switch from the normal ladder of a patriarchal society.

The status of the gay community in Turkey is fragile. I have many friends who are happily 'out' and in a same-sex relationship which is known about in their particular social circle; many of them, however, have not come out to their families, who will usually be hoping for a nice daughter- or son-in-law and the pitter-patter of tiny feet. Apart from the most artistic of professions (film makers, architects, photographers or designers of some description), it is not a subject to be mentioned at work, unless one is lucky enough to work in a liberal international company. Having said that, once you are in the circle of trust, as it were, the gay scene in Istanbul is famously good fun – clubs featuring the best DJs and performers on the clubbing circuit are hugely popular with gay and straight locals alike, and gay art and film making in particular is thriving.

An extraordinary film, *Zenne* (*Male Dancer*), came out in 2011 and swept the board at the Turkish equivalent of the Oscars. It was originally intended to be a documentary about the life of a modern *zenne*, a relic of the Ottoman practice of using male dancers to perform in the public quarters of the Sultan's palace, because women were confined to the harem. At an early point in production, however, the directors' friend Ahmet Yildiz came out as gay and was subsequently murdered by his own father, which stalled the film and gave the directors, Mehmet Binay and Caner Alper, a more serious ambition. They decided to turn the documentary into a feature film which follows a trio of gay men in Istanbul and Eastern Anatolia – the original *zenne*, their murdered friend Ahmet, and Ahmet's German boyfriend Daniel, all played by actors. Sadly, the film is very true to life. I interviewed Mehmet Binay after watching the film, and it was humbling to hear him talk without bitterness about his friend's murder, and all that he had gone through to hide his sexuality from his family.

One of the most shocking parts of the film follows the procedure that Ahmet and Can the *zenne* have to undergo in order to be granted exemption from compulsory military service on the grounds of homosexuality, which is technically classed by the army as a psychological disease manifesting itself as 'unnatural intimacy' (meaning that the military powers that be and the former Turkish Family Minister disagree on the finer points of its medical classification). Not only do gay conscripts have to provide graphic evidence of their passive participation in gay sex in the form of film or photographs, they must also be smiling to show that they are willing participants. In *Zenne*, there is an almost unbearably sad scene in which Ahmet and his boyfriend set up the video camera to film this contrived 'evidence'. The film also depicted the way gay conscripts are subject to humiliating medical examinations and are pressurised to attend their review dressed in drag. In November 2012 the army made official their previously unofficial practice of expelling career soldiers (as opposed to conscripts) on the grounds of homosexuality, classing it as a disciplinary crime.

As is generally the case not only in Turkey but the world over, when extremes of society rub against each other, tolerance is stretched and ultimately snaps. I have already mentioned Galata as an area which has suffered a rapid gentrification in recent years, leaving traditional locals out of sync with the growing influx of modernity and its free and easy ways. There is an empty house just off Galata Square that was used until a few years ago for the monthly meetings of the LGBT Mothers' Support Group of Beyoğlu. In much the same spirit as Alcoholics Anonymous, the mothers of lesbian, bisexual, gay and transgender people met secretly to help each other through the stress of their children's chosen path in life. Not for long – the crazed xenophobe who so ruthlessly persecuted Andrew Boord's tenants was soon on the scene with a bevy of homophobic followers, hurling abuse and missiles at the house until the poor mothers called the police. When the police arrived, they made no move to arrest this violent gang but instead demanded to see the rent agreement for the flat and requested the mothers to leave.

While disgusting, this incident was, at least, relatively isolated. Much more worrying are situations like the one in Avcılar, a far-flung suburb of Istanbul filled with what in Turkish are known as *gecekondu* houses (literally 'built in the night') – ramshackle but, by now, well-established slums. Because Avcılar is so far out and hitherto unpopular as a neighbourhood, it gradually became home to a large number of transvestite prostitutes – the area was cheap and no one bothered them. This all changed in recent years with the city-wide rise in property prices, the general seeping of Istanbul's resident population further and further from the centre, and the dawning realisation among Avcılar landlords that they could charge a lot more for their properties if they got rid of the unsavoury transvestite population. In the autumn of 2012 this spurred a landlord-led anti-transvestite movement, joined by homophobic locals, but vociferously opposed by the transvestites themselves, LGBT activists and, impressively, a good number of fair-minded Istanbullus with no particular concern about the area but a conviction that the evictions were not just.

It is depressing that the root cause of this movement appears to be money – everyone got on reasonably well before prospective rent prices changed – but not nearly as depressing as it would be if the movement had been solely driven by prejudice from the start. As is evident in Tarlabaşı, there is a certain amount of tolerance for the homosexual and transgender community in Turkey, but it would be too much to hope for blanket acceptance; there will always be a few bigots everywhere, in Western countries as well as in Middle Eastern. To match the Avcılar scenarios of this world, there are cheering cases like that of the support for Halil İbrahim Dinçdağ, a gay football referee who has been consistently cheered on by fans during his legal battle against the Turkish Football Federation for dropping him on the grounds of his sexual orientation (a charge they deny).

Beyoğlu is, as I mentioned, a hunting ground for prostitutes of all variations of gender and sexual appearance. However, there is another interesting scene in a neighbouring area called Aksaray, which is full of a very idiosyncratic kind of establishment called a *pavyon*. Unlike brothels, you can find *pavyon*s all over Turkey, but they have changed almost unrecognisably from their original incarnation. Traditionally – in fact, until about twenty years ago – a *pavyon* was a kind of wholesome nightclub, where Turkish girls would sing classic love ballads and where lonely or misunderstood men came to listen to them sing and later talk to them over a drink. The original Pavyon (French *pavillon*) was the first such place, in Taksim, Istanbul. They later spread all over the country and were, in fact, more popular in isolated Anatolian towns than in the hub of Istanbul, because of the relative lack of any other excitement. Old-fashioned *pavyon* girls were not allowed to leave the premises with customers; they were good singers and conversationalists, but they were not prostitutes. They were also all Turkish. Now, the idea of a *pavyon* has drastically changed – it is still tame compared to the strip clubs of Europe, but it is much more about ogling and, in some cases, taking the girls home: an optimist's hunting ground. There might be a token Turkish singer, but the girls are mainly Russian or Ukrainian, no older than twenty-four, dancing en masse and speaking

just enough Turkish for basic transactions. Conversationalists they are not.

The Turkish man's fascination with exotic women is well
known – and by 'exotic' I mean Russians, Eastern Europeans
and, bluntly, blondes of all descriptions. Some Turkish men
make pilgrimages to the seaside resorts of Antalya especially
to pursue Russian women looking for a holiday romance.
Academics insist that this stems from Ottoman times, when
the celebrated concubines in the Sultan's harem were all from
distant, northern reaches of the Empire, notably Circassia
(modern Ossetia). Alternatively, it can be more simply explained as an example of the universal trait of desiring what
is unusual. Belatedly, this particular racial preference is being
granted full outlet in the modern revamping of the *pavyon*.
In keeping with the old Ottoman tradition, contemporary
Russian prostitutes initially come to the Black Sea region in
the north of Turkey, mainly through the border with Georgia, before travelling further south. In the town of Hopa, near
the Georgian border, there is a very high concentration of
brothels where 'Natashas' (Russian prostitutes) work, knowing there will be high demand for them just inside the border
of Turkey. The sudden proliferation of prostitutes in Hopa
reminds me of the towns in Holland full of sex shops, just
across the Belgian border. One woman from Hopa gave an
interview in which she spoke of the problems these brothels
posed for Turkish families, how they were destroying family
life. She had even formed an association for the maligned
wives of Hopa, but to very little avail – it was no match for
the sheer scale of the brothel business in this strategic town.

My knowledge of the *pavyon* scene comes from first-hand

experience. Normally women are not allowed into a *pavyon* as spectators, but I went with a persuasive man of the world who is a valued customer in Ankara – currently the most celebrated city for *pavyon*s in Turkey. I was immediately disappointed by how shabby and kitsch the place was – swirling disco lights, cheap velveteen booths and the most unbelievably overpriced, bog-standard *rakı* (this is, of course, how all these establishments make their money). The veneer of glamour was even thinner than I had expected. The whole performance was farcical to the appraising and sober eye of a female researcher: a small stage cluttered with young girls dancing to average club tracks with the minimum show of enthusiasm. It was, frankly, embarrassing in its lack of any pretensions to sensuality. Nevertheless, I persuaded my chaperon to invite one of the girls over, which requires more overpriced drinks, of which the girl drinks a thimbleful. Angelica was Ukrainian, twenty years old. She told us in fairly fluent English that she and her friends had all been imported en masse by their agency in Ukraine. Unsurprisingly she was very bored in Ankara, speaking very little Turkish and with nothing to do during the day. She said the money was good but she dreamed of going to central Europe. Later, she thanked us graciously and went back on stage to dance under a bucket of water in what turned out to be an attempt at the famous performance scene from *Flashdance*.

The atmosphere and agenda of the current scene are totally antithetical to the original idea of a *pavyon* and show a marked cultural shift in Turkish society. Thirty years ago, it was hard even to find a girl who would talk to you outside the family home (hence *pavyon* chats) – now, as society frees up, it is more about sex. Girls used not to leave the *pavyon* with a customer; now in many cases they do.

Like everywhere in the world, Turkish society is getting more explicitly and commercially sexualised. Because sex is more visible and purchasable than it used to be, the growing conservative contingent of society has more to object to. This exponential tension leads to conflicts like the Avcilar trans-vestite–landlord stand-off and the imminent eviction of transvestites from Tarlabaşı as it becomes gentrified. It is safer for gay people or bisexuals in Turkey to go under the radar, joining the considerable number who are quietly conducting their affairs uninterrupted. I'm not saying this is a morally correct system, and in a liberal society everyone should have the right to express themselves just as they like. But Turkey is in many ways a religiously conservative Middle Eastern country, and it is clear that in the struggle to achieve equal rights for openly gay people, there is a long way to go and the path is not only difficult but violent. It is not easy to change the deep-seated prejudices of a nation, indeed a region, and while it might be right and worthy to attempt it, I can't help being struck by the relative normality of casual, hidden ro-mances and the low-key nature of homosexuality as an accep-ted mode of behaviour in this country.

Andrew says that he loves being gay in Turkey, because it is his own business. In England he would have to be 'out', and this would immediately give him a dictated identity in the eyes of a Western audience. In Turkey, he is a delightful charmer, or flirt, however you choose to look at it, queen of his castle. He has had several long-term, fondly remembered relationships with Turkish men, and now, as a more senior

'Alpha Female', as he puts it, has the exciting prospect of a new encounter round the corner in the fruitful hunting grounds of Istanbul or Bodrum (or wherever he happens to find himself). His gay circle of friends are the best company in Istanbul, and Andrew loves discovering hidden kindred spirits – 'I think he's a bit of a whoopsie, Alevia darling, don't you?' (This question is entirely rhetorical – Andrew always knows his man.)

Andrew would be quite wasted in England.

6

Digiturk

Betrayal, jealousy and family conflict: these are the ingredients of all successful Turkish soap operas, or *diziler*. Sex and money are the inner sinews running through their cores and holding viewers captive. Fittingly, the worlds of TV production and commercial acting warrant scripts of their own – dark tales of strategic censorship, politics, the druglike pull of celebrity and, above all, money. Digiturk, while sounding like a subversive metaphor, is in fact the reigning satellite provider, holding the monopoly of almost all national and international channels broadcast in Turkey bar Sky and the state channel, TRT (Turkish Radio and Television). It is available worldwide, and is arguably Turkey's most powerful PR agent.

In the past six years, televised melodrama from Turkey has taken over countries in the Middle East and North Africa, central Asia, the Balkans and Eastern Europe in dubbed or subtitled format, and is wildly popular in unlikely countries like Iran and the Ukraine, sometimes even more so than in Turkey itself. Enthusiastic teletourists, mainly Arab, have flocked to Istanbul to visit familiar locations from their favourite shows, whole families trooping over on a giddy pilgrimage of pop culture. This TV tourism is so profitable that in October 2012 the Turkish Ministry for Culture and Tourism decided to stop charging certain countries for the broadcasting rights to soap operas, specifying a desire to shower audiences as remote as Kyrgyzstan with freely available blockbuster shows like *Aşk-ı Memnu* (*Forbidden Love*), *Ezel* (*Eternity*) and *Muhteşem Yüzyıl* (*Magnificent Century*). Considering that the annual income from foreign broadcasting sales had reached nearly a hundred million Turkish lira from a total of 150 series sold to seventy-three countries, this was a striking testament to the more valuable potential of *dizi-turizm* and the anticipated boost to trade.

Of course, money is a big motivator but there would have been more important strategic and long-term financial motives behind this decision. Until the AKP came to power, the Middle East was largely suspicious of Turkey, seeing it as an extension of the West with its secular ways. Now, under the Islamic auspices of the AKP, these countries can view Turkey more as part of the fold, and over the past decade the country has become what the Turkish Foreign Ministry carefully calls 'an inspiration' rather than 'a model'.

The proliferation of Turkish soap operas in the Middle East pushes an image of Turkey as a modern, socially inspirational example without alienating the viewers in these countries. In central Asia and Eastern Europe, Turkish soap operas far outshine their nearest competitors on Russian television channels and the sheer volume of Turkish TV spread over international airspace speaks of progress and prosperity. The shows have a regular, captive audience and media hype constantly fed by a growing online audience obsessing over the attractive Turkish stars of the series. The sphere of influence stretches from Oman to Uzbekistan to Bulgaria; it is a digital renaissance of the Ottoman Empire.

The popularity of Turkey in Middle Eastern countries is such that during the Gezi protests of 2013, many Arabs could not understand why Turks would be protesting. People in the Middle East, and North Africa in particular, are big fans of Erdoğan. Often they cannot fully articulate why, but he seems to be a feel-good regional leader with strong Muslim credentials. If pressed, these Erdoğan fans talk admiringly of his protective stance on Palestine and fearless criticism of Israel. This is a hugely emotive subject and the kudos of a strong position on Palestine cannot be underestimated in the Middle East. Erdoğan has hit that exactly right, and strengthened his position with a tour of 'liberated' Middle Eastern countries post-Arab Spring in September 2011, in which he encouraged optimistic Arabs to copy Turkey's example of a moderate Islamic democracy. Arabs are simply perplexed by the attitudes of Turks who might have concerns about his leadership.

As domestic and international media began to show footage of Turkish protesters being attacked by police in 2013, the government responded by describing the protesters as dangerous looters manipulated by an 'interest rate lobby' whose mission it was to bring down the Turkish economy. Turkish soaps began broadcasting propaganda-style episodes in which brave policemen resisted unprovoked attacks from protesters and responded only unwillingly with tear gas. In one memorable episode, the interest rate lobby group are unconvincing villains represented by a couple of snappily dressed businessmen who cackle as they watch protesters and police fighting from behind a fence, high-fiving each other as the clashes get out of control. Incidentally, the channel that aired this was Samanyolu, a nationalist channel with links to the Islamic movement headed by the cleric Fethullah Gülen. While these soaps were obviously aimed at a Turkish audience, I'm sure they were seen by a fair number of Arab viewers too.

The popularity of Turkish soap operas in Arab countries has caused problems over the years. Prominent Saudi clerics, including the Grand Mufti himself, complain during the holy month of Ramadan about too many people watching programmes glorifying loose morals in the evenings after their *iftar* (fast-breaking) dinner. In November 2012, Macedonia's Information and Society Minister announced that the broadcasting of Turkish soaps would be reduced on national channels, as Macedonia's own programmes were being pushed past midnight while Turks hogged the precious primetime slots. 'To remain under Turkish rule for five hundred years is quite enough,' apparently.

This has done very little to dent the mass viewership of these soaps. One particular series, *Gümüş* (*Silver*), a sentimental rags-to-riches cliché that ran to one hundred episodes over two years, was renamed *Noor* (*Light*) for its Arab audience and became far more popular abroad than in Turkey, reaching 85 million viewers in Arab countries alone for its final episode in August 2008. Part of its success was explained by the fact that the programme was dubbed into the widely spoken Syrian dialect of Arabic, rather than classical Arabic, which had previously been used for imported soaps such as Mexican *telenovelas*. *Noor* was the real breakthrough in the phenomenon of Turkish soap operas' popularity abroad, and set the standard high: the lead actors, Kıvanç Tatlıtuğ and

Songül Öden, were catapulted to cross-continental fame, their characters inspiring a generation of baby names, their onscreen wardrobes copied and sold in the most far-flung souks. A feature-length film starring the original cast is in production as I write.

It would seem that the semi-liberal yet not-too-alien lifestyles idealised in Turkish *diziler* are perfectly pitched for an Arab audience yearning for a world to which they can both relate and aspire, an audience which cannot necessarily identify with Western TV. Turkey is, after all, recognisably Middle Eastern while having many of the attractive trappings and fashions of a European country. There is more freedom for women, crucially, and most of the storylines involve some kind of romantic intrigue designed to be pleasantly shocking for the average housewife.

Aşk-ı Memnu is a wildly popular modernised tale of secret lust adapted from an Ottoman-set novel of the same name, and seems to me the quintessential *dizi*. It centres on the claustrophobic situation of a young wife conducting an affair with the handsome nephew of her old, rich husband under the noses of everyone in the house. Worse, the heroine's scheming mother has designs on the old husband, and towards the end the dashing nephew gets engaged to the heroine's stepdaughter. The heroine duly kills herself. Stolen embraces, laden silences and guilty glances fill every episode. When the credits start to roll, one realises that hardly anything has actually happened in ninety minutes, but the tension has been pulled ridiculously, unsustainably high. It is like an elongated, meaningless cliffhanger with all the qualities of a tooth being drawn. But it is somehow very watchable, and Middle Eastern housewives cannot get enough of it. The atmosphere of stifled lust and the pressure of social restrictions prevalent in so many communities in the Arab world are dramatically reproduced on screen with improbably daring characters playing out the housewife's wildest dreams. More often than not, the onscreen femme fatale is fatally punished, but the aproned spectator has lived through her for scores of episodes.

This breed of TV is brilliantly simple but sensational escapism, typically gilded by a luxurious setting (or the promise of luxury), social competition and cathartic falls from grace. Many of the soaps are set in wealthy houses on the banks of the Bosphorus; the female characters wear designer dresses and full make-up to breakfast, the children have governesses, and there is usually an *Upstairs, Downstairs* scenario going on, with the kitchen staff or local salesmen providing comic relief in the interludes between the glitterati's wrangling. To a Western eye, it all seems totally over the top, grotesque even. And yet a lifestyle which is patently several million dollars beyond what most Turks could afford is not seen as improbable and alienating but rather, impossibly exciting, the stuff of dreams. Producers such as Ay Yapım, the production company behind *Aşk-ı Memnu* and other successful shows, have developed a magic formula and are pursuing it doggedly.

I began watching the soaps to improve my Turkish. I had initially started off watching cult films like *G.O.R.A* (a sci-fi spoof by much lauded Turkish comedian Cem Yılmaz), but the lightning pace of the dialogue defeated me. Instead, soppy classics such as *Aşk-ı Memnu*, *Muhteşem Yüzyıl* and *Kuzey Güney* (*North, South*) became my linguistic bibles. I can highly recommend these soaps to anyone wishing to improve their Turkish, because they are invariably filled with pregnant pauses (allowing the looking-up of new vocabulary) and the kind of acting which renders dialogue largely superfluous – sadly not in an Alec Guinness kind of way, but more like a nuanced mime artist. The plot is reinforced yet further by the heart-rending strings and sinister percussion of traditional Turkish music, expelling any remaining confusion over what is going on. This is of course a slight exaggeration, and I have often worried about the intricacies of which character knows what details about the secret betrayal/affair/switch of allegiance currently unfolding; luckily these mysteries have, if anything, added zest to the exercise. I remind myself of my grandmother, who spoke not a word of English, but would never miss an episode of *Dallas*, providing her own specialised interpretation of the plot and chiding the characters in animated Turkish as she watched.

For the *dizi* dilettante there is an extensive underworld of niche, budget soaps which are almost more fascinating than the mainstream ones, if less watchable. Many of them follow similar lines of ill-fated romances, but often draw their inspiration from real life. One particularly unfortunate series was inspired by the true story of Sarah and Musa, the stars of a scandal which the *Daily Mail* and *Mirror* covered with ghoulish tenacity, as did most of the Turkish media, in the summer of 1996. Unlikely thirteen-year-old heroine Sarah Cook accompanied her parents on holiday to Kahramanmaraş in southern Turkey, and ran away with an eighteen-year-old waiter called Musa Kömeağaç. As the world watched, aghast, the two got married. British papers decried the disgraceful neglect of everyone responsible while Turkish papers, although officially shocked, rather enjoyed the romance of it all. Sarah fell pregnant and was finally whisked back to England.

Sara ile Musa (*Sarah and Musa, Together*) was the series that drew its inspiration from this cause célèbre. It was not a roaring success, lasting only five episodes, but it is astonishing that someone thought it was a good idea to serialise the story at all – it would be like making a soap opera out of the British schoolgirl Megan Stammers running off with her maths teacher in September 2012. Turkish papers occasionally revisit the Sarah-and-Musa story, some sixteen years on, printing sadly nostalgic pieces about Musa missing his distant son, but declaring himself happy with his new Turkish wife. This, to my mind, is absolutely typical of the Turkish trait of dramatising and romanticising everything, no matter how inappropriate in the eyes of the rest of the world.

For sheer genre variety, I am very glad that such series exist but it cannot be said that they have the same mass appeal as the glamorous blockbusters like *Aşk-ı Memnu*. The actors involved in these are huge heart-throbs, in a way that is almost old-fashioned now in the West due to the proliferation of transient talent-show stars and the myriad avenues of celebrity. Turkey has its fair share of minor celebrities, but there are a handful of astronomically well-paid actors who take on most of the lead parts in the top soaps and who are real megastars as a result. One actor in particular, Kıvanç Tatlıtuğ (the male lead in *Gümüş*, *Aşk-ı Memnu* and *Kuzey Güney*), has cult-like status across the Arab world, where he far outranks Hollywood types like Brad Pitt. Tatlıtuğ was once sighted in the mall in which I worked, and I went to the office bathroom at lunchtime to discover it packed with near-hysterical ladies daubing themselves with war-paint rouge, ready to go and hunt down the poor man like sexually charged Bacchic priestesses. Although most soap viewers and fans are female, Middle Eastern men are equally dedicated star worshippers. The equivalent of Tatlıtuğ is Beren Saat, the actress who plays his adulteress lover in *Aşk-ı Memnu*. There are forums devoted to Saat in which Arab men post odes to her eyes and chastity. It would seem that there is a degree of separation in the minds of fans between onscreen characters and the actors themselves, which is charming.

The stardom and money involved in TV has completely changed the world of acting in Turkey, and has been the death knell of theatre. The Golden Age of Turkish theatre peaked in the seventies and eighties, before the dramatic emergence of popular culture in the nineties and the mushrooming of singers and well-paid celebrities of every kind. Theatre was politicised and relevant in a pre-TV era where people went there to hear a story. Touring Anatolian troupes earned money, like British theatre in rep, and new plays were a talking point. An industry existed.

That is, for the most part, lost now. There is a relatively poor tradition of philanthropy in the arts in Turkey, which is partly the product of decades of turbulent politics and economic uncertainty, but it is also just not a big part of the culture. The result of this is that, when not prioritised by the state – as is the case now – theatres are crippled. In Britain, despite much vilified Arts Council cuts, theatre is still going relatively strong. One has the sense that it is still important, that it can affect people's conversations and concerns and be part of the popular voice. Many young people in Turkey don't even know what theatre is any more. It is a word vaguely connected with actors, so people think it is a genre of television series or film. Many of those that do know of it think it is a slightly effete waste of time.

If theatre had been replaced by good TV, this would not be such a catastrophic loss. As it is, *diziler* dominate prime-time TV and a *dizi* is emphatically not a TV series, but a soap opera. They are completely based on ratings, episode by episode, and if they get a negative response from the public, the plot is rewritten or the show is simply pulled. There is no equivalent of BBC drama on the national channels in terms of artistic integrity or vision. The name of the game is profit, and each production company is a moneymaking powerhouse riding the crest of a six-year boom.

Serdar Bilis is a Turkish theatre director based in London, but he occasionally works in Turkish theatre despite the constant frustrations involved. He also teaches drama at private universities Kadir Has and Yeditepe, both in Istanbul, which is pretty much the only avenue for theatre directors to earn money these days. According to him, Turkish actors feel obliged to pretend they want to be involved in stage productions, but only because they are guiltily aware that theatre used to be a noble art. Serdar has been frequently subjected to the frustration of beginning rehearsals for a play only to have his actors answer calls from their agents mid-rehearsal, claiming to be available and agreeing to offers of parts in the newest TV series. Their priorities are clear, and the figures make sense: TV actors earn the equivalent of £7,000 a week, on average. Huge stars get about £12,000 a week while lower, plot-filling actors get about £2,000. That is big money in a country where the minimum wage is less than £100 per week. Not only is there no money involved in theatre, the glamour and popular support it used to enjoy have now vanished. As a result, there is very low morale among the few stage actors who still try to make a career of it.

Young actors are rarely stage-trained these days, heading straight for TV or film, but it is interesting to note that most of the successful *diziler* have a couple of ageing stage legends to lend gravitas to a cast otherwise comprised of nubile youths with patchy talent. These are generally male, and no younger than fifty-five. In the UK, it would be like watching Derek Jacobi or Ian McKellen on screen with the cast of *Hollyoaks*, uttering crass lines with sonorous subtlety.

A striking example of a stage legend who never featured on glitzy TV soaps is the late theatre actor Erol Günaydın, whom I met a few weeks before his death in August 2012. The once lauded thespian star spent the last years of his life in relative poverty, ill health and obscurity in his daughter Ayşe's house in Bodrum, with frequent stints in nearby hospitals. I remember watching *Kuzey Güney* with him in a stuffy room one night during a heatwave, and asking him what he thought of the acting. His answer was unprintable. A successful celebrity of the seventies, his only income at the end of his life consisted in paltry royalties from a couple of TV commercials, although he had played the lead in *Çiçek Taksi*, a low-budget, low-profile soap about taxi drivers. One day, out of the blue, his AKP-despising daughter Ayşe received a call from Prime Minister Erdoğan in her Italian restaurant in Bodrum. Mr Erdoğan had heard of Günaydın's plight and wished to offer his personal help to such a distinguished icon of the stage. Günaydın was immediately airlifted from his hospital in Bodrum (where he was more feared than adored by the staff due to his furious temper and foul language) to a hospital offering the best care possible in Istanbul. When he died, a few days later, Ayşe received condolences from AKP members and a call offering to send refreshments to the wake. Ayşe's requests for beer were quietly ignored – crates of soft drinks were sent to the house. These were left untouched in a corner as mourners drank in happy memory of the great man.

Erdoğan's concern for Erol Günaydın is confusingly at odds with his attitude to modern theatre practitioners, whom he has vilified in the national press as alcoholic lowlifes, but this instance of respectable old-world celebrity is an interesting precursor to the current, stratospheric stardom of commercial TV actors. According to Serdar, Turkish actors are unique even among the international acting community for wanting to be the Star – of everything. As he put it, wryly, 'In a production of *Hamlet*, there would have to be six Hamlets. The most common question I get asked is: "Have you got a one-man show?"' The obvious outcome of this attitude is that there is no sense of ensemble in a cast. This egocentricity is no doubt an inevitable result of the rise of TV – when there is the opportunity for one's face to be known by millions of people, it is understandable to crave that kind of recognition and respect. Theatre, by comparison, offers very little in that department. In all probability, a combination of factors within the industry and society in general has resulted in this fame-hungry approach, but it also fits with the stereo-typical personality of a Turkish actor, according to those who know them best.

I was once waiting in the passport control queue at Atatürk airport when I spotted a familiar face in the snaking line behind me: Martin Turner, a British actor with whom I had worked a couple of years previously in London. He was bearded and tanned and I was astonished to learn that he had been in Turkey for the last six months shooting a series called *Son* (*End*). Martin looks a lot like Jeremy Irons and has distinguished himself as a stage actor under directors like Rupert Goold and Declan Donnellan – what on earth was he doing in a Turkish soap opera that would do nothing for his career? The answer was money. The hard truth is that an act-or who has played principal roles for the RSC and the Globe can earn far more as a peripheral character on the set of a re-latively unsuccessful Turkish soap opera than on a West End stage. His agent had been delighted with the offer.

In the ample time afforded us in the passport queue, Martin confessed that he was sad but relieved to be leaving an uncomfortable working routine where he had floundered in the midst of an all-Turkish-speaking cast and crew, mainly in the eastern town of Mardin. He had been playing the part of a roguish English ex-spy in Iran, and the first few epis-odes had required him to speak in English, plus some broken Turkish. As the series progressed, the producers (none other than Ay Yapım) had worried that the subtitles were turning viewers off, and he had to master subsequent dialogue in Turkish and Farsi. Although the production team had been welcoming the only person Martin could communicate with was the actor Philip Arditti, who trained at RADA and was in rather the same boat as him, but with the benefit of Turkish as a mother tongue.

I had previously heard of Philip through the drama scene in London and phoned him up to ask him what it was like working on *Son*. To my surprise, he told me that *Son* had been a risk for Ay Yapım, who had earmarked money especially for a slightly braver, mould-breaking *dizi*. They had drafted in a playwright in place of the usual formula-churning scriptwriters, and the gritty themes of drug smuggling, espionage and cross-border mafias are a far cry from the usual fare of unsuitable love matches and domestic wrangling. *Son* is relatively cutting edge – and correspondingly unpopular with the average housewife viewer.

Did the mould-breaking nature of *Son* mean that the actors were excited to work on a meaningful project? Did they view *Son* as a career-building opportunity, a chance to test their craft on meatier material? Perhaps, says Philip, but the money was still good. In other words, the career-building opportunities were right on the money.

Turkish soaps rarely include controversial material (at least by European standards) and, despite the fact that many of the plots revolve around illicit affairs, never explicitly show sex scenes or nudity. In Turkey, as in much of the Middle East, even kissing is sometimes seen to be inappropriate in a programme that could be seen by children, and is often cut in the dubbed Arabic versions. The mere fact that women are uncovered and illicitly in love is a problem for some authorities. In Turkey, the conservative government is particularly unhappy with the 'anti-Turkish' nature of some plots and characters. Erdoğan has repeatedly called for the axing of *Muhteşem Yüzyıl* (*Magnificent Century*), on the grounds that its characterisation of Ottoman Sultan Suleiman the Great is overly sexualised and historically inaccurate. Suleiman's on-screen incarnation has a vicious harem of women who compete for his attention, and this is, according to Erdoğan, malicious and unpatriotic slander. In November 2012 Erdoğan took the opportunity while opening a regional airport to voice his concerns and issue a warning to the show's producers: 'Those who toy with these [Turkish] values should be taught a lesson within the premises of law.'

TV regulating authorities are very much influenced by the government and interfere not only in the form of fines but also directly in plotlines. A prime example is *Behzat Ç*, which features a policeman anti-hero working within an inept police service in the capital city, Ankara. The production company of this unusually vocal anti-government series was fined 273,000 lira for the last episode, apparently because the anti-hero is 'an unsuitable role model to the youth of Turkey due to excessive consumption of alcohol, pre-marital cohabitation and foul language'. This was the charmingly old-fashioned wording of the official offence, and explained the fine, but the unspoken and indeed unspeakable reason would have had more to do with the terrible picture painted of the Turkish police force. In addition to the fine, the plot had to be changed so that Behzat married his girlfriend, making an honest woman out of her and an example of the programme's production company.

The threat of TV censorship must raise an interesting quandary for production companies: how to toe the line between keeping authorities happy and keeping viewing figures high? A lot of these programmes' popularity is based on racy storylines and sexual intrigue, however tame by Western standards. Erdoğan has not managed to mete out any punishment to the makers of *Muhteşem Yüzyıl,* despite his blustering (although there have been noticeably more scenes of Suleiman reading the Koran and praying since Erdoğan's outburst), and it is possible that the reason has something to do with its extraordinary commercial success. An Arabic-speaking friend of mine stopped to help a lost Yemeni family on the Istanbul metro in the autumn of 2012. Speaking to the father, she learned that he had saved up to bring the whole family to see Topkapı Palace, where the series is set, and was very proud to have done so. His wife and children were over the moon to be in the former Ottoman capital. The extraordinary influence of this show might be the clue as to why it has gone unpunished while the relatively unpopular *Behzat Ç* has been both fined and censored. It remains to be seen whether the popular shows will continue unchecked, or whether government disapproval will win out.

Newly commissioned programmes often cater to the political flavour of the moment. *Avrupa Avrupa (Europe, Europe)* is a recent series produced, significantly, by the state channel, TRT, whose main motif is to ridicule the idea of joining the EU. It posits bizarre, hypothetical scenarios like a mandatory number of toilet flushes to comply with EU standards – not satire at its most biting, but an interesting indication of the changing tide of opinion with regard to the desirability of EU accession, and most importantly the perceived interest, or lack of interest, from the government in keeping up with EU demands.

If the government is limited in its interference on privatised TV channels, it can be far more vocal in the realm of state theatre. Serdar Bilis tries to steer clear of state projects after a peculiar experience at the Izmit City Theatre. When pitching for his show, he had a meeting with the artistic director and the general manager of the theatre. Normally, the artistic director decides whether to accept a play proposal and the general manager is there to confirm that putting on the show is practically possible. In Turkey, this is not always the case; when Bilis presented his show and suggested its billing as a *kara komedi* ('black comedy'), the general manager immediately vetoed the decision and walked out of the room. An embarrassed silence followed, and the artistic director went to confer with his apparent superior. It turned out that the general manager felt that *kara komedi* could be construed as a subversive wordplay on the popular acronym of the ruling AKP – *Ak Parti*. In Turkish, *ak* means 'white' or 'clean', so the party's acronym sounds like 'White Party' – this would be set unfavourably against the 'black' comedy that Bilis was proposing. The mind boggles at the extent of suspicion necessary to entertain this rather subtle association. Bilis was not allowed to pursue that marketing idea but went ahead with the play anyway. Apparently the farce was ill received, as it involved drinking and bare legs on stage. Bilis seems permanently discouraged from trying anything of that ilk again with a state theatre.

Even if Bilis was undeterred by this experience and wished to continue down the state route, he would find it difficult, and not just because of the decline of theatre in general popularity. In April 2012 the bizarre Battle of Erdoğan vs State Theatre unfolded, culminating in a polemic by the prime minister against theatre practitioners and a vow to privatise theatres. At a youth meeting of the AKP in Istanbul he claimed: 'There is no such thing as a theatre being funded by the state in most developed countries.'

Why? Several Turkish papers – and indeed the *Guardian* in the UK – printed a story which sounded like the script of a badly written play but was plausible given the characters involved. The story was that Erdoğan's youngest daughter had attended a performance at the Ankara state theatre in 2011 and had walked out of an interactive performance because one of the actors, Tolga Tuncer, had apparently picked on her for wearing a headscarf and chewing gum. Tuncer was summoned by the Culture Minister and told that actors 'had no right to interact with their audiences'. Tuncer said he had no idea that the lady in question was Erdoğan's daughter and he had only singled her out because she was chewing gum in the front row; it was, he added, an integral part of the play to involve audience members. In March 2012, the mayor of Istanbul responded with explosive anger to a Chilean play, *Daily Obscene Secrets,* which had been condemned by a religious playwright who had never seen it as 'vulgarity at the hands of the state', and demanded its closure. Following that, Erdoğan took the lead and vowed to cut funding to state theatres. Under his proposal, special provincial councils would follow the lead of a council already set up by the mayor of Istanbul, deciding which plays should or should not be shown in formerly self-governing state theatres. The response from the theatre world was understandable outrage, but accusations of political interference and downright censorship fell on deaf ears. Erdoğan declared that the days of 'despotic intellectuals' lecturing the masses were over, and had very much the final word: 'I am privatising the theatres. This is what I am going to propose: stage whatever play you want after privatisation, but you cannot get your salary from both the municipality and city theatres and then criticise the management. Sorry, but there is no such absurdity.'

If theatre is dead, then inevitably television must take its place. While the vast majority of Turkish television is vapid and depressingly irrelevant to real social concerns, there is a small but important corner of the *dizi* world which is rising to the challenge of tackling serious issues. *Hayat Devam Ediyor* (*Life Goes On*) is a primetime soap opera about an underage girl forced to marry a seventy-year-old man in Cappadocia, in central Anatolia. Underage marriage is a topic which is known about in Turkey but not usually part of public discourse. This particular series seems to be a labour of love by one man, Mahsun Kırmızıgül, a former Kurdish singer who has more recently become known as a serious film director. He sought the help of a women's rights activist group called Flying Broom, which campaigns against underage marriage and has submitted reports to the Turkish parliament about girls as young as thirteen being forced into marriage in some parts of Turkey – far below the legal threshold of seventeen, or the 'special dispensation' age of sixteen. Flying Broom provided a lot of the data for the series, and it is to be hoped that a primetime soap opera will reach millions of viewers, far more of the population than activists can influence. *Hayat Devam Ediyor* is undoubtedly melodramatic, involving many tears, arrests and recriminations, which will leave it open to criticism from cynics saying these are viewer-grabbing tactics. I don't see this as a problem. The real-life situations are equally dramatic, and it is established by now that the Turkish public respond well to melodramatic TV – I very much hope the show gets a huge following. I watched one scene in which former 'child brides' have a group therapy session, voicing total mistrust of their families and men in general. It is not comfortable viewing but it is important that people take in the reality of what it must be like, beyond the sterile statistics that can be found easily if one wants to – five and a half million women living in Turkey had been forced into underage marriage in 2009, for example, and in May 2013 the women's committee of the Turkish Lawyers' Association went so far as to say that one in four marriages in Turkey involved child brides. Perhaps some of them will watch the programme and realise they are not alone. Perhaps others, as yet unaffected, will see this 'tradition' in a new light. Most of all, I hope men watch it.

The general trend in the soap opera world is not for socially challenging or controversial programmes, unfortunately. But this is the case the world over; popularity is achieved by familiar, universal themes of love, social and familial conflict, played out in recognisable settings by beautiful people. What is interesting is that Turkey has got the formula so right that everyone wants access to it. Beyond the current sphere of influence in former Ottoman areas, there is interest from even further abroad – the Far East and the Americas, most significantly. MIPCOM is a commercial TV festival held at Cannes every autumn. In 2012, Turkish production companies represented at MIPCOM received interest from China and Korea, and American production company NBC Universal bought the rights of *Aşk-ı Memnu* in order to distribute it to Latin America, once the most prominent series exporter in the world. It seems that Turkey has triumphantly taken that title.

Turkish companies seem to be increasingly aware of the influence they have in the world. Like the Turkish soap opera industry, the national airline, Turkish Airlines, is a hugely important commercial ambassador for the country – it flies to more countries in the world than any other airline, carries around 39 million passengers a year and has made clever sponsorship choices with football clubs with its annual revenue of $13 billion. It has been interesting to watch the airline Ottomanise its image: first, the design for a new, Ottoman-style of uniform for flight attendants complete with kaftan and fez was 'leaked' to the public, only to meet with general outrage. Then, red lipstick and nail varnish for female flight attendants were banned – the same outcry ensued, and the airline quickly overturned the ban. Most controversially of all, the airline announced in early 2013 that it would no longer serve alcoholic drinks on domestic flights and eight international destinations, apparently because of lack of demand.

While I make no claim that these changes were instigated by the AKP, or are part of any kind of behind-the-scenes policy, it is interesting to see the Middle Eastward trend of the last few years in sectors as diverse as television and air travel. Just as Turkish Airlines is appealing to a hungry Arab audience with its not-so-subtle image change, so are Turkish soap operas with their glamorisation of Ottoman sultans and reworkings of Arab love stories. These changes make commercial sense, but they are part of something bigger. Turkey seems to be managing the extraordinary feat of modernising with a retrospective twist.

7

Business à la Turca

After the Californian gold rush of 1849, a new American Dream emerged. As opposed to the old, Puritanical ethos which had inspired people to accumulate a modest fortune year by year, the new aim has been described by the historian H. W. Brands as 'the dream of instant wealth, won in a twinkling by audacity and good luck'.

There are no equivalent gold reserves in Turkey, but there are infinite business opportunities, and people hungry and audacious enough to seize them in an economy developing at speed. Turks are a curious mix of big dreamers and risk-averse, middle-class plodders. There are nearly as many billionaires in Turkey as there are in France and Japan combined, and the number of lira millionaires in Turkey rose from seven thousand to more than fifty thousand in 2012. There are also many Puritan equivalents, the religious lower middle class, who are happy to ensconce themselves in traditional jobs like tailoring or shopkeeping, modest but secure. When big dreamers succeed, their success is all-embracing, attended by huge celebrity.

İbrahim Tatlıses ('Abraham Sweet Voice') is a Kurdish Arabesque pop singer and alleged mafia king who has created a massive business empire from nothing. He is a hyperbolic example of the potential of Turkish entrepreneurship, a man with very little education and boundless ambition who came from a working minority background, made shrewd decisions and manipulated his music celebrity to create a one-man conglomerate. 'Ibo' is a national icon, loved for his unapologetically sentimental music and revered for his commercial success. His wealth has also made him serious enemies – in 2011 he survived being shot in the head, having been the victim of two earlier assassination attempts during his extraordinary career.

Aside from selling millions of albums in both Kurdish and Turkish, Tatlıses has acted in scores of films and has his own weekly chat show. In his hometown of Urfa, fans flock to the İbrahim Tatlıses Museum to ogle shiny waxworks of the great man. His businesses are varied, but the most famous are his eponymous kebab chain and coach company, both of which dominate the entire south-eastern region of Turkey, where Ibo fans abound. He has construction interests in Kurdistan, northern Iraq, and unsuccessfully ran for parliament in the 2007 general election. Despite this rare personal failure, he has political support when it counts – after the latest assassination attempt in 2011, Prime Minister Erdoğan visited Tatlıses in hospital before the latter was whisked off to Germany for treatment. Photographs and footage of this visit were widely circulated in the press to advertise a friendship that came as a surprise to everyone but the most cynical.

It might seem that Tatlıses has overcome extreme obstacles to achieve his success, and in some ways this is true – certainly in the case of assassins' bullets. However, his Kurdish background and lack of education were, in some ways, part and parcel of his success. Formal education is not the natural springboard to mass celebrity; certainly in Turkey, people with degrees tend to follow reliable but unspectacular careers as engineers, technicians and lawyers. Tatlıses was originally a construction worker with nothing to lose and everything to gain, and that was a crucial part of his road to fame as well as sustaining his appeal in the long term as a man with whom millions of working Turks and Kurds could identify. He is, significantly, a rare example of a celebrity who thrives on his Kurdish identity. He has the devotion of a minority which accounts for nearly twenty per cent of the population, and the only Kurdish celebrity who rivals him in fame is Abdullah Öcalan, the jailed leader of the PKK. From 1989 to 1991 public music performances and recordings in Kurdish were censored, so when Tatlıses erupted onto the radio waves again in 1991, it was a triumphant return, almost a personal celebration. He is the champion of a demographic who claim him as one of their own, but he has been very careful not to over-identify himself as a Kurd. He sings in Turkish and is loved equally as a Turk. He is also very popular in the Arab world and Iran – his music has been the ultimate vehicle to national and regional fame.

Tatlıses is a prominent reminder to Turks that you can have it all. Far from discrediting his business gravitas, his popular music persona has been crucial to the success of his commercial ventures – people have an emotional attachment to the man and his art which makes them loyal to his products. In America, celebrities sell perfume and produce designer clothes. In Turkey, they sell kebabs and bus tickets. Here, as nowhere else, success is not nuanced or compartmentalised –

it is achievable and desirable in all incarnations and combinations.

Turks may not all be such ambitious dreamers as Tatlıses, but there is a strong family ethos which inspires many of them not only to provide for their immediate relations but to accumulate wealth for future generations. Prominent family dynasties who hand down their wealth from father to son are minor gods in Turkish society; they are few, but mighty, and everyone knows them.

Back in the 1920s two major family businesses took root: the Koç and Sabancı holding companies, which between them now seem to run most of Turkey's business. They dominate the construction, energy and finance sectors in particular; they each have founded prestigious universities and run world-renowned private museums in a spirit of mild rivalry. The grandfathers of the current, managing generation both started from nothing; Hacı Ömer Sabancı started working as a penniless cotton picker in the early 1920s, while Vehbi Koç sold vegetables from a cart in 1917. They both built business empires so successful that today all of their grandchildren are billionaires, holding top positions in their respective companies at the same time as running side businesses of their own. None of these men and women or their children or children's children will ever need to work, but their role in carrying the baton of the family business is as symbolically important as the co-operation of any Turkish family.

The Koç and Sabancı families have had several decades to accumulate and consolidate their financial and social power. Families who came later to the game are not so fortunate, and very few family-based companies are allowed to achieve such influence these days. The Doğan family, who founded their media and food company in 1980, are rumoured to have fallen foul of the government in the late 1990s and were fined 3.3 billion Turkish lira (£1 billion) for tax 'irregularity'. This is the standard accusation levelled by Turkish authorities at individuals or organisations that are in disgrace for something else, and is a convenient way of financially hobbling an overly successful company. In the case of Doğan, the perceived reason was that their media channels did not depict the government favourably. Now, after the protests of 2013, Koç Holdings' taxes are being investigated, predictably enough, following the family's support of protesters and perceived animosity to the government.

For the past few years Turkey has been universally described as an 'emerging economy', and its natural entrepreneurial spirit has thrived – most visitors notice this buzz as soon as they arrive in Istanbul. Everyone wants an empire of their own, in some shape or form. From small kebab joints to massive banking syndicates, there is an energy and drive to business life here that is comparatively lacking further West. Turkey is a massive country, more used than most European countries to economic crises, and Turks have buckled down where others have whinged and rioted. Mass production in particular is thriving, though this has dwindled slightly from its heyday ten years ago as wages have risen. It is a very young country – sixty per cent of the population are under thirty, and they are busy getting married, raising families and spending money on a far greater scale than the older populations of Europe.

This unprecedented level of spending is partly due to concerted efforts to lower interest rates – at the time of writing the interest rate stands at around six per cent, an all-time low. The current government has worked hard to achieve this, and is very sensitive to perceived threats. AKP ministers have repeatedly claimed – as during the Gezi protests of 2013 – that an 'interest rate lobby' is jealous of Turkey's economic growth and seeks to drive up interest rates to cripple the Turkish economy.

While the six per cent interest rate is still high compared to the UK, for example, it is low for Turkey, so people are borrowing freely. Banks encourage this, pushing credit cards relentlessly onto a people who are not traditionally comfortable with owing large amounts of money. They are also not conventional savers, which is equally problematic for banks. Turks are hoarders, specifically of gold. The government is currently encouraging families to collect the vast quantities of gold hidden away under mattresses all over the country, and bank it for the good of the economy. The total amount is estimated at $302 billion (more than Ireland's gross domestic product) and comes from a tradition of storing tangible capital, which can be transferred into cash in an emergency. It is a habit fuelled by mistrust of conventional banking after decades of economic unpredictability due to hyperinflation and political drama, a mistrust which peaked in 2001 when the inflation rate rose to seventy per cent. More importantly, gold is a big part of Turkish culture – at weddings, births and circumcision ceremonies, gifts are always given in the form of gold coins or jewellery, and stored for future family life.

I found out the importance of gold by bitter experience, turning up to a traditional Turkish wedding with a generic wedding present instead of the requisite gold coin. To my horror, the bride and groom stood by the door as guests left the reception, holding a large bag to collect the coins as they wished everyone goodbye with beatific smiles. With my wretched photograph frame in hand, I could not bear to join the queue; instead I found myself in a glass elevator escaping to the staff parking lot upstairs, probably seen by all the guests queuing below me.

The government is desperate for this stash of gold to ease the nation's current-account deficit of $60 billion. Foreign creditors are waiting, and the nascent boom must be sustained. The extent to which the Turkish economy is dependent on foreign investment and tourism was brought dramatically to light during the Gezi protests, when the lira fell every time Erdoğan talked about how negotiation with protesters was out of the question; as a consequence, the government was forced to sell nearly US$3 billion to keep the lira afloat. Hotels were left empty as tourists avoided a country which suddenly began to look more like its beleaguered neighbours, Syria and Egypt, and the government had to reimburse local businesses affected by the protests to the tune of fifty million lira. The protests exposed a more fragile economy than many people had thought, and the protesters' surprisingly successful boycotting movement threatened it even more. Major businesses like Garanti Bank and restaurants in the Doğuş Holding Group were boycotted because they were deemed to have links to people in government; Garanti alone lost a reputed $10 billion in the first few days of unrest.

Many Turks are pessimistic about the future and the protests have swelled speculation about an imminent crash. Having said that, the Turkish economy has been doing well for years and Turks are slowly altering their spending habits, giving momentum to growth. Banks advertise their credit cards like sweets – delicious, harmless and readily available – and many people go for the bait. The average Turk has a clutch of credit cards which they flash impressively as they open their wallet to pay for their friend's lunch – a selection of cards still suggests wealth rather than debt. The proud owner won't use all of them, but the option to spend is always there. In fact, so great is the proliferation of credit cards that the government has had to step in to stop banks advertising them so aggressively. In July 2013, Erdoğan delivered words of wisdom: 'Those credit cards, don't have them. If everybody spends as much as they [the banks] want, they would not even be able to earn that income. They could never be satiated.'

Turks are being offered more and more ways to pay for previously unrealisable dreams. Everything for sale, bar groceries, is available via monthly or even quarterly instalments. Since I have been living here, there has been a noticeable increase in the number of men undergoing hair transplants – they generally go in pairs, and I often see them wandering around on major shopping streets with matching hats or post-op headbands. Intrigued, I went online and discovered most clinics offering credit options for treatment, with links to specific Lebanese and Swiss banks in partnership with the clinics in question. I am sure there are two-for-one deals too, which would explain the pairings more satisfactorily than mere moral support. After a little more research, I found that certain companies offer special package deals to overseas clients which include the transplant procedure with short tourist trips. Medical tourism is a huge business in Turkey, attracting Arabs in particular to come for cosmetic surgery, combining their visit with a skiing holiday or a few days wandering around the Blue Mosque and Aya Sofya. The most intriguing cosmetic speciality in Turkey is moustache transplant surgery, for men who want a more virile-looking moustache. Arabs are particular fans, probably inspired by the well-endowed upper lips of celebrities like İbrahim Tatlıses.

Despite the overenthusiasm of banks to give out loans, many Turks don't seem to have bank accounts, especially small business owners. Traders in particular always want cash, and do not declare their earnings unless absolutely necessary. It is the same with my landlord, who claims not to have a bank account, so I give him wads of cash every month like a drug dealer, to ensure that he avoids paying tax on the rent he earns. This has been a huge problem for Turkish governments past and present, so they build in tax to necessities like petrol – which costs five lira (£1.70) a litre, the highest price in Europe – so that people have no choice but to pay it. If a Turk does pay tax legitimately, he is effectively double-taxed when he fills up the car with extortionate petrol.

Turkish consumerism is changing swiftly in big cities, but there is still a culture of face-to-face business that persists, especially in less developed areas. Despite the encroachment of bank loans, online shopping and malls, there is plenty of old-fashioned salesmanship on street corners, and an entrepreneurial energy as obstinate as the hawkers that I have already described. In the UK, the individual salesman spirit has declined almost to extinction. Everything is done via registered companies, and you can price-match online and deliberate as much as you like before parting with your money. In Turkey, a *carpe diem* attitude prevails, encouraging impulse purchases, and more importantly the chance to sell anything if you have enough enthusiasm and persuasive power to grab people's attention and credulity. Certainly, people shop online, but Turks enjoy living in the moment. More than that, they are comfortable with down-to-earth human interaction in a way that Western Europeans often are not.

One hot Sunday in September, I was on an oppressively crowded ferry to the Prince's Islands from mainland Istanbul, watching a man trying to sell metal spouts ('patented juice extractors') to an audience of grumpy, sweaty Arab tourists. Remarkably, the initially sceptical crowd showed interest and he had sold at least three spouts that I witnessed by the time we reached land. What I admired about this man was that, faced with the prospect of a potential customer base, albeit on a Sunday, albeit among tourists who probably had no interest in random kitchen apparatus, he seized the opportunity to work the crowd and, against all odds, managed to win himself some customers. In Britain, an embarrassed and cold reception would have awaited him, because it is just not the done thing to buy unorthodox juice extractors from strange men on ferries. Where's the warranty? Where's the instruction manual, where's the receipt?

There is a noticeably laissez-faire attitude to business here, despite all the hustle and bustle. A thin line separates friends and business associates, and there is a great deal of nepotism, which is an alternative way of looking at the culture of sustaining family businesses. Most annoyingly, lax payment is totally normal, although this has become less common since the days of sky-high interest rates and the corresponding profit one could make simply from sitting on cash for as long as possible. The Russian great-grandfather of a Turkish friend of mine was the tsar's pastry chef in the early twentieth century; he emigrated to Turkey and set up a successful wholesale bakery which, until the 1990s, used to supply some of the main supermarkets in Turkey. Eventually, the family business was sold because they could not cope with the cash-flow problems caused by late payments. Their debtors were companies with multimillion-lira turnovers, but they operated in the same way as any other opportunistic enterprise.

On the upside, Turkish business is very direct. If you want to trade with a Turk, you ring him up or walk into his shop and pitch an offer. My boyfriend sells British fabric to Turkish tailors and it is all very straightforward on the Turkish side – what really matters is money, so the conversation gets straight down to business. When my boyfriend deals with British companies, he must ring the purchasing manager at a certain time on a certain day of the week and an order will depend on the decision of this manager's regional manager. The whole process takes weeks. In Turkey, the same decision would be made within a single conversation, which makes business far more flexible. The lack of protocol can sometimes be a problem, but single traders and small businesses find it liberating.

I do not think it is a coincidence that Italian companies do very well in Turkey, with their Mediterranean adaptability. They manage to win huge contracts here, for example the £1.6 billion third Bosphorus bridge project, which is being carried out by an Italian company called Astaldi who also built the second bridge and the metro system in Istanbul; in addition Astaldi is beginning work on an enormous hospital complex in Ankara. Turks traditionally see eye to eye with Middle Eastern companies, as is evident from the current shift in business away from the EU and towards the Middle East and North Africa. Turkish construction companies secure multi-billion-dollar projects in countries like Qatar and Saudi Arabia, while these countries are rumoured to invest heavily in Turkey. Rightly or wrongly, people assume that there are important political reasons for this shift, which has been happening over the last ten years or so of AKP rule. Certainly, the AKP are overtly Islamic, and so are the governments of these countries. Commonalities like this do not automatically lead to strong business ties, but they suggest a closeness which in this case is complemented by Turkey's increasing disillusionment with the EU.

Turkey is popular among Arabs for all the reasons I explained in the previous chapter, and Turkish–Arab business is going well. Turks understand the way business is done in the region, so much so that British and American companies are seeking their help when trying to win contracts in the Middle East. I talked to a lady working at the UK Trade and Investment department in the British Consulate whose main mission is to ensure that British and Turkish companies work together in countries like Libya, Iraq, and Turkmenistan to get deals with local businesses.

As she described it, Brits and Turks have complementary strengths and weaknesses. Brits have their global reputations to prop them up; once an agreement is in place, the company and local authorities in, say, Iraq, will honour it because they respect the aegis of the United Kingdom. But Brits do not understand the way business works in Iraq and rarely get the deal in the first place if left to their own devices. At a meeting with a junior associate of the target company, the British delegation will politely state their terms for the deal, send a follow-up email, and then complain that no email has been sent in return. 'They haven't responded to our offer. The ball is in their court.' Turks have no such hands-off approach. They wait in person, for hours if necessary, to see the director of the company they are petitioning for the deal. They cajole, persuade, harass. If they are bidding for a construction project and the CEO wants lighting design and landscape gardening thrown into the bargain, the Turks agree without hesitation and make it happen. They are quintessential yes men, impressing their partners with apparent omnipotence, building bridges for future work. The trouble is that Turkey does not have the international political clout that Britain does, and the Iraqi or Turkmen authorities will not treat a Turkish contract with the respect they would afford a British one. To make the most of the strengths of both Turkish and British companies, the British Consulate has started this new initiative to supervise collaborations between the two.

It is less risky for Turks to exploit the Middle Eastern affinity with Turkey on home ground, and the tourism sector has been very responsive to the recent influx of Arabs. Increasing year by year, these tourists come in their millions and head straight to historic sites and museums which celebrate Turkey's romantic Ottoman heritage. In 2012, one opportunistic Turkish entrepreneur decided to test just how keen these tourists were, so he offered them something a bit special: air. They loved it. In fifty-six museums across the country, proudly branded Turkish and Anatolian air is on sale in tiny cans for sixteen lira (about £5) a pop, and these are now one of the top souvenirs sold in museum shops.

The visionary behind Airstock is a man called Halim Karslı, who obtained separate patents for Turkish and Anatolian air in 2011. He has marketed his air as something between a health product and a nationalist commodity – 'Whatever happens to the air of the world, let the air of Turkey remain good!' reads the blithe slogan on the can. Having travelled all the way from Morocco or Oman, Arab tourists no doubt feel that they should take home something unique, a physicalised portion of the hallowed atmosphere of Turkey. In shops in Istanbul, there is another product for sale – Istanbul Air, which presumably holds the patent for the polluted air of the sixteen million-strong metropolis. Airstock and Istanbul Air struck me as wonderful evidence for the apparently infinite capacity of the Turkish business mind to make something out of nothing. The sale of air has more than a whiff of the Emperor's New Clothes about it, but that is what makes it so commercially brilliant.

Turks are very skilled advertisers. The zeal of the individual salesman is carried over to the commercial sector, and to less mainstream avenues of marketing. In particular, the Turkish market is remarkably good at adapting to restrictions placed on it by the government, mostly in the forms of taxes or censored advertising. Put simply, Turks can sell anything, no matter what the obstacles.

As I've explained, the mainstream advertising of both alcohol and tobacco has been steadily prohibited throughout the

AKP's decade in power. Combined with increases in taxes that have made cigarettes and alcohol considerably more expensive, the result has been the growth of a hugely successful underground promotion scene in Istanbul in particular. A few years ago, in an attempt to overcome 'regulatory challenges', alcohol and tobacco brands started approaching individuals on the arts scene in Istanbul to host private parties, sponsored by the brand. These parties target a prime audience of young professionals far more effectively than mainstream advertising. Despite the obvious nature of the sponsoring, the parties still manage to retain an exclusive, glamorous atmosphere, as though the guests are lucky to count themselves part of what is essentially a giant advert – this is mainly down to the genius of the Turkish promoters who organise them.

Zeren Aslan was the particular mastermind of the 'guerrilla' party I attended. One of the top promoters and social sultans of Istanbul, his parties are legendary. Unusual venue choices like car parks, cellars and rooftops, multimedia entertainment and a network of the best contacts in Istanbul make him a far more valuable asset than any billboard space for clients like Absolut and Jameson Whiskey. Aslan is well aware that the exclusive nature of his parties encourages the elitist image the foreign brands are trying to promote, and we had a frank discussion about his methods in his sleek downtown office. 'I invite my guests personally by text message, and send out the details of the event only a week before. They are flattered. The party is not to be missed.' It is the sense of modern-day Prohibition-style secrecy, with an added dash of sophistication, that makes the parties so attractive. There is also no doubt that the relationship between Aslan and the brands is mutually beneficial. He used to earn €35,000 from selling the front cover of his monthly listings magazine to alcohol companies. As this is now illegal, he asks guests at his parties to design their own, which his staff then subtly seed with alcohol or cigarette branding. This scheme both pays for the party and creates the artistic factor that appeals to the typical 'guerrilla' partygoer, who likes to feel part of a creative community while secretly being rather thrilled at the element of free alcohol.

The huge growth in sponsored parties and festivals has not gone unnoticed by the AKP. In January 2011, a new bylaw made it illegal for those under the age of twenty-four to attend any event sponsored by an alcoholic brand, apparently an attempt to protect the young from free alcohol. This represented, of course, a sizeable percentage of the guest list for these events, and the law was received with widespread derision and outrage before it was repealed several months later. As of June 2013, any public sponsoring whatsoever is out of bounds to alcoholic brands, which means promoters like Aslan have to make absolutely sure their parties cannot be construed as public. Turkish alcohol brands in particular are adept at coming up with ever more inventive promotional methods. Efes Pilsen is at the forefront with its launch of Efes Alkolsüz, a non-alcoholic version, which now allows the company to advertise freely, with massive EFES lettering and the words 'non-alcoholic' in tiny print somewhere at the bottom of the advert.

On the other extreme of the marketing spectrum is the kind of conventional mainstream advertising that is designed to appeal not to the individualistic middle-class ego but to the mass mentality of the average Turkish consumer. One advert in particular caught my eye on the Istanbul metro, which is in some ways more advanced than the London Underground, the Paris Métro or the New York Subway. It may only have three lines (the third having recently opened), but it has slick stations and video advertisements in every carriage and station. From Şişhane to Taksim, bored commuters are treated to an advertisement for Istanbul Halk Ekmek, 'Istanbul People's Bread'. This three-minute film features a kaleidoscope of scenes from a huge, shiny bread factory, teeming with white-coated technicians and thousands of identical loaves churned out on conveyor belts. To a Western eye, the obvious mass production is repellent, almost an anti-advert. We are used to products being marketed as handmade, organic, farm-bought, artisan – as wholemeal and wholesome and far from a factory as possible. In Turkey, shiny technology like this is still impressive and attractive, something that attests to the advancement and quality of the brand, and by extension the product. Most of this particular advert is focused on the smooth workings of the gargantuan factory and the digital thermometers of the space-age ovens (billed as 'the largest in Europe'), rather than on the bread itself. The finished loaves simply whirl by like a utilitarian nightmare. The brand has the seal of the Istanbul Municipality, which means that it is *the* official bread of Istanbul. In Britain, it would be equivalent to Gregg's the Bakers teaming up with the City of London and giving itself the moniker 'The Londoners' Loaf'.

The most arresting moment of the advert, however, is saved until the end, when the camera zooms into a map of the world, magnifying an image of Turkey which glows red and turns into the Turkish flag before quickly spreading over the whole globe in a sinister, fiery blur of nationalism. The red globe then merges seamlessly with the emblem of the bread – IHE (Istanbul Halk Ekmek) – associating the brand with Turkey itself. Playing on Turkish national pride is absolutely key to securing the trust and good feeling of a wide consumer base. The marketers at IHE are clearly hoping that when people buy an IHE loaf, they feel they are buying a part of Turkey, becoming a cog in the wheel of the Turkish economy and its world-conquering greatness. The fact that this is a constantly running film on the central metro line shows that big returns are expected on a substantial investment. IHE stands are everywhere in Istanbul; nearly two million loaves are produced every day.

I used to watch this advert on my way to work in the financial district, where I learned a number of surprising things about the way Turkish businesses work, shortly after arriving in the country. The first lesson was that a successful company based in a shiny skyscraper in the middle of the City might well be employing a significant proportion of its staff off the books, while awarding them big bonuses. When I started working at a rather glamorous publishing company, I was handed an envelope full of cash at the end of my first week and taken for lunch by the editor in chief. A friend of mine works for a business data publication based in Istanbul, which claims to be based in Dubai for tax reasons, and she is paid in cash which comes via an account in the Virgin Islands. What I thought at first was highly dubious tax evasion in my individual company turned out to be pretty widespread policy. I went on to work freelance in other companies – banks, marketing companies – and discovered the real meaning of 'normal' business practice here.

Over forty per cent of Turks are employed off the books. This is because for every employee in Turkey, their employer must pay the equivalent of their salary in tax and social security to the government; an official employee is twice as expensive as an unofficial one. Many companies cannot afford to put people on the books, so employees often accept a slightly higher hourly rate but have to pay their own social security. They will also have no pension or insurance provision, of course, but for many Turks, this is not as terrifying as it might be for a Brit. A pervading belief in *kismet* (fate) usually means that Turks will chance it whenever necessary: 'What will be, will be,' they say. '*Kismet.*' If God decides to strike them down with flu or redundancy, that is His will, but it is more than a religious belief. It is an attitude: Turks live in the moment.

The AKP are believers in *kismet* but they are also believers in tax, so they are trying hard to encourage people to employ or be employed on the books. This usually takes the form of scare tactics; for example, a British consultancy company called WYG, which has a big presence in Turkey, is currently managing a government campaign of this kind, using cartoon leaflets with appealing characters and simple storylines. These characters endure disasters like broken limbs, redundancy and high medical bills all at once. They repent and, guided by the government's slightly spooky pixelated mascot, sign up for legitimate employment with happy smiles. The end of the story is a flash-forward scene of their cosy, pensioned old age. The leaflet is clearly aimed at the poorer, religious demographic who work for small businesses and are usually the prime candidates for tax evasion as both employers and employees.

As I have mentioned, there is a problem with underemployment of women in Turkey and the government has recently offered generous incentives to businesses to employ female staff: for example, no tax is paid for female employees for the first year, and after that only fifty per cent of the regular employment tax. There is a similar arrangement for young people, but no one seems to know about these incentives. Either the government has not done enough to spread awareness, or the financial pay-off is not enough to tempt most employers.

Some incentives for female employment are ridiculous. There is a law allowing a married woman to resign from her job at the request of her husband, within a year of starting work, with a full redundancy package. I found this out by accident when I questioned the puzzling presence of unclaimed mugs in the office kitchen cupboard where I worked. It turned out they belonged to women who used to work at the firm, but who had resigned recently, leaving unloved personal items behind. The law that allowed their paid resignation panders to the conservative tradition of a wife not being encouraged to work or being required to concentrate on childrearing. The law does not stipulate any kind of checks on women who make this particular resignation request, and so it is possible for a woman to repeatedly start a job, receive training and resign within the year, claiming the redundancy package as her legal right. There is very little a company can realistically do to combat this practice. The sobering downside to an otherwise quite amusing social phenomenon is that it makes companies less open to hiring a female over a male applicant – who knows if she is secretly a Serial Quitter? Better not risk it.

The macho business environment is being gradually balanced by more female promotions, as I mentioned, but sometimes this is done in a way which feels embarrassingly condescending to someone used to the Western version of equal employment. When I was working freelance at a major investment company, I arrived at the office on Valentine's Day to an atmosphere of jubilation. Five female employees had been promoted in honour of this most cherished of dates in the female calendar. Pink posters hung on walls; flowers had been placed on desks. The ladies in the office were all delighted, and of course promotions are great – but something in me felt deeply patronised and resentful at this exaggerated circus of pandering to the female stereotype. I'm sure it was done with the best intentions, and no one was offended but me. I am not sure, however, that J. P. Morgan's London branch would have reacted well to the Ladies' Valentine Special Treat.

The backbone of the Turkish economy is still mass production, despite the growing importance of the financial services and tourism sectors. Turks are brilliant at copying things and producing huge numbers of these copies. There are obvious, practical reasons for the success of this sector in this country – relatively low wages compared to Europe, plenty of workers and space for big factories among other things. Helped by a move towards 'fast fashion', Turkey continues to challenge China as the main exporter of mass-produced clothes to

Europe, mainly because it is much closer, significantly reducing shipping costs and delivery times. Chinese factories operate on such low profit margins that it is only worth their while to take orders in the thousands of tonnes; Turkey will do smaller orders, which means that high-street chains can order a new season's worth of stock, receive it on time, and order a different batch a few months later for next season. Dealing with China involves the risk of having thousands of late, outdated stock items sitting in warehouses accruing dust and storage fees, while Turkey is a relatively low-risk business partner. Having said that, only the biggest of Turkish companies succeed in the world of mass production – several of the independent clothes factories in central Istanbul have gone bust in the last few years because competition is so fierce and cash-flow problems are usually fatal.

Turks are the most enthusiastic followers of international designer brands outside of the Far East, so one of their most successful clothes-related markets is the replica designer industry. Foreign designer items are prohibitively expensive, so there is a roaring trade in what are often called 'genuine fakes', good reproductions. While genuine fakes may raise some interesting metaphysical questions in the mind of a native English-speaker, they are straightforwardly real when it comes to hard cash: from the 'Channel' perfume bottles sold in street bazaars for two lira (about sixty pence) to the exquisite Mulberry handbag replicas displayed in reputable shops for a comfortable seven hundred lira (£250), the Turkish passion for copying foreign designer brands is ubiquitous. The market value of Turkish-produced fakes has increased from one billion lira (around £320 million) to two billion lira in the last ten years, making it the second biggest counterfeit market after China, and the subject of thousands of lawsuits brought by individual brands as well as Turkey's long-suffering Registered Brand Association.

Big brands are the gold standard of quality, dizzyingly desirable, but why pay a fortune when you could have effectively the same product for so much less? In the most chi-chi parts of Istanbul one can find authorised Prada, Louis Vuitton and even Diane von Fürstenberg outlets; far more widespread are shops with names like FAME and LUKS selling pretty much the same products at a fraction of the price. The better the fake, the higher the price, but the discerning Turkish fashionista is still saving several hundred or even thousand lira apiece on good-quality products which are supposedly made in the same Turkish factories which produce the originals. The salesman's story is that the 'fakes' are made after normal working hours in, say, the Prada factory with exactly the same materials and are, to all intents and purposes, the same product. More probably, a single item is bought and copied by a 'designer' who studies its details like a clever painter forging a Caravaggio.

A few months after arriving in Istanbul, I went with my glamorous friend Leyla to a 'genuine fake' boutique near the Blue Mosque – the critic's choice, if you will. As I watched, Leyla ignored the prominently displayed shiny Prada models and moved swiftly to the Bottega Veneta section, where she picked out a classic criss-crossed tote. She opened it, ran a finger across the lining, squinted at the stitches and finally rejected it on the grounds of the size of the inside zipper. The owner, acknowledging a pro, brought out the superior stock, and eventually another bag passed her rigorous scrutiny and was purchased for four hundred lira (£150), about £2,500 less than the original. Leyla wears her bag proudly, without fear of discovery, even when she goes to a Bottega store to check out their new-season ranges in the name of research. The Bottega assistants note her bag and treat her like a queen, hoping for what they fondly imagine will be repeat custom.

A step above this kind of boutique store is the private seller who operates his business by invitation only. In the manner of an exclusive members-only club, new potential clients must be brought by an existing patron to an arranged viewing of the very best fakes available. Apparently (I am still hopeful of an invite), most of the clients are wealthy Arab women who could easily afford the original but get a thrill from buying several versions of a bag or favourite pair of shoes for the same price as one original purchase. There is quite a trend for this kind of retail tourism, and the net sales of desirable under-the-counter businesses like this probably make up a high percentage of Turkey's considerable undisclosed income.

The few Turkish designers who make it to international fame, like Nicole Farhi or Bora Aksu, are well respected and indeed commercially successful, but unfortunately there does not seem to be a huge appetite to follow in their footsteps. Designing copies for mass production is more lucrative in the short term than going to design college, but I think there are more important reasons than mere practicality behind the Turkish appetite for copying existing models and playing it safe.

The real reason is education. In Turkish schools, children learn a great deal by rote and regurgitate it for big exams in high school. Independent thinking is not encouraged, and creativity consequently suffers. For such a large country, there are not as many designers or inventors as there should be, because Turkish ingenuity is largely focused on new business ideas rather than invention for its own sake. Turkey is one of Europe's biggest car producers, with massive Renault factories in Bursa and outside Istanbul, but there has been no Turkish-designed car since the demise of the Anadolu marque in 1986. One still sees a few on the streets of Istanbul today but they went down especially well in rural Turkey, where their fibreglass bodywork was eaten ravenously by roaming farm animals.

I had never quite noticed the correlation between education and industry until I had a conversation with the owner of one of Turkey's biggest construction companies and got an insight into the Turkish business mind. As we talked, the man who had made billions from building roads and energy plants idly picked up his coffee cup: 'Look. A Turk picks up this cup and thinks, "I can make this." And he does – he makes hundreds of thousands, exactly the same. But it does not occur to him to design his own. This is Turkey's problem.' I found it both impressive and depressing that a man who had made his money by constructing things on a bigger scale than his competitors had such a clear insight into Turkey's problem with creativity. He was dazzlingly successful proof of his own theory.

8

The Dickensian Model

Turkey is a developing country – which is easy to forget when you're living in the cosmopolitan buzz of Istanbul – and it needs to concentrate its resources on building up its economy. That is not done by arts and crafts and individuality but by big industry, banking and construction. Turkish schooling is utilitarian. It prioritises useful, science-based subjects over useless arty subjects and is characterised by box-ticking examinations: ends-based, mechanical and deeply unattractive. There is so much creativity in Turkey, and it is almost always directed towards moneymaking. Many other countries could be charged with the same crime, but I have never before seen it so institutionalised as in Turkey. There is a tendency here to concentrate on the big picture in both business and schooling – overambitious returns on minimum investment, maximum marks from the most efficient cramming. This utilitarian 'big picture', while rewarding for the economy, is incredibly short-sighted for society as a whole.

Governmental and municipal neglect of the supposedly superfluous concerns of the arts and the environment, among other things, has a sense of impending tragedy about it – what will be the point of a flourishing economy when Turkey's landscape is entirely marred by ugly architecture and rubbish-strewn countryside? Who wants to live in a country thronged with houses expensively but hideously furnished, where people watch glossy soap operas on television, and theatres and libraries stand empty? I taught at a university in Istanbul and saw the products of the Turkish schooling system – grade A, uninspired and uninspiring students; I marched in the Gezi protests and saw these students transformed by a cause – courageous, creative and excited by the future, they were shining examples of what young people should be. The creative output of the protests was astonishing: strangers composed song lyrics together on the streets at night, dancers performed in Gezi Park and people of all ages and backgrounds scrawled poetic graffiti and cartoons on walls and roads everywhere. The contrast made me realise the tragedy of unfulfilled potential in Turkey, and why it is frustrating that a rapidly modernising country is held back by stuffy, outdated institutions and a lack of trust in non-mainstream sectors.

I wanted to work out what fuels the Turkish obsession with volume, repetition and uniformity. Turks are, traditionally, great believers in safety in numbers. If asked where they would live in a perfect world, most would probably answer: 'In a *site*.' A *site* (from the French *cité*) is a characterless gated community, with identical apartments, security guards and a token patch of garden within high walls. Pre-installed on all televisions within the apartments is a direct link to the building's security-camera screens. It is very telling that Turks are generally less concerned with where they live and more concerned with the building in which they live – provided, of course, that the neighbourhood is respectable (which is to say, full of similar *site*s). Apparently, people feel safer in the environment of a *site*, but what exactly they feel safe *from* was a mystery to me for some time. Today, crime is impressively low in urban areas and there are no obvious reasons to feel threatened.

The political upheavals of Turkey's past have a lot to do with the apparently baseless paranoia common to the Turkish middle class. In the years preceding the military coup in 1980 in particular, politically fuelled violence was common in cities and people at large were in considerable danger from various warring political gangs, most of all the extreme nationalists. A friend of mine, now in his fifties, remembers being beaten up by members of the National Front in the late seventies simply because he went to a high school at which German was the main language. The memories of these times live on, and although there is no equivalent physical persecution on the streets any longer, the fear remains, and has most recently been fuelled by the Gezi protests. Even before the protests, the old lady who lives on the fourth floor of my building had steel shutters on her (definitely inaccessible) back window, which I found amusing in a depressing way, like watching a hypochondriac swaddled in wool on a fine summer's day.

Turks still feel vulnerable on the international stage, and are arguably insecure at the epicentre of a conflicted geopolitical region. Much of their insecurity is historical, ingrained. The lingering sense of unease which persists from past troubles has resulted in a conviction of safety in numbers. On top of that, there is a swiftly growing middle class, which brings with it the old-fashioned, middle-class brand of paranoia that manifests itself as curtain-twitching in English suburbia, and is certainly not particular to Turkey.

As I described earlier, a village-like sense of community is still obvious in traditional neighbourhoods in Istanbul. While the relative novelty of supermarkets appeals to many city-dwellers, in small neighbourhoods people often prefer the daily visiting vegetable seller, not from any kind of individualistic consumer stance but because everyone else in the vicinity buys from him. He is a trusted part of the community, and in a strange way more unifying than an anonymous supermarket. On the other hand, malls are hugely popular. Galleria Atakoy in Istanbul was the first, modern mall built in Turkey, in 1988 – the Grand Bazaar of 1461 was the labyrinthine, long-lived precursor to the security-checked, concrete constructions of today. There are now 366 malls in Turkey, new ones popping up all the time for locals who crave their comforting, highly polished vastness. A mall delivers a reassuring sense of community in its own way; like a *site*, everything is contained within walls, other respectable people of middle to high income are buying from the same shops, and nothing is unknown or threatening. More than anything else, a trip to a mall is a fun day out for a Turkish family, especially in Istanbul, where there are hardly any green spaces.

I have never been to school in Turkey, so for a while I did not appreciate the link between the mass mentality I have been describing and the Turkish education system. However, about nine months in to my stay in Istanbul I was offered a post teaching Latin at the Boğaziçi (Bosphorus) University, situated next to Mehmet II's 'Throat Cutter' fortress on the European side of the Bosphorus. I had no formal teaching experience, I was in fact younger than some of my students, and my only qualification was that I had studied classics at a British university. Why did they hire me? Partly because there are very few Latin teachers in Turkey, but also because no one else would accept the ridiculously low level of pay offered by a state university. Ceyda Seçim, the charismatic don who persuaded me to take the job, was very honest about the state of things: 'Our teachers are here because they love it.' Fair enough, I thought. The following week, I represented the entire Latin staff of the university.

Boğaziçi is a puzzling paradox; currently ranked the top university in Turkey, it is modelled both architecturally and academically on an Ivy League university, while receiving totally inadequate funding from the state. It looks like Princeton from the outside and Wandsworth prison from the inside and follows the American style of courses composed of majors and minor options. It also follows a highly inflated grade system, which led to a fiasco when I came to mark my students' papers at the end of the year. Dealing out the kind of marks normal to an English university (where anything between sixty and seventy per cent is average), I awarded my students a clutch of what I considered unremarkable grades. A couple had done surprisingly well, a couple not so well. Within a few minutes of publishing their grades, I had received a deluge of emails from my students demanding an explanation for my outrageously low marking. One student asked, with chilling politeness, whether perhaps I had not received one of her answer sheets? Others were frantic, and one student, whose major was in genetic science, declared that I had ruined his life. I realised – rather late – that Boğaziçi followed the American system where anything below the eighty per cent mark is shamefully low. What I did not understand was why they felt entitled to demand that I increase their grades in such a hysterical and entitled manner. A fellow teacher explained: 'They think of you as a civil servant. They are studying in order to improve their chances of getting a good job, and they won't let you stand in the way of that.'

Boğaziçi picks the very best high-school applicants from national exam results, and boasts some great teachers, despite the ludicrous state salary. The department heads live in constant fear of their staff decamping to private universities like Koç, Sabancı, Bilgi or Yeditepe, where private funding is plentiful. I fear it is only a matter of time before Boğaziçi runs out of the historical cachet which currently ensures its top position.

I was so impressed when I first walked onto the campus for my interview: grey stone, ivy-wreathed buildings around a sun-dappled quad, an oasis of Ivy League sophistication in the middle of Istanbul. Inside the buildings is a different matter – the unmistakable smell of industrial detergent in dark corridors, walls badly in need of paint and no lift in a building of six storeys. Just like the rest of Istanbul, lazy feral dogs command the outdoor realms of the campus, and cats occupy most rooms – curled in library shelves, under desks, begging at tables in the canteen.

On the first day of term, I strode confidently into class, books in hand. To my dismay, I was faced by rows of expectant students, pens at the ready, who looked at least as old as me. In an effort to impress upon them my infinite knowledge of all things Latin, I began to talk airily of Catullus and fifth declensions, but was soon interrupted by a tortoiseshell tom-cat who completely ruined the gravitas of my teaching style by leaping onto my desk from nowhere. When I shut him out of the room, he mewed pitifully until allowed back in. From then on, I learned to embrace all manner of teacher's pets.

Boğaziçi is woefully underfunded. At the beginning of December in my first term, I arrived on campus one day to find the Western Languages building covered in scaffolding and workmen; the inside had been partly gutted already, and drills pierced the usual scholarly hush. I picked my way through exposed piping and buckets of paint to find the registrar, Yelda. She told me that all my classes had been relocated to the engineering department on the other campus for the foreseeable future.

'I see. Why?'

Yelda gestured at the rubble encroaching into her office and looked at me wearily. 'The department still has some of its budget left and has to use it by the end of the calendar year. They decided to renovate the building.' The unbending rules of state funding meant that the university would lose this portion of the money unless they used it before January. Instead of being saved for the next order of books for the understocked library, or added to the teachers' salaries at the end of the academic year, it had to be used now. So the run-up to December exams was blighted by noisy renovation; students struggled to find relocated classes and fought for precious library space as exams loomed, but the departmental budget was safely spent.

By contrast, the atmosphere in private universities like Koç is heavy with wealth and privilege. Renovation is the last thing needed, for one thing, the university having been built in 2000 by the multibillionaire Koç family. Car parks are full of Porsches, books spill out of Gucci handbags, and its fees ensure that – with the exception of a few scholarships – only the graduates of expensive private high schools can attend. The universities boast correspondingly expensive teachers, for example the celebrated historian Norman Stone, who has now left Koç for Bilkent University in Ankara, another private institution. Stone is a superstar among history buffs, former adviser to Margaret Thatcher and a bestselling author of genuinely gripping historical tomes, and yet he has been lured to teach on a remote university campus in central Anatolia. It is a significant and impressive choice, and partly reflective of the standards of private Turkish universities.

Teaching the products of the Turkish educational system at university level made me realise what the system was all about. My students were very bright, and had been picked for their exemplary grades at national high-school entrance exams, but their lack of interest in the subject was disheartening even for an accidental Latin don. The course was an elective rather than a core subject, so the students could be excused for not being as invested in Latin as in their major courses, but it was still rather sad that the most common question I ever got asked was: 'Will this be in the exams?' The answer 'Yes' would be met by a frenzied scribbling of notes, 'No' by a vaguely reproachful blankness.

Only one of my students asked anything in the spirit of enquiry rather than for exam-focused information. He was a unique individual in more ways than one, and my first introduction to his particular breed of intellectualism was a quasi-

Shakespearean email he sent in response to a businesslike query about weekly timetables that I had sent to the entire class before term started. His reply was clearly the product of much toil with a dated dictionary, his style both elevated and constrained by a concern to be as polite as possible to a new and potentially draconian teacher. I copy it below:

> Good Night Milady,
>
> I am indeed sorry if I bother you with my misunderstandings, but the group to whom you've sent the underlying message has already taken both Lat 111 and 112, hence are they all the would-be members of the 211 class.
>
> As for me, my schedule is totally available on Wednesday, thus it is a perfect niche for me to fill in with the Latin classes. Lastly, I would like to manifest that I might come to see you any time you find appropriate after 13:00; but if that would be beyond conveniance for you, I might as well chime in to the remaining party at 5 o'clock, at the place assigned.
>
> With my respects.
>
> İbrahim

I was of course delighted with this email and looked forward to meeting its author; he did not disappoint. A leftist, despite his formal English, he would stay behind after class to discuss Marx and the Beatles with me, and one memorable afternoon he delivered an awkwardly phrased but impassioned polemic on the atrocities committed by America on the English language. According to İbrahim, Americans should not be allowed to speak English, because it is a language fit only for the elegance of traditional English expression, as delivered by proper English people. İbrahim despised phrases like 'I figured' and 'That sucks' and refused to watch any Hollywood films on principle; previous exposure to the movie genre had instilled in him a hatred of actors like Tom Cruise and other prominent examples of the American Uncouth. İbrahim reminded me of my old-fashioned English grandfather, and yet here was an earnest nineteen-year-old Turkish boy, unshakeable in the charmingly snobby literary convictions which he had picked up from a childhood of reading English classics. He applied his pedantic rigour to Latin, demanding etymological explanations for all new vocabulary and asking expansive questions about the rule of Augustus. The rest of the class found him a great nuisance, as did I on occasion, but he kept us all on our toes, and actually I think he overdid the smart Alec act to prove a point – he had an intellect, and he wanted to feed it. İbrahim was a shining exception of curiosity and individuality among a class of clever young people dulled by their Dickensian school years.

At school I studied *Hard Times*, and thanked my stars that the likes of Mr Gradgrind, the fact-obsessed schoolmaster, and Bitzer, the chillingly well-informed teacher's pet, were a thing of the past. In Turkey, they are not. Dickens describes the young victims of Utilitarian education as 'little pitchers to be filled up with facts', and this is a disturbingly apt metaphor for Turkish schoolchildren, uniformly grinding their way through years of fact cramming to one exam they sit at the age of eighteen: the national university placement exam. This 180-minute exam consists of 160 multiple-choice box-ticking questions, which means the papers can be easily marked by computers; even Dickens's gloomy exaggerations are trumped by the digital age of assessment. The Dickensian enemy of Fact is Fancy, which is equally detrimental to the Turkish education system. Imagination is an unhelpful distraction when it comes to cramming for exams – accurate memorisation and regurgitation of the correct answers is all that really matters. Turkish teenagers are so used to these methods that when it comes to university, they are firmly set to cramming mode, unused to critical thinking and almost past the point of learning anything in the spirit of discovery. I began to feel guilty whenever I taught my students anything that wasn't on the syllabus that, ironically, I myself had set (Latin is an extremely niche subject in Turkey). I was not, in fact, teaching – I was merely talking while they looked at me as if to say: 'Why are you wasting our time?'

Turkey's university and high-school attendance is relatively low: 31 per cent of adults aged between twenty-five and sixty-four have earned the equivalent of a secondary school qualification, much lower than the OECD average of 74 per cent. Those who do continue, however, work extremely hard, to a prescriptive and exhaustive curriculum, and they are mercilessly examined. Turkish schoolchildren go straight from school to the *dershane* – a private 'lesson house' – to cram a few more hours of study in before bed, and these are not just the children with pushy, moneyed parents. Examinations are tough and increasingly competitive, with 1.6 million students fighting for four hundred thousand university places. The *dershane* exists solely for the purpose of exam preparation and has become the norm for every schoolchild, regardless of wealth. On a bus in Urfa, south-east Turkey, I met a man who worked as a caretaker for a German archaeological team. He told me about his family – his daughter was blind and, while the state helped pay for a braille teacher, he spent more than half his income on sending her and her brother to the *dershane*. So even though the state provides free schooling in Turkey, effectively it is not free for those aiming for university because normal school hours are not adequate to keep up with the required standard. There is a similar situation in Taiwan and Hong Kong at the moment, where parents spend disproportionate percentages of their salaries on their children's education. It has become a sordid mathematical equation of money + extra schooling = some ambitious % increased chance of university entrance.

The Turkish *dershane* reminds me of my own experience of the Japanese *juku*, a comparable kind of cramming school which is as widespread in Japan as the *dershane* is in Turkey. I attended a state primary school in London, with patchy levels of teaching, especially in the maths department. Aged nine, I had a Japanese friend called Aki who was brilliant at maths, and who often declined my offers to play after school as she went to an after-school study centre called Kumon, a hugely popular Japanese crammer now available worldwide. My parents decided this was the thing for me, and I attended, miserably, for a few weeks. Hour after dreary hour of symmetrically aligned, repetitive sums was only made worse by looking around the silent 'classroom' at the heads of my more studious peers bent over their individual work. Academic progress was measured by the ratio between the speed at which we could complete a page of sums and the number of mistakes we made in that page, as though we were computers of variable efficiency. Aki was, indeed, brilliant at maths, as are most Turkish schoolchildren, but at what unquantifiable, Kumon-defying cost?

There are those who accuse *dershane* and *juku* owners of excessive profit seeking, exploiting parents' fears of their children's failure for their own financial gain – there is almost no price a parent is unwilling to pay for their child's education. Kumon alone is worth $650 million, and it is impossible to estimate the value of the market as a whole. There are even darker rumours circulating in Turkey about collaborations between religious *dershane*s and the government; it is said that the education ministry secretly feeds the answers of national exam questions to *dershane*s run by Islamic groups, to ensure that religious children get places at top universities. As with all conspiracy theories in Turkey, this has a high likelihood of being false. What is certain is that the market for after-school crammers is hugely profitable and, sadly, as open to corruption as any other institution anywhere in the world.

The commercial competition between various *dershane*s can be vicious. The average Turkish town in the run-up to September will have several large billboards advertising the top students of a particular *dershane*, their photographs emblazoned with exam percentiles and names alongside: local teenage superstars arranged in first, second and third place like Olympic champions. In Istanbul and Ankara, the adverts might have a clutch of names followed by famous American universities to show off the number of students who achieved the Holy Grail of parental ambition thanks to the efforts of this particular *dershane*. Every July when results come out, newspapers and television channels descend like vultures on the top few students in the country and conduct interviews with these rather dazed child prodigies. If the struggle for university places is a war, then the *dershane* is a form of warfare, and the war will continue until more university places are created.

The Turkish Education Ministry says it cannot afford the extra teachers and examiners necessary to reduce class sizes and broaden the national examinations, given the volume of applicants. One of the attractions of the national university application system is that it is actually very fair, because it is based entirely on multiple-choice questions, the answers to which are either right or wrong: clinical and dry, perhaps, but straightforwardly quantifiable, unlike arbitrary essay marking. Turkish students are graded and placed within a national percentile which determines which universities will accept them. The scheme is totally anonymous, so no one knows who you or your parents are, as opposed to the system in Britain and America, where personalised applications – including personal statements and interviews – give the admissions department an accurate estimation of your socio-economic status, whether they use that information or not. Ivy League universities are notorious for accepting a handful of average students whose parents have been generous to the school's coffers, justified by what they call the 'legacy' system of favouring the children of alumni. This arrangement ensures future donations to the school, which are used for the benefit of all students. There are pros and cons of this system, but it is not something that Turkish universities engage in, at least on an official level. If you are clever, that is reflected in the calibre of the university which accepts you in a relatively uncomplicated way.

The Turkish system of assessment, while technically fair, does not encourage or reward critical thought. Some of my brightest friends from school and university in England would probably be classed as simpletons if they took the national exam, because while they can write brilliant essays on the imagery of James Joyce, their knowledge of simple algebra is lost in the mists of time, thanks to the British system allowing subject specialisation from the age of sixteen. It gives one food for thought – thousands of high-school dropouts in Turkey may be stuffing kebab buns as they ruminate on Rumi, literary geniuses thwarted by their own one-sided intelligence and bumped off the conveyor belt of Fact to make room for duller, more mouldable students. Given this background, one can see how İbrahim the Shakespearean eccentric was such a unique individual. He was not cleverer, but merely more independent-minded than his peers, and that made all the difference to his approach to life.

A question remains: why are Turks so obsessed with doing well in exams? On a material level, entry to a high-ranking university will lead to a good degree and a well-paid job, which everyone wants. But beyond that, there is an acute concern with the status that comes with all of that. The top five per cent of students in Turkey study electrical or industrial engineering as a matter of course, simply because it is considered the most demanding subject. Even if a top-grade student has an intellectual appetite for architecture, literature or psychology, they would be extremely unlikely to choose any of these courses because they would be passing up the opportunity to be recognised as the best of the best. Their family would be horrified, for one thing.

In Turkey you do not study for yourself or for the subject itself, you study for the respect and money it will earn you. Young professionals follow the dictates of their milieu when it comes to education, but this crowd-pleasing instinct is true across Turkish society – in commerce and social attitudes as well as education, as I will discuss in the next chapter. It is a very dangerous thing when it comes to education. It means that there is a lack of outstanding professionals in sectors like mental health and architecture, because these careers are considered secondary to engineering and conventional medicine.

On a brighter note, careers in the arts are gradually getting more popular in Turkey. I talked to an arts management director who has worked in Turkey for thirty years, and who was very excited that school-leavers in Turkey are increasingly enrolling in graphic design and music colleges, defying the limits of mainstream education, and opening up galleries or starting film companies. There is a significant underground music scene in Istanbul, with a particularly large French following who come for particular DJ nights at niche electro clubs. It is not really fair to compare Istanbul to London or New York on the arts front, because it is simply not such a well-established cultural capital. The fact that it is even considered in the same class is a huge compliment given that, until recently, it was the biggest and most problematic city of a turbulent country beset by huge economic problems. Now it is catch-up time, and many curators and festival organisers I have spoken to predict that Istanbul will soon be able to contend with major international cities for genuinely cutting-edge arts and design. Turkish artists like Cannes Grand Prix winner Nuri Bilge Ceylan, artist Tracey Emin and Nobel Literature Prize-winner Orhan Pamuk – to name a few of the über famous – are in some cases more famous abroad than in Turkey. Emin, for example, who is half Turkish Cypriot and grew up in Britain, would never have gained the prominence she currently has if she had pursued her career in Turkey, or indeed Northern Cyprus. Whatever you may think of unmade beds and sketches of anthropomorphic genitalia, they represent a kind of art more warmly received in Britain than in Turkey. Perhaps, with a growing number of brave young artists, this is set to change.

While criticising the herd-like mentality of the average Turkish classroom, it would be wrong not to mention the incredibly brave individuals who protested on university campuses against the suppression of freedom of thought, long before the Gezi protests swept the country. Turkey has the highest number of imprisoned journalists in the world, and it is notoriously dangerous to have any kind of link to anything in the manner of Kurdish rights or leftist-sympathising groups – the mildest of connections to either of these is construed as sinister 'anti-Turkish activity'. While I taught at Boğaziçi, there were several protests on campus, but the most memorable was that stemming from the arrest of a female student who was discovered by police to have made a job application to a leftist thinktank. Her boyfriend organised a protest against her arrest, collecting signatures from his fellow students to petition for her release. As I arrived for work one Wednesday, banners demanding 'Free Özge!' were being strung up outside the undergraduate common room by her friends. On Friday, Özge's boyfriend was arrested and this was duly protested against by the friends who remained, in a sad cycle of futility.

Students who dare to question state university fees are equally at risk; fees are low by British standards, but cause much controversy. In June 2012, two undergraduates, Berna Yılmaz and Ferhat Tüzer, were sentenced to eight and a half years each for unfurling a banner which read 'We want free education and we will get it' in front of a building in which Prime Minister Erdoğan was holding a meeting. Initially held for eighteen months in custody during the trial, the two were finally convicted of membership of a terrorist organisation. This organisation was not, to my knowledge, identified by the court, probably because there was no such membership. Yılmaz, a student of archaeology and Tüzer, an engineer, are in prison as I write. When they are released they will be in their early thirties, without the degrees they started ten years earlier.

In July 2013 Erdoğan announced that police would be re-placing private security at state universities. This came in re-sponse to the Gezi protests where, according to Erdoğan, young protesters were wandering around 'with Molotov cocktails, machetes and whatnot'. The image of Boğaziçi University's leafy campus dotted with armed police is a terri-fying one and prompts the question: whom exactly will po-lice be protecting, the students or the state?

Terrorist links and 'insulting Turkishness' have always been convenient excuses to lock up troublemaking students and intellectuals, and the desire to avoid these charges has greatly influenced the development of academia. Broadly speaking, leftist-leaning academics are vilified, while dons who write papers along acceptable nationalist lines are promoted – in the eighties, for example, professors were sacked because they refused to shave their bohemian (and therefore leftist) beards off. This is changing now as nationalism becomes less *de rigeur* under the current government. Schools, too, are getting less nationalistic, though not by European standards. Most Turkish schoolchildren still take a regular oath of national allegiance; they learn in great detail about the life and teachings of Atatürk and his face is on every wall. A primary-school teacher I spoke to told me that she gets her children to write letters to Atatürk thanking him for his life's work, to personalise their Turkish history lessons. This teacher told me with pride that one child expressed her regret that Atatürk's mother never lived to see his full achievements. Another letter contained a paragraph dedicated to the beauty of his blue eyes. This is more than a little strange for a European who comes from a country with no equivalent background of hero worship – when it comes to the Turks' relationship with Atatürk I often feel like I am intruding on a private relationship that is, in fact, confusingly public. The Atatürk-centred education of Turks does not stop at school. In the first term of every university degree, no matter what it is, there is a mandatory course on the founding father of modern Turkey.

A strong nationalist and secular bent has characterised Turkish schools since the 1920s, but in the past few decades this has been quietly but insistently challenged from the sidelines by various religious organisations, some of them the

Sunday-school equivalents of local mosques. The most influential and far-reaching of these religious organisations is the Gülen movement, which runs a thousand schools offering an unobtrusively religious education in Turkey and abroad, as well as many of the *dershane*s which supplement Turkish schools. The Gülen movement, known as Hizmet or 'The Service' to its followers, was set up by the Turkish Islamic cleric Fethullah Gülen in the 1970s and now runs schools in 140 countries, as well as several media companies including *Zaman*, a popular Turkish newspaper. Quite often its workings are not officially linked to Gülen, but his influence is unmistakable. There is something of the Freemasons about the movement, but it is much less fussy and exclusive – it casts the recruitment net far and wide. Gülenists refer to themselves as the *cemaat* ('gathering of the faithful'), and there is a sense that once you're in, you're in a supportive environment for life. As cults go, it is definitely on the benign end of the spectrum, but lots of people feel uncomfortable about the extent of its influence and the simple fact that it is an Islamic organisation, moderate or otherwise. The *cemaat* mentality extends to business circles too, and is not specific to the Gülen movement, although Gülenists are notable businessmen. In many circles in Istanbul and cities in the middle of Anatolia, pious individuals gather to perform charitable works, and in the process, they build social networks which give their members an advantage in business. These are not intentionally exclusive communities, but in effect, a sole businessman can get nowhere until he has paid his respects to the leader of the local *cemaat*. If you are willing to do that, you have immediate contacts and channels open to you, because you are a trusted member of the community. If not, you might be rather stuck.

Fethullah Gülen himself is a rather mysterious figure, despite his faux-modest personal website. He is an ex-imam turned Islamic scholar who would use tears to great effect when addressing his Izmir-based congregation, generating the kind of emotional hero worship not common for Turkish imams. He is heavily influenced by the relatively mystical branch of Islam, Sufism, which encourages a personal relationship with God, and is revered by his millions of followers across the globe, who call him Hoca Efendi, 'Master Teacher'. He reminds me slightly of Sai Baba, the controversial Indian mystic-guru who was adored by millions but became dogged by rumour towards the end of his life, leaving behind hundreds of ashrams, schools and a legacy of near-divine status in India and abroad, as well as a great many critics. Gülen is a decidedly more mainstream figurehead, promoting the kind of moderate and responsibly organised Islam which many see as preferable to the fanatic fringe groups springing up over the Middle East, and indeed the West.

Gülen is still too religious for many people's tastes, including the previous Turkish government's. In 1999 he fled to the US and in 2000 was tried *in absentia* for plotting to overthrow the government. As he left, he entrusted the schools he had started to his key followers, telling them to 'be vigilant'. He used to be very friendly with the current AKP government, and was in fact acquitted of the state charges against him in 2008, a few years after the AKP came to power. However, Gülen is still in self-imposed exile in a gated compound in Pennsylvania and chooses to remain there, despite

Erdoğan making a public call for his return in 2012. There is a very intriguing power balance between the two men.

Gülen's souring relationship with the AKP belies his claims that religion has no place in politics. It is widely accepted that Gülenists hold many of the most influential positions in the judiciary and police forces in Turkey, and that Erdoğan used Gülen's help to curb the power of the military in the first decade of AKP rule. Since then, the power vacuum left by the military has led to wrangling between Gülenists and the AKP. This is all conjecture among journalists and academics, because Gülen's public announcements are about peace and harmony and there is little to go on beyond significant events like his rejection of Erdoğan's appeal to return to Turkey, and unexpected shakings-up in governmental positions. It is difficult to get to the bottom of things, particularly when most Gülenists put complete trust in 'The Service' and refuse to countenance the idea of any untoward political goings-on.

Either way, schools are the real root of the Gülenist movement. The interesting thing is that most of them have no explicitly religious teaching, and schools in the US, Africa, Japan and elsewhere have a wide range of students of various ethnic and religious backgrounds. Having said that, there is a strong Islamic ethos nurtured by Gülen's personal rhetoric, and the schools instil incredible loyalty in their students. Many of the Turkish students come from poor, religious backgrounds, and therefore feel they owe everything to the Gülenist school which made it possible for them to go on to university and have subsequent successful careers. Ex-Gülenist students typically give back a portion of their earnings to the movement, similar to the charitable donations (*zekat*) required by Islamic law. This payback scheme generates a cycle of loyalty and commitment, and this has led to accusations that the whole movement is a profit-seeking one: critics say that Gülenists poach clever children, train them up to get high-paying jobs and then plough the 'gratitude money' back into the organisation. Other people are convinced that Gülen is working with the CIA (how else would a religious scholar have access to billions of dollars?) and that the extensive network of Gülen loyalists working within the judiciary and police are in fact serving an American agenda of keeping Erdoğan's power in check while promoting moderate rather than extreme Islam in Turkey, a key ally of America in the Middle East. Frustrated by never-ending conspiracy theories, I tried to find someone to talk to who actually had dealings with a Gülen organisation.

I interviewed a philosophy teacher at Fatih University in Istanbul, a very conservative university that has ties with Gülen but is not officially affiliated. He told me that the content of his course is entirely up to him, and his teaching of Descartes's questioning of God is totally unmonitored by the university authorities, as is the course taught by a colleague on Sexual Deviancy. Other, more religious teachers teach their own way. Sometimes this is confusing for students, particularly when they are taught the same subject by two different professors. One student in a sociology class questioned a teacher who called himself a member of the *cemaat*, asking him about a definition he had given of 'family' which contradicted that given by an evidently secular teacher. 'Ah,' said the Gülenist. 'That is a Western formulation. It is different from ours.' There was no attempt made to dictate a 'superior' definition, but a subtle point was made. This subtlety seems to define the Gülenist modus operandi.

Undergraduates at Fatih University often come from Gülenist schools in Africa or the Balkans and are, according to the philosophy professor, very bright, fluent in English and much more analytically minded than the average Turkish student, because the Gülen method is not shackled by the nationalist bent of conventional Turkish education. Having said that, I am sure it places its own subtle parameters on its private curriculum; I have noticed, for example, that in the Gülenist newspaper *Zaman*, certain events like gay rights parades are never mentioned, and a couple of columnists have been dropped for veering from the editor's line: nothing too overt, but enough to catch the eye.

Many people praise Gülenist institutions because they are actually very inclusive. They welcome female students both with headscarves and without, stressing the importance of study above the issue of religious practicalities. Institutions like Fatih University provide girls-only dormitories so that religious girls can come and study with the blessing of their families. There is nothing ostensibly wrong with the Gülenist movement, and a great deal of apparent benefit: a high standard of education is provided to children who might otherwise not get it, girls from religious backgrounds are encouraged to study and a tolerant, moderate form of Islam is promoted in a world where fanatical Islam is becoming more and more of a problem. These are all good things, but there is still something that makes me uneasy about a schooling system that has at its heart a highly opinionated figurehead with a mysterious involvement with politics. There is something about the movement that is shifty, particularly its method of attracting teenagers from non-religious backgrounds via a network of *abiler* and *ablalar* – 'big brothers' and 'big sisters' – young Gülenists typically in their early twenties who befriend the teenagers before introducing them to the movement. Perhaps it is all for the good, but it is underhand.

While it is an interesting sign of the times that Turkey's nationalist education is moving almost imperceptibly towards a more religious bent, it is still education with an agenda attached. It would be nice if Turkish classrooms were unfettered by a biased curriculum of any kind, nor terrorised by mind-numbing exams. Assessment is a necessary part of education, but it should be secondary to learning, not an overshadowing goal in itself. I left Boğaziçi mainly because there was no money to pay temporary staff, but I might have stayed had there been less of a preoccupation for mark-hungry note taking among my students. İbrahim, while charming, was too solitary a counter-example to the norm. He brought to mind a fourteen-year-old scholar taught by my grandfather at Winchester College, who complained that 'College is a walled garden, and I, a wild rose.' This rather nauseating sentence is an example of something a Turkish student would never, ever say – the Turkish classroom is all wall and no garden.

9

New Look

All wall and no garden: the same could be said of Turkey's recent concrete transformation. The construction boom of the past twenty-odd years has distorted the country, adding swathes of concrete to existing towns, sprinkling apartment blocks on mountainsides and inserting ill-judged monuments in city centres. Turkey is, in fact, breathtakingly beautiful, and has probably the most varied of landscapes in either Europe or the Middle East. The aquamarine coves of the Mediterranean are humbler cousins of the Amalfi coast; the stark, prehistoric plains of the Central Anatolian Plateau suggest the moors of north Yorkshire in baking heat, and the Caucasian wilderness of the Black Sea mountain ranges is softened by the greenery of an Alpine summer. Turks are rightfully proud of this beauty, but unfortunately a lucrative and hungry construction sector is hard at work, ably assisted by the government, hacking away at the countryside and bulldozing the last scraps of urban parkland and surrounding forestry into dust. The Mediterranean coves have been partly preserved, parly ruined for the sake of package tourists but the greenery of the Black Sea region will be history if water-diverting dams are built at the rate they are now. No one cares much about the Anatolian plains so maybe they will be left alone and unmolested in millennia-honoured tradition.

The furore over Gezi Park proved the extent to which green spaces are under threat in Turkey. Gezi is one of the last remaining parks in the centre of Istanbul, precious for locals and developers alike, which is why locals had to fight so hard for it. The AKP regularly trumpet the fact that they have planted more trees than previous governments, but they seem to cut them down at a fairly rapid rate, in more important areas. AKP municipalities plant flower beds and small parks, generally in the suburbs, where land is cheap. Out by the airports there are plenty of herbaceous motorway borders, which no doubt impress first-time visitors to Turkey as they taxi into town, but prime real-estate potential in the centre is always dealt out generously to developers, especially those with good connections. Sometimes, considerations other than money are involved, for example personal ego. Gezi Park was standing in the way of the prime minister's personal project to rebuild an Ottoman barracks of great Islamic significance. Erdoğan has a number of grandiose plans, such as a thirty-mile-long canal (which he has personally named the 'Crazy Project') to be built to the west of Istanbul, connecting the Black Sea to the Sea of Marmara and thus transforming Istanbul into an island city. It has the express purpose of diverting shipping away from the Bosphorus, because Turkish authorities cannot charge ships going up the Bosphorus thanks to the Montreux Convention. The canal will, supposedly, be very lucrative. The Turkish treasury has said it will cost $10 billion to build, and has already set aside the money, vowing proudly that no foreign loans will be taken. Land around the canal site shot up in value years ago, leading to speculations of government tip-offs. The canal's projected

opening is 2023, the centennial of the founding of the Turkish Republic, and if Erdoğan's presidential aspirations go to
plan, he will be finishing his second term as president in style
that year.

The mind boggles at projects like these, but there are
plenty of instances of smaller, less significant building projects or municipal attempts at beautification that smack of
the same kind of pretension. One example is the faux-grandiose monuments that have been imposed on city centres across
the country. Most of Turkey's cities are steeped in history and
graced with the architectural relics of the Roman, Byzantine, Selçuk and Ottoman periods. These cities have unique
histories and characters which need no embellishment, so
the 'municipal symbols' that have been erected in the last
few years are both undignified and puzzling. The officially
chosen symbol of the city of Diyarbakır in south-east Turkey, for example, is a watermelon, so an oversized concrete
watermelon has been deposited in the central square atop a
fake castle, an absurd object masquerading as a serious edifice,
like a GCSE arts project deposited in Trafalgar Square. In
Inegöl, a mighty hand holds a four-metre fork upon which is
brandished a monstrous concrete *köfte* meatball – half intimidating and wholly unappetising; in the city of Van, the municipal mascot is a Van cat with one eye painted green, the
other blue, in true pedigree style. Edirne's city centre features
a celestial hand holding a bowl of garishly painted fruit; another statue depicts two oil wrestlers grappling on high. With
some notable exceptions, these symbols are fairly arbitrary.
Most cities claim as their official symbol something that is
common across many regions in Turkey – Nizip, for example,

claims the pistachio, which is grown prolifically across the whole Antep region. Watermelons, while admittedly abundant in Diyarbakır, are ubiquitous across the southern half of Turkey, and certainly not the first thing that springs to mind when one hears 'Diyarbakır' (troublesome PKK spot, yes). These monuments are artificial in every sense, conceptually and visually meaningless. They are symbolic not so much of the cities they supposedly represent but of the tasteless and self-important 'planning' that goes into urban construction in Turkey today.

Construction here is excessive, frenzied: cranes swing above young men hauling gravel on busy roads and drills interrupt thought and conversation every day in every city. Istanbul is under siege, and Erdoğan's 'crazy projects' do untold damage to its environs. Work on the £1.6 billion third Bosphorus bridge started in 2013, the £19 billion third Istanbul airport will be completed by 2017 (*if* financial backing is still to be found after the Gezi Park debacle), and all the while thousands of new apartment blocks are built on the peripheries of a city swelling in an unprecedented and precarious property bubble.

Driving through the rapidly expanding towns and cities of Anatolia, one has the ominous sense that the construction boom is getting out of control, like the spread of randomly coloured Lego blocks a toddler assembles haphazardly over the floor of his playpen. As the economy expands and construction magnates get ever more ambitious, short-term concerns are painfully evident: big concrete tower blocks with low ceilings fit in as many tenants as possible; many of them lie empty, sad relics of an overambitious developer. Gardens are rare, despite the fact that Turks love open, green spaces. There are so few parks in urban areas that on weekends you see ridiculously overcrowded little pockets of green almost obliterated by huddles of picnicking families – occasionally I pass a traffic island in Fener, Istanbul, where a token scrap of lawn gets completely filled by families on their day out, rugs and barbecue sets spilling out over the floral border practically into the path of passing cars. For a nation that so enjoys the outdoors, it is a horrible irony that construction has got to its current level.

This may be upsetting, but it is not surprising: land equals property potential, which equals money. Turkey is a developing country and profit is paramount. Construction generates a lot of money, giving employment to a young workforce, but not, it would seem, to a skilled body of architects. Preserving the existing landscape or respecting original architecture are secondary concerns that only the rich can afford to heed on private land – forget about the public domain.

Wandering through cities like Istanbul, Antep and Izmir, where elegant old *konak*s and mosques are flanked by brutally square concrete blocks, I am reminded of the awkwardness of a chronologically confused Oxford college, its fourteenth-century cloisters marred by seventies accommodation blocks protruding outrageously amid the quiet of the original architecture. The difference between the two cases is that those seventies constructions were designed by someone with aspirations to taste, however terrible, whereas taste did not even enter the drawing board of recent architecture in Turkey. New buildings here are primarily characterised by disproportioned right angles painted in garish colours, wherever they happen to be; the ubiquity of this kind of building almost suggests a trend, but not quite.

This kind of excessive, ruthless construction is not a crime particular to Turkey. It is a trait of developing countries, and European states, now so smug, were all once guilty of it. Ugly buildings crop up everywhere, all the time. Nevertheless, in places like Britain an overdue appreciation of old architecture has emerged relatively recently, resulting in Grade A listings and, in some areas, draconian planning permission laws. Europe is just a little further down the line than Turkey in understanding the adverse effects of over-hasty urban 'development'. She has the regret of an ageing grande dame who didn't appreciate her youth and ruined her body with excessive sun exposure and heavy boozing. Now, older and wiser, she deplores her past follies and yearns for what she no longer has, belatedly funding National Trust and Heritage sites. Turkey is her beautiful but reckless younger counterpart, who will come in turn to realise her mistakes.

These mistakes are already being noticed in a few pockets of Turkey, for example in Mardin, an ancient town near the Mesopotamian border. Old Mardin stands on a hill, an intricate ants' nest of very old sandstone houses, churches, mosques and monasteries topped by a citadel on the crest; an ugly new town of concrete apartments skulks at the bottom of the hill. Tourists love the Old Town, which still has a hodgepodge of long-standing residents (Muslims, Christians, Arabs and Kurds), while the majority of the town's population live down the hill in identical new apartment blocks which are cheaper and more convenient than those on the steep, cobbled streets above. Recently, municipal authorities have started an extensive project of restoration in the Old Town, pulling down modern buildings and repairing the original architecture. While an excellent decision, it is not a spontaneous or agenda-less one; the restoration project is fuelled by the authorities' realisation that tourists are much keener to visit ancient sites which look the part. Local residents who are being turfed out while renovation is underway have requested permanent accommodation in the newer part of town, preferring to live in a modern, functioning apartment rather than a stone house built hundreds of years ago. Old Mardin is getting a makeover, but its inhabitants want out.

This is a common story. The chasm between what Western visitors appreciate and what residents of a developing country appreciate is widening as the former yearn for the romance and beauty of the Past and the latter strive for the comfort and kudos of the New. This goes for accommodation, art and anything that can be bought, acquired or shown off. While tourists will spend $100 a night staying in a renovated 'authentic' house in Old Mardin, the locals who live in the authentically draughty old house next door see nothing romantic in their situation, and long for central heating. I remember wandering in the outskirts of the town just under the citadel and coming across a donkey munching hay in the doorway of one of these old houses. 'How charming,' I thought, and then felt ashamed to have been charmed by the sight of livestock living just next door to their owners.

A similar thing happened when I was taken by a friend to see the remote mountain village on the Black Sea where he grew up. As we walked up the mountain we would occasionally pass homes unlike any I had ever seen in Turkey – eighteenth-century houses with the date of their construction inscribed in Arabic numerals under the eaves, hay stored under the roof, smoke curling out of a rickety chimney and a storehouse alongside, built on stilts to keep the grain safe from mice. These stone houses fitted the simplicity of the surrounding apple trees and cabbage plots, unpretentious but with a gravitas born of rural longevity, like a Thomas Hardy character. As we passed one of the houses right on the side of the mountain we stopped to admire the view, a moment that was almost instantly shattered by the startling appearance of an enormous *kangal*, an Anatolian guard dog, who charged round the side of the house and whose barking brought a stooped old lady out of the interior. Initially wary, she soon recognised my friend and joyfully invited us in for tea, all the time apologising for her 'old, old' house and making us promise to come back next year when her lovely new house would be ready. Gesturing up the hill, she pointed out the concrete skeleton of a half-built house jutting ominously from a cloud of apple blossom – her treasured new home would be a monstrosity like every other newly built house in the area.

Much as it pained me to contemplate her spending her pension on this charmless blot on the horizon, I also recognised that it was unfair of me to blame her for wanting to live there. After all, the farmhouse I saw as delightfully old-fashioned was probably exhausting to look after – it would have been a constant chore for this lady to wipe away the grime from the coal stove, keep the earth floor damp to stop dust from rising, clean the nooks and crannies and stuff rags in the walls to stop the wind whistling through. I had been privately scorning her aesthetic insensitivity while being correspondingly insensitive to the difficulties of living in an antique of a house.

In reality, Turkey's devotion to the New is not confined to matters of convenience, but is often a matter of principle. A preference for the comforts of an all-mod-cons apartment is totally understandable, but Turks will lust after the modern decor of a new apartment just as much as its advanced appliances, drawn to the undefined but ever alluring aesthetic of the New as well as its practical benefits. The current craze among rich Turks is to employ an interior designer to modernise their homes at great expense – these kinds of houses all look the same, cluttered with ornate but identical lamps and vanilla-coloured leather. On the walls is the kind of awkwardly insipid 'art' which is bought by a designer to impress her client's visitors – the homeowner is completely and willingly sidelined in this process. The less wealthy but still commercially lascivious Turk scorns objects of the past, ignoring antiques that most Westerners would treasure, in favour of Ikea and all the exoticism that its Scandinavian blankness has to offer. They aspire to what is new – whether that is a house, an Apple product or an opinion – because it symbolises what is popular and progressive.

I am aware these aspirations are not unique to Turkey; they are, and have been, a feature of society across the world for ages past. However, I feel that in the West there is a counterbalancing appreciation for what is timeless, or classic, in commercial circles as well as ideologically. I see very little of that appreciation in Turkey, at least in commercial aesthetics, and it is usually reserved for the splendour of Ottoman history. Turkish tourists visit sites like Topkapı, the Ottoman palace in Istanbul, and love books or TV shows like *Muhteşem Yüzyıl* which glamorise the Ottoman look, but they stay well clear of it in their own houses. The past has a time and a place which is decidedly not here or now – nostalgia has absolutely no place in modern Turkish aesthetics.

When I was kitting out a new flat last year, I screwed my courage to the sticking point and headed to Ikea for a new mattress. It was absolutely heaving, and as I queued in the cavernous warehouse to collect my mattress like a body from a morgue, I had the slightly surreal experience of watching two ladies in traditional dress having an argument over the merits of two near-identical black laminated cupboards. The ladies occasionally consulted a catalogue, prodding emphatically at two entries and repeating 'BIRKELAND' and 'KOPPANG' in the unmistakable Arabic tones of Turks from the southeast. What really puzzled me was the fact that these two equally hideous cupboards were not even cheap – the average item of furniture from Ikea is way beyond the average Turk's budget. They want them all the same, probably even more so because of the expense. Ikea is foreign, with a totally un-Turkish aesthetic, and its high prices probably affirm the Turkish expectation that these intimidatingly bland objects are Eminently Desirable and worth saving up for.

In my old neighbourhood of Tarlabaşı, there are many shops which call themselves *eskici* – literally 'sellers of old stuff' or junk shops. In any city in Europe, they would be called antique shops, because they are full of the most beautiful old furniture, either thrown out to make way for the plastic cupboards or simply forgotten. Most of the pieces I have seen in these shops have come from Greek and Armenian houses abandoned in the 1950s and 60s after the race riots in Istanbul, all being sold for a song. In place of the mean, angular cupboards I could have bought in Ikea, I found in the *eskici* a statuesque, aged wardrobe made of walnut wood, with carved feet, little brass keys in the doors and old newspaper cuttings lining the lower shelves inside. It cost a third of the Ikea cupboard price, because no one else wanted it, and smelt like a distinguished library. I also got a couple of ancient wooden chests to cover with cushions and use as sofas to replace the horrible sofas blighting the flat I was moving into.

My landlord, Turgay, is a thoroughly nice man. His wife is an officer in the Turkish army and he has a profound respect for women. He told me I could change any of the furniture that I didn't like in the flat, but could not hide his bewilderment when I rejected the grotesque twin leatherette sofas which faced each other in grim confrontation across the living room. They were a nauseating off-white, with matching cushions, but Turgay thought they were great. In an attempt to persuade me of their merits, he sat on one of them, stretching his arms out to demonstrate its expansiveness as though he were explaining something very obvious to a small child. 'You see? Very comfortable. Very *şık* [chic].' I nodded politely but stuck to my guns. Now, when Turgay visits, he pretends to like the divan-style chests I have set up but clearly thinks I am mad to have rejected a respectable pair of sofas in favour of some old wooden chests.

Again, Turkey is not alone in this social trait of wanting to keep up with the leather sofa-owning Joneses, but there was a watershed moment in Turkish history when the country was reborn as a republic in the 1920s. This national rebirth sped up the shedding of old-fashioned Ottoman ways that was already taking place, and formalised the embrace of Western sophistication, which was seen as synonymous with a desire to progress, to modernise. This has only intensified with the march of globalisation in the last century. Who wants old wooden wardrobes your grandmother owned when brand new ones are available, imported from Germany or Sweden? Ikea wardrobes are a form of ostentation in Turkey, a sign to guests that you are attuned to foreign commercial trends, and, crucially, that you can afford the trappings of Western modernity. While in the UK Ikea symbolises uniformity and consumer laziness, in Turkey it sums up all that is desirable – how can you go wrong buying a brand with worldwide appeal?

While Turks like Turgay cannot understand the Western fondness for old things, others are very much attuned to it and have exploited it to make a lot of money. In areas widely patronised by foreigners, opportunistic and well-informed Turks call themselves *antik* (antique) sellers and charge prices approaching the European norm. These crafty men buy the 'junk' from *eskici*s and sell them in foreigner-beloved areas like Çukurcuma to expats at five to six times the price. They get even more money for trinkets – old watches, cameras and sunglasses – which they can pass off to passing tourists as *otantik antik*s. In one *eskici* I saw an enormous Kodak movie camera, about the size and shape of a calf, hiding away at the back of the shop. It must have been incredibly old, a real collector's item, and the *eskici* owner was rather unsure of what it was – it had simply come in a haul from an abandoned house, he told me. The camera had probably been overlooked by the *antik* vultures because it was too big to sell to tourists, and too niche to be worth the bother of transportation anyway. I still regret not buying it.

Just as the antique dealers in Çukurcuma have learned to profit from foreigners' appreciation of the past, so too have the Turks who own property in the little pockets of Beyoğlu that seem to be the areas of choice for expats moving to Istanbul. The so-called neighbourhoods of Cihangir and Galata are the best examples of areas which have been transformed almost beyond recognition into overpriced, foreigner-filled bubbles. Until fifteen or twenty years ago they were quite disreputable but fun, especially Cihangir – a mixed community of gypsies, Christians (in particular Armenians) and transvestites who would wander untroubled around this uniquely quirky neighbourhood, filled with beautiful Italian houses with grimy neoclassical facades. Quite quickly, the area became popular with artists and hippies, drawing foreigners who liked this slightly kooky side of Istanbul; it soon underwent an ironic process of gentrification to suit the elevated budgets of the foreigners who insisted on living there, and the original residents quietly left. Property has skyrocketed and expensive shops have opened everywhere. Cihangir has become *the* place to live, if one is a relatively bohemian, moneyed expat, but the irony is that most foreigners like living there because other foreigners already live there – it is one of the least authentically Turkish areas in Istanbul. While retaining some long-standing residents and Turkish artisans, the place is largely an artificial expats' wonderland, where they feel safe and unthreatened, surrounded by home comforts. It is full of New York-style coffee shops selling wheatgrass smoothies, boutique ateliers and shops like Carrefour, so the adventurous Turkey-dwelling expat can still buy Western staples like peanut butter and ham. In Cihangir, you can have the best of both worlds – you are in Turkey, with the fringe benefits of home. I would be a hypocrite to claim that it is not a nice place to live (it was the first place I moved into when I arrived), but there is something a little fake about it. For one thing, the area also attracts the kind of Western-aspiring Turks who love the New York/Parisian vibe – you see them sitting at café tables in the street, drinking frozen lattes all day, there to see and be seen.

Cihangir is crawling with celebrities who rent renovated apartments that were, until fairly recently, inhabited by families of eight. The owners of these houses have become millionaires by sheer good luck, and if they renovate the interiors to Western style norms they can charge rents which are unheard of by Turkish standards. Foreigners always compare house prices to those of London or New York, so they accept sale prices or rents which are actually way above what a Turk would pay. The whole area is a bubble inflated by hot air and ultimately, fear. A foreigner will often be afraid to live anywhere else but Cihangir or perhaps Nişantaşı or Bebek, because they can't face the prospect of an area without skimmed milk options, or scary Turkish menus without English translations.

While I like to think of myself as different from the average bumbling expat, the uncomfortable truth is that, to most Turks, there is not much discernible difference between us. I

found this out when I went through the torrid process of trying to find a flat to rent with the 'help' of a string of progress-
ively charmless estate agents, all of whom were convinced
that they had struck gold when I showed up, another yummy
yabancı.

One incident in particular made crystal clear to me the
perception that the average *emlakçı* (estate agent) has of the
average foreigner. It was a rainy day, and Ahmet the Cihangir-
based agent insisted that I take his umbrella as we trudged
off the main road of Çukurcuma, away from the overpriced
antique shops and down what could only be described as a
muddy garden path (the irony escaped me at the time). A few
hours earlier he had rung me to tell me of an exciting property just released onto the market, a three-storey house in
Çukurcuma offered for the price of an apartment. He had not
seen it himself, but was assured it was magnificent. Sceptical, I showed up and was initially impressed when we reached
the beautiful *konak* at the end of the garden path. It was made
of dark wood, one of the rare nineteenth-century houses still
(just) standing in Istanbul. The hall smelt of damp but I was
cautiously curious; we ventured inside to find a dusty kitchen
with a huge fireplace fringed by broken tiles and a spiral staircase disappearing intriguingly into the gloom. Feeling like
Alice taking the plunge down the rabbit hole, I took the lead
as we creaked our way up the staircase. At the top, I opened
a door into the face of a bearded man in a woolly hat – we
both yelled. I apologised. He stared, wordlessly. A movement
on the floor caught my eye, and I saw another man stirring on
a mattress amid a confusion of guitar cases, mouldy mugs and
what might have been another person's limb. Whispering my

apologies this time, I turned to find Ahmet behind me, staring at the scene.

'Ah. There is some mistake.'

'Yes,' said the bearded man. 'We are living here.'

'I'm so sorry, we must leave,' I said. By now I had recognised the men – they were buskers who often played Algerian jazz on the main shopping street in Beyoğlu. Much as I admired their musical abilities, I did not want to linger and question their status as legitimate tenants of this house. Ahmet, only moderately embarrassed, led the retreat, all the while pointing out features like the height of the ceilings and the curvature of the bannisters. 'Disgusting tramps – but look! Such ceilings! Such bannisters! Do you know how rare these features are, Madam Alev? It is an excellent price, really.'

As we set out into the rain, he was still trying to persuade me that these squatters were only a temporary problem, that the damp was a minor matter, and that I would be mad to miss out on such a splendid property. I am absolutely certain that no Turk would have set foot in the house, let alone retain any interest after a disquieting encounter with smelly buskers. The fact that I was a foreigner wanting to live in this area was enough to convince Ahmet that I would love this dilapidated old wreck because it was old and atmospheric. No doubt I would spend vast sums renovating it. That was not his concern – he wanted his commission and those buskers were not going to stand in his way. I do not blame him. Based on a quick appraisal, I was a clueless foreigner: fair game.

Turkish estate agents are in no way a reflection of Turks in general. The world over, estate agents plumb the depths of low cunning, and the agents of Istanbul are only doing their modest part in the whole. They have neither the pinstripe suits nor the shiny company cars that add the extra oily sheen to a Foxtons employee but they are just as ruthless in the pursuit of their cut (typically twelve per cent), and foreigners are particularly easy prey.

It is a far bleaker picture further south than Istanbul, where tourists flock to towns on the Aegean and Mediterranean coasts and even less principled estate agents lurk to welcome them off the plane. Dazzled by the sun, happy to be on holiday, British tourists can be talked into almost anything – including buying property. Having spent a bit of time in towns like Bodrum, Kalkan, Ölüdeniz and Marmaris, which welcome hundreds of thousands of tourists in the summer months, I know the drill in the Costa del Turk.

Walking down the high street of Kalkan, one is assailed by the distinctive, practised tones of tourist-soliciting locals: 'Hello, lady, nice fish for you. Delicious chips. You like beer?' Every shop, restaurant and bar bears the unmistakable stamp of a community which depends on and caters almost solely for its summer influx of Brits on Tour. To my left, Tesko's supermarket has a newspaper stand displaying imported copies of *Hello*, *OK!* and the *Daily Mail*. To my right, Ali Baba's All Day English Breakfast has a large plasma TV showing *Match of the Day*. At night, the marina comes alive with the sweet strains of Rihanna and other UK chart-toppers, and Mojito's Bar is doing a roaring trade in Jägermeister shots and Red Bull cocktails. Sterling is welcome, and the local economy is thriving. To give some idea of the bubble which is Kalkan, a few miles up the road in the Taurus mountains are villages with names like Islamlar ('The Muslims'), where no one speaks English and Ramadan is strictly observed. A loaf of bread costs half what it does down on the coast, and your proffered English fiver will be met with bemusement.

Kalkan is unfortunately not an anomalous community, vying with places like Bodrum, Ölüdeniz and Marmaris for top spot as package-tour destination of choice. Today, these towns are the Turkish equivalents of Malaga and Marbella, where the sun shines just as brightly, and, moreover, kebabs are on offer. Despite the setback caused by the protests in 2013, Turkey's popularity among tourists is pretty high. This goes not only for seasonal tourists, but also for foreigners looking to buy a holiday home in the sun – real estate here, unlike Spain, is booming. Unfortunately, the eastern utopia is not all it seems.

Bodrum airport is one of the busiest in Turkey, with more than 1.5 million tourists arriving just in July and August. A steady stream of Thomas Cook, Easyjet and Pegasus planes disgorge their contents into the balmy Aegean air, and hordes of stocky Brits trot off happily with their package-tour guides onto a bus that takes them on the 'scenic' route into town. This route inevitably passes brand new, glittering holiday villas which the tour guide will plug as the best buys in town. The guide happens to be a friend of the building contractor, and yes, perhaps there are some more deals on the market. And so it begins; gullible Brits caught fresh off the boat by very seasoned scammers.

Charlie Gökhan is an investment fund manager who sorts out property scams in the Bodrum area in particular. Charlie is a financial magician with a shadowy past and an intriguing scar across his face, who moved from Britain to Turkey thirty years ago and took Turkish citizenship (his English name is a mystery). His Turkish wife, Serin, is a lawyer and together they run a smooth enterprise helping conned British tourists, for a fee. Gökhan cannot hide his scorn for those who fall for the typical scam: 'These tourists leave their intelligence on the plane.' Newly arrived, excited to be on holiday and spurred on by low prices for units in purpose-built apartment blocks or 'holiday villages', Brits are all greedy ears when it comes to attractive property deals, especially when it seems like they are getting a good deal from a friend of the developer (who is often a crooked subcontractor or a commission-hungry estate agent). Any remaining doubts are quelled by an apparently independent lawyer, who lets them sign a contract which leaves them with no rights, no title deeds and ultimately no property. They put a deposit usually worth €20–40,000 in a bank account later cleared by the estate agent or subcontractor, who then disappears. The Turkish court system is far too intimidating to tackle, especially with the expenses of an interpreter to consider, and most foreigners give up then and there. They will never recover their stolen money, and the most they can hope for is the affirmation that they were misled. For a lucky few, Gökhan saves the day by coming in to slam down some injunctions, redraft the contracts with Serin and carry the project to completion, meaning that the hapless Brit at least gets a property at the end of everything, albeit at a rather higher price than anticipated.

In 2012 in the Bodrum and Milas areas alone, over €400 million of real estate was sold, predominantly to non-locals. Of these sales Gökhan estimates about five to ten per cent have been scammed, to the tune of €20–40 million. The scammers 'disappear', only to come back richer and more brazen than ever; and while local authorities are wise to them, tourists are not. One notorious Bodrum-based construction company is family-owned, and their website makes this astonishing claim: 'We believe in COMPLETE HONESTY, VALUE OF PLANNING and WIN-WIN BUSINNES MODELS, which we think are the natural rights of our clients.' Despite their notoriety, the son managed to open a very successful boutique Ottoman-style hotel in London five years ago.

Kalkan locals are pragmatic about property scamming, even when not directly involved themselves. 'These aren't scams; they are business,' I was told by Hasan Bey, a pharmacist who keeps a store well stocked with sunburn treatments for his fair-skinned Anglo-Saxon clientele. Tourists get burnt in all kinds of ways down on the south coast of Turkey, and it is because they have a naïve and rather patronising, orientalist view of this part of the world as a sort of paradise – sun, sea and smiling locals, what could go wrong? The same rules apply here as in the rest of the world when it comes to offers which are too good to be true: if you are foolish enough to put a large amount of money in a private bank account without due investigation, you are considered fair game, wherever you are. Of course, there are plenty of opportunities to legitimately buy a property in Turkey, and much of the coast is stunningly beautiful and unspoiled. Kalkan is an eyesore without parallel, with a fan base to match.

Kalkan locals become completely different people when you speak to them in Turkish. So used are they to performing the eager-to-please act with tourists ('Yes, can I help you, nice fish?') that I think it is with a profound feeling of relief that they talk honestly, in Turkish, about the reality of dealing with an annual deluge of tourists. For the local economy these tourists are, of course, a blessing, but it is not easy working in the tourist sector. One particularly gloomy and, I think, alcoholic sea captain talked to me about how the development of Kalkan had stripped him of all self-respect. From May to October, he drives drunken, braying, half-naked English people round the bay in his little boat and lives off the income from that for the rest of the year. He is not religious or prudish, but he is worlds away from his passengers and clearly hates his job. Yet he is arguably in an enviable position, earning more and working less than the average Turk. No one is forcing him to work as a tourist boat operator, it is his own miserable choice. There is something sad and sordid about the whole tourist scene on the south coast, but it is the way of the world – people follow money, which is why there are Colombian economists and Filipino PhD students working as nannies in London.

Fleecing tourists is one thing, but there are more sobering examples of the Turkish preoccupation with making a quick buck; namely, short-term, cheap construction work and a blasé attitude to natural disasters. In 1999, the town of Izmit in north-western Turkey was the site of an earthquake that killed twenty thousand people and left half a million homeless. Six earthquake taxes were set up after the disaster, which were meant to go towards repairing the damage and funding projects to protect areas at risk across Turkey. Since then, tens of billions of Turkish lira have been raised thanks to these taxes, but when the Van earthquake struck in 2011, there was no sign of any funds. When questioned, the Finance Minister, Mehmet Şimşek, said that the money had been spent on roads and construction which mattered 'to all seventy-four million people living in Turkey', and that the notion of collecting taxes for a sole purpose was internationally condemned. He claimed that the AKP government was simply using these taxes as previous governments had done. General outrage ensued, of course, but nothing was achieved, and no one was named or shamed.

Despite modern regulations concerning earthquake-proof foundations and buildings controls, only rich people care enough and can pay enough to buy properties which conform to quake-proof standards. These standards are, by and large, completely disregarded, with millions of Istanbullus living in shanty towns on the peripheries of the city, and average housing in areas like Van being built as it has been since the sixties.

It would take a library of books to cover the problems facing Turkey's environment and the threats towards communities all over the country, and I certainly cannot cover them in one chapter of this one. From urban over-expansion to massive hydroelectric dams present and future, relocations of whole villages, destruction of archaeological sites and local ecosystems, there is a catalogue of woe written into Turkey's 'development' over the last few decades, and its over-eager push to reconstruct the country materially as well as politically. While attempts to protect an environment under threat on this scale might seem sadly inadequate, they are still important – as Gezi Park showed us. Locals often become accidental environmentalists when the pitifully small greenery on their doorstep is threatened. Others are aware of the bigger picture and fight to protect large areas of land or indigenous species.

One person in particular deserves mention, an English lady who has almost single-handedly preserved the Mediterranean habitat of an endangered species: her name is June Haimoff, she is ninety years old and she is the guardian angel of the Mediterranean *Caretta caretta* turtle. I stayed with June in 2011 when she was celebrating being awarded an MBE down in her home in Dalyan, on the south coast. She is known as Kaptan June by the locals, partly because she arrived in magnificent style by boat back in the 1970s, and partly because of the masterful way she has campaigned for the protection of the turtles in the area. In 1988 she successfully lobbied for İztuzu Beach in Dalyan to become a protected site. A beautiful, pine-fringed crescent of uninterrupted golden sand, it is the breeding ground for the *Caretta caretta* of the surrounding Mediterranean area and in 1987 was set to have a gargantuan package hotel built at one end and a holiday village at the other. June put an end to that with a huge international lobbying effort, set up a rehabilitation centre for injured turtles near the beach and in recent years has thrown herself into a project to attach propeller guards to tourist boats, in an effort to save the unfortunate turtles being cut up as the boats cruise around their feeding grounds.

June is in the wonderful position of being completely unafraid of Turkish authorities. She lives in a ramshackle house called The Peaceable Kingdom, surrounded by semi-feral cats and dogs, majestically issuing instructions to her aged maid in fluent but atrociously accented Turkish – a confusing mix of colonial and hippy. Delighted to have an English guest, she sang Gilbert and Sullivan songs to me as we chugged around the bay of Dalyan, and told me about her life as an artist in Gstaad before she sailed herself down to Turkey in her ex-husband's boat.

I wish there were a thousand Kaptan Junes at work in Turkey, but unfortunately it seems that only little pockets like İztuzu Beach get this kind of attention and care. On a grand scale, construction sites and dams will prevail unless an environmentally conscientious political party gets elected, but no such party exists. On a minor scale, there have been some efforts to sugar the pill of over-construction; AKP municipalities have made some belated attempts to create green spaces in overdeveloped cities, but as I mentioned at the beginning of the chapter, these tend to be far from the centre of town, simultaneously showy and insignificant. The government's cleaner energy efforts are a bit more impressive. A recent initiative has aimed to match any money spent by factory owners on cleaner manufacturing up to the tune of a million lira in grants, an offer that has already been taken up by a particular cotton manufacturer near Ankara to whom I talked last year. The municipality of Trabzon, on the Black Sea, is also introducing incentives for residents to switch from their favoured coal to natural gas in an effort to improve air quality. These are of course changes for the better, but the preservation of habitats and ancient sites is even more urgent than clean air, at this stage.

The Turkish landscape is not yet completely ruined, and many areas retain a great deal of original beauty, despite the best efforts of so-called developers. Turkey is in the sad position of relying on the admiration of foreigners and the determination of local environmentalists for the preservation of a landscape which serves as a playground for greedy, Lego-wielding toddlers. Gezi Park showed us that extreme measures are needed to stop the march of over-urbanisation in Turkey. It achieved extraordinary celebrity for a transient cause – what is needed is greater awareness for the rest of Turkey's threatened spaces.

10

A Continental Love Affair

After nearly thirty years, Turkey's courtship of the European Union is in its death throes. The Gezi protests might well have been the nail in the coffin. Strong condemnation by EU ministers of the Turkish government's overreaction to the protests created a diplomatic danger zone, into which charged the EU minister, Egemen Bağış, all guns blazing. He released a statement with all the defiance of a Shakespearean rogue biting his thumb at the European powers that be: 'The eagerness of some members of the European Parliament to make absurd statements merely for media attention is obvious. We respect the freedom to make these kinds of statements. We hope that they regain their reason as soon as possible.'

This supercilious attitude was not always in evidence. Since first applying to join the European Economic Community in 1987, Turkey has been constantly knocking on the door of Europe and has never been let in, though it has not explicitly been turned away. The relationship between the two brought to mind an over-keen suitor constantly being rejected by a coquettish mademoiselle, as she led him on a never-ending game of kiss chase. One had to admire both her powers of manipulation and his optimism, but it was fundamentally an undignified situation. Now, fed up with rejection and criticism, confident in its rosy economic horizons and scornful of recent Euro crises, the neo-Ottoman Justice and Development Party has started to concentrate its efforts elsewhere.

In the wake of the Arab Spring, Foreign Minister Ahmet Davutoğlu described Turkey as 'the master, the leader and the servant of the Middle East'. This was an interesting insight into the psychology of Turkey's foreign policy. Like everyone, Turks enjoy feeling respected and needed. Traditionally, they have been ignored and patronised by the EU, so it must be nice to return to a position of Ottoman-esque prestige among countries in the Middle East. The AKP want to show their voters that twenty-first-century Turkey waits for no man or political body. In April 2013 the deputy prime minister, Cemil Çiçek, declared, 'We no longer want to wait forever', noting that the EU had lost the attraction it once had.

This is not to say that Turkey's efforts to join the EU have been in vain. Its candidate status, the work it has done to meet EU standards of human rights and an all-important trade agreement and Customs Union have ensured a great deal of foreign investment in Turkey, the lynchpin of the economy. On top of that, Turkey gets over €700 million a year from the EU just for being an accession state, and they spend the money on things like training prison staff in an ongoing effort to comply with EU standards related to the justice system. Turks also have recourse to the European Court of Human Rights. There are both direct and indirect benefits to Turkey's long-lasting courtship of the EU, but in recent years it has run out of steam – for the last two and a half years there has been no progress in talks which have become increasingly lacklustre. The great myth is that Turkey's membership of the EU is attainable, just round the corner, but everyone knows – on both sides – that this is simply not true.

The chill between Turkey and the EU is largely mutual – important European states have traditionally been extremely unenthusiastic about allowing Turkey to join. France and Greece refuse to allow certain accession chapters to be negotiated, due in great part to lingering mistrust of a large Muslim state officially joining 'Europe', and historical enmity, respectively. Germany is also very ambivalent about Turkey; Angela Merkel is a notable critic and the German Finance Minister, Wolfgang Schäuble, a fellow Christian Democrat, said to supporters at an election rally: 'We should not accept Turkey as a full member [...] Turkey is not part of Europe.'

Cyprus is a complete stalemate. No one in the world recognises the existence of the Turkish Republic of Northern Cyprus apart from Turkey, and until they do, Turkey will not recognise (Greek) Cyprus or open air and sea ports to Cypriot trade. This non-implementation of the EU Mediterranean trade pact has led to the EU council freezing eight chapters in accession talks, but Turkey will not compromise, saying they will always choose Cyprus over the EU: 'Turkey's choice will forever be to stand next to the Turkish Cypriots. Everybody should understand this,' said Deputy Prime Minister Çiçek in 2009 and he reiterated this in 2013. It's non-negotiable, a dead end to the Turco-European relationship.

The EU is not in the best financial shape and, unsurprisingly, many Turks are jubilant that the lira is doing comparatively well. When you have been excluded from something for so long, and made to feel inferior, there is a particular elation in a reversal of fortune. I was speaking to an old, wizened fisherman recently, and asked him what he thought about Turkey joining the EU. He was unapologetically scornful of the idea: 'Why should we want their measly Euro?' he asked, quite reasonably. 'The lira is strong! Let *them* ask to be part of Turkey!' Turkish officials reacted in a similar spirit to the Cypriot economic crisis of March 2013. When it became clear that a serious, multibillion Euro bailout was needed, Egemen Bağış, the EU minister, magnanimously offered Cyprus the prospect of sharing the Turkish lira used by North Cyprus, on the condition that Cyprus leave the EU. To rub salt into the wound, he added that this crisis would never have happened if Greek Cypriots had accepted the Annan plan of 2004, which would have unified the island, as the Turkish Cypriots had done. Bağış made a valiant effort not to gloat. 'It's not proper to kick someone when they're down. God save them,' he said, which no doubt comforted his intended audience no end.

This is, in any case, largely irrelevant to Turkey's current interests, which have been drawn ever eastward. The Middle East is beginning to open up again and even Israel is eager to be friends. Gas deals are being signed with Azerbaijan and trade agreements with the Ukraine. Japan is a high-profile business partner. The EU, while remaining an important trade partner for Turkey, is no longer a promising political ally.

At the same time, the middle-class Turkish consumer is embroiled in a European love affair which shows no signs of abating. Turkey's relationship with Europe is complex and long-standing; since Ottoman rule, there has been a historic fascination with Europe and all its Western sophistication, counterbalancing Turkey's more natural geographic and religious association with the Middle East. Correspondingly, Europe has long been fascinated by the exoticism of the East. Both orientalists and occidentalists have often unrealistic and misguided pictures of the other.

It has traditionally been wealthy, secular Turks who want to associate more with the West than the East. One of the most striking public examples of European influence in Turkey is Dolmabahçe Palace on the western bank of the Bosphorus, built in 1856 by the last Ottoman Sultan, Abdülmecid I. Until then, the Sultan's residence had been the magnificent but decidedly un-European palace of Topkapı, on the southern peninsula of the Golden Horn; in the fading autumn of the Ottoman Empire, Abdülmecid felt that he should show his European neighbours that he could compete with them in pure pomp and extravagance, as dictated by the style of the times. Dolmabahçe was built at a cost of thirty-five tons of gold, a riot of rococo style and pseudo-Baroque architecture, gold leaf-covered ballrooms and Victorian crystal conservatories. The central hall contains the largest Bohemian chandelier in the world, a gift from Queen Victoria, and is reminiscent of the Doge's palace in Venice, in the same way Versailles is reminiscent of a French chateau. The palace is an exaggeration of European influence, with no coherent style of its own, a striking sign of the Sultan's desire to prove that Ottoman Turkey was on a par with (the rest of) Europe.

Unconvincing as that attempt was, there were more considered efforts to emulate the best that Europe had to offer.

In the last days of the Ottoman Empire, it was obvious that the Ottoman system of government was outdated, the coffers were empty, the world had moved on and Turkey had become, in the words of Nicholas I of Russia, 'the sick man of Europe'. No one wanted to be associated with the old ways of doing things, and European influence was welcomed in Istanbul and further afield. Italian architecture graced city streets, French and German engineers designed funicular and railway systems, British bankers controlled a sizeable portion of the financial sector, and schools and hospitals were built by major European powers. In the early 1920s Atatürk embraced the Western ideology of secularism and encouraged modern dress, as I described in earlier chapters. By banning the fez and veil, and promoting suits and fedoras, Atatürk was giving the Turkish people themselves a Western makeover.

The influence of European powers has always affected Istanbul first and foremost – the most historically significant half of Istanbul is technically in Europe, along with Thrace. The eastern half of Istanbul lies across the Bosphorus in Asia, along with the vast geographical majority of Turkey. The now defunct Orient Express began her journey in London, steamed through Paris and Vienna and ended her European leg in Sirkeci, a train station on the western side of Istanbul. Passengers who wished to continue to Baghdad took a ferry over the Bosphorus to Haydarpaşa train station on the eastern side of the city, a transition which very clearly marked the literal (and littoral) separation between West and East with symbolic ceremony.

Many people visiting Istanbul for the first time expect there to be some great change when they cross to Asia by ferry or drive across one of the bridges, but there are no turbaned camel traders waiting to greet you on the eastern shore; it looks much the same as the western shore, without the great Ottoman landmarks. It is true that the western side still has a clutch of consulates, foreign schools and churches, but these make up a very small percentage of this side of the city. Crossing from West to East or vice versa is all about the journey itself, the excitement of passing over a historic stretch of water thronged with ferries and tankers from far-flung corners of the earth. Once you reach the other side, you are back to urban normality. The truth is that European influence in Turkey these days is more conceptual than actual; it is not stamped on the landscape but in the minds and aspirations of the middle class. It works behind the scenes – in finance, on television and most of all in what people can buy.

From a commercial viewpoint, European popularity in Turkey is gloriously profitable. Turks fork out disproportionate prices for European – and American – brands, paying considerably more for suits, face creams or the humblest saucepan than they would pay for the Turkish equivalents. The high prices of these foreign products are only partly justified by import cost; even factoring those in, the prices are grossly inflated, because the market panders to Turks' expectation that foreign brands are superior. Main roads and malls in big cities are full of restaurants and clothing chains like Zara and Caffè Nero, and there are an increasing number of boutique, Parisian-style bistros and English or Irish 'pubs' in the expensive parts of town where foreign-loving Turks live. European influences crop up everywhere; on menus in high-end restaurants, *şnitzel* (schnitzel) and *sufle* (soufflé) will feature, even if the majority of the food is Turkish. European culture symbolises refinement and progress, and people who identify themselves with European products and words are considered terribly *şık*, at least by themselves.

This is not new, but it is more visible than a couple of decades ago because of the explosion of chains and the exposure to Europe in the form of tourism, in both directions. However, European desirability runs much deeper than commercial enterprises, and is not, of course, unique to Turkey. The charm of European or 'Continental' sophistication can be felt in America or the Far East, or indeed Britain, just as it can be felt in Turkey. However, Turkey is in the position of being caught between two worlds, and the pull of Europe is particularly attractive to those Turks who want to associate themselves with the Continental capitals and all the undefined but apparently superior trends and standards contained therein.

The superior social status that seems inherent in a European-facing perspective is reflected in language. In Ottoman times, French was spoken by the nearest Turkey has to an aristocracy – the 'White Turks' – and in administrative circles. French-derived words have formed a considerable part of the Turkish vocabulary, and many are now ordinary, everyday terms: *kuaför* (coiffeur, hairdresser), *şöför* (chauffeur), *bulvar* (boulevard). Some, however, still carry an air of sophistication. Words like *nostaljik* (nostalgic) and *otantik* (authentic) have rough Turkish equivalents that do not convey quite the same thing as the French-derived terms. There seems to be hierarchy even among foreign-derived words in Turkish; for example, the Italian-derived *lokanta* (*locanda*) means 'restaurant' but in reality, establishments calling themselves *lokanta* are usually more modest affairs than those calling themselves *restoran* (a transliteration of the French *restaurant*). Once upon a time, all restaurants were probably foreign-owned, and indeed a relatively foreign concept in Turkey, hence the comparative lack of Turkish equivalent words. The *meyhane* (literally 'wine house' or 'tavern') is a truly Turkish concept, but it is less about idle eating out and more about concentrated fun.

It would be wrong to assume that all this means that Turks are dissatisfied, or would want to trade a Turkish lifestyle for a foreign one. They like to have *egzotik* options open, but in reality they often prefer their Turkish way of doing things. I am always struck by restaurants which are, in fact, Turkish, but aspire to Continental glamour. To the middle-class Turk, these restaurants represent the zenith of foreign sophistication. The House Café and Kitchenette are prime examples of successful hybrid Euro-Turkish chains; with English names, expensive Shoreditch café-style tiled interiors and deafening elevator music, they offer menus in both Turkish and English and a mix of all kinds of cuisines at much higher prices than your average Turkish restaurant. Wealthy Turkish ladies who have nothing to do but lunch scan a menu full of eggs hollandaise, schnitzels and linguine, but usually order *dolma*, *simit tost*, *menemen* or *köfte*. They enjoy coming to a place with European pretensions, and seeing these items on offer makes them feel that they are buying into an exotic way of life. When it comes to what they will actually eat, they choose Turkish over foreign dishes most of the time.

It is the same phenomenon with the oft-proclaimed wish

of Turks to live abroad. So many of my Turkish friends complain about living here – the government has gone to pot, they don't earn enough, the traffic is terrible, they would be much better off in San Francisco or London or Berlin. When I ask them when they are actually going to move, the answer is always evasive, and some are honest enough to admit that they would never actually leave Turkey. It is where they belong – their family and lifelong friends are here, they couldn't leave them, nor could they bear life without Turkish food and the summer sun. Their attitude makes me think of an old man constantly complaining about his wife, who would never contemplate life without her. He threatens her with divorce, but these are empty words. The two belong together.

Turks may not be prepared to jump ship, but they like to buy into a European lifestyle. Turkey's aspirations to Western business models have varying degrees of success; some things, like fast food delivery companies and mid-price fashion chains, have done extremely well. Other things have not taken off so quickly, but could feasibly be popular in the future. One striking example of a European model requiring a period of adjustment is the new skiing resort which opened in 2012 in Erciyes, Kayseri, in the very heart of conservative Anatolia. Until relatively recently, skiing was not particularly popular in Turkey, but the sector is growing every year. At more than three thousand metres above sea level, Mount Erciyes is covered in snow six months of the year and is in the process of being made into a 'world-class' ski resort at the cost of £260 million. Ski instructors and tourism consultants have been imported from Austria, state-of-the-art chair lifts installed and a gourmet restaurant which can only be reached by gondola is already extremely popular not only with skiers but Kayseri locals who make a family outing of it on the weekend.

The resort has obviously been a huge investment, with considerable funds from the government, although the Kayseri municipality is very much the proud face of the project. When I went, the resort was closed – not because of blizzards, but because there had been so much snow in recent days that the snow cats had been unable to clear the pistes. It seems to be a tragic flaw in many Turkish projects such as this that, even with huge investment, expert foreign advice and plenty of ambition, unforeseen events (like excessive snowfall) can destroy the best-laid plans. The Erciyes resort will obviously pick up and improve in coming years, but not as quickly as hoped. A fundamental problem is the atmosphere of the place; the hometown of President Abdullah Gül, Kayseri is a famously conservative city, where an uncovered woman is a rare sight, and alcohol is only sold in one or two hotels and a few clandestine bars (one is The Black Rose, should you ever go). There is a mosque right next door to the Zümrüt resort, so that I had the surreal experience of hearing the call to prayer as I made my way down a slope crowded with a confusing mix of expert skiers and excited children being pulled along in toboggans. I doubt this resort will ever succeed with foreign tourists – an unmistakably Islamic feel, the absence of beer in the après-ski programme and a rather worrying shortage of snow cats are all elements which will not go down well with skiers used to the professionalism of Chamonix or Zermatt. Moneyed Turks themselves always go to Europe to ski, leaving Erciyes to rookies like me.

How to spend one's money in Turkey is, as everywhere in the world, a way of placing oneself within a specific bracket of society. Wealthy, secular Turks almost always associate themselves with foreign travel and foreign purchases, because these things ensure membership into an elite club. Expenditure seems less and less like a question of personal choice and more about socially dictated expectations – one acquires, and judgement follows accordingly.

The obsession with status-granting trends is particularly obvious in the art scene. There is almost an a priori prestige attached to art, because only the rich can involve themselves in it. This is mainly because contemporary art, in particular, is fuelled by private money; there is very little government support for the study or practice of art, or the general public's enjoyment of it. As I have described, the Dickensian Turkish education system does not encourage artists in any significant way – masters courses in fine art, for example, do not really exist in Turkey. The closest courses are design- or craft-orientated, such as the course in 'visual arts and visual communications design' at the private Sabancı University. Even within the arts, utility is paramount – design courses enable you to get a job, but learning for the sake of learning about art is not profitable.

This is not to say that the arts scene is not flourishing in Turkey. Thanks to private donors and collectors, usually big banking families and industrial superstars like the Koç, Sabancı and Eczacıbaşı dynasties, there is a great deal of exposure to Turkish artists both mainstream and fringe, and they are proving very popular. In 2000 there were only three galleries in Istanbul; since then they have multiplied a hundredfold, and many privately owned museums and galleries offer free exhibitions to the public. The growth in the arts scene in the past fourteen years has been exponential, and Istanbul is now competing with the big European capitals, particularly with big events like the Biennial. There are five art fairs a year here, and Istanbul has the edge on cities like London and Berlin because of its geographical position – not only do artists, collectors and curators come from the West, there is also a wave of artists from the Middle East and further afield. The 2011 Istanbul Biennial referenced the work of the Cuban artist Félix González-Torres, featured pieces by politically motivated artists like the Lebanese photographer Akram Zaatari alongside Turkish artists, and was housed in a building designed by the Japanese architect Ryue Nishizawa. It was the epitome of multinational collaboration, eagerly anticipated by art collectors and curators across the world, proof of the heights to which the Istanbul arts scene is ascending. The showing of Turkish art alongside international art was symbolic of Turkish artists taking their place on the international scene. They are ready to compete, to impress and to be purchased by a worldwide audience, not just a handful of patriotic Turkish art collectors.

The question is, what is fuelling this? Undoubtedly, private sponsors provide a great service to the public, and to Turkish artists, a service that should be provided by the state. But there is also a sense that building a name as a major player on the arts scene in Istanbul is the ultimate display of peacockesque ostentation. 'I am so rich I can afford to throw my money away on paintings' seems to be the intended message of some billionaire patrons of the arts. Kerimcan Güleryüz, the founder of the Empire Project Gallery in Istanbul, has been quoted as saying, 'Art is the new Ukrainian top model on the arm of the fat man.'

It would be unfair to paint all collectors in this light; there are several anonymous benefactors and unobtrusive patrons who genuinely want to make art more accessible to the public, with minimum fuss and zero self-promotion. A good example of this is Arter, a private arts space discreetly funded by one of the prominent business dynasties, which shows brilliant exhibitions of Turkish and foreign artists at no cost to the public. It is right on İstiklal Caddesi, the pedestrian thoroughfare in central Istanbul, and passers-by regularly wander inside out of idle curiosity and become engrossed in whatever happens to be on – usually something provocative. The last exhibition I went to, *Envy, Enmity and Embarrassment*, featured Turkish porn film posters from the seventies, and the one before that, *Wounds*, starred a series of disturbingly realistic horse carcasses.

In recent years, government views on art have not been encouraging. On 30 December 2011, the Minister of the Interior, Idris Naim Şahin, described the arts and cultural scene as the 'backyard' of terrorism. 'Sometimes it's on the canvas, sometimes in a poem, in daily articles, in jokes,' said Şahin. 'These too legitimise and support terror.' Ridiculous as this seems, the rest of his speech was yet more so. He talked darkly of people in terrorist organisations eating pork and practising homosexuality and Zoroastrianism. He had the grace, at least, to apologise for mentioning the dirty word 'homosexuality'. While providing a laugh for the sane listener, this kind of paranoia is very depressing. It speaks of a deep fear of free expression, and all that that entails on the cultural scene of Turkey.

Artists are painfully aware of this. In February 2013 visitors stepping through the door of Arter entered a maze of X-ray images of street protests and riots, police beating protesters and scenes of chaos, brightly displayed on luminous walls like the forensic evidence of a crime-scene investigation. This was the work of a Turkish artist, Hale Tenger, who is concerned about the suppression of free speech in Turkey – and rightly so. Even today, when military rule and nationalist paranoia is meant to be over, suppression of protests is violent, because that is the mode in which Turkey still operates. I am no longer shocked by the sting of tear gas in my nose and throat, the sight of police massing in gas masks and riot gear, armed with sub-machine guns and batons, and commuters hurrying home to avoid getting caught up in crowds of protesters. I am even faintly amused by the sight of a protester being chased by a policeman being chased by a journalist down an alleyway. The fact that the Minister of the Interior can publicly equate art with the nurturing of dangerous forms of terrorism speaks for itself, and Arter is to be applauded for prioritising the works of artists like Tenger who draw attention to the status quo in a public forum.

It is not only contemporary art which is under threat. In April 2013 the historic Emek Sineması, a much loved cinema built in 1924, was demolished to make way for a shopping and entertainment centre in the heart of Beyoğlu. Prominent actors, directors and film critics gathered in front of the cinema to stop the demolition. Unfortunately their normally show-stopping celebrity status did them no good here; they were water-cannoned and teargassed, in what was to become a totally normal routine after the occupation of Gezi Park, and then prosecuted, despite high-profile appeals to Erdoğan himself. The day after the Emek Sineması protests, the director of the Arter gallery put up red cinema curtains in its windows as a sign of solidarity. In June, one hundred prominent artists and intellectuals put their names to a notice in national newspapers calling on the government to stop polarising society and oppressing artists in the wake of the Gezi Park protests. It is telling that, in Turkey, artists and intellectuals of all kinds have to band together in an unprecedented coalition to oppose restriction of freedom of expression. It is not their individual artistic sphere they are concerned about – it is the fate of outspoken people everywhere.

The primary reason for the demolition of Emek Sineması was of course private development, but it is not a coincidence that it had always been a bastion of outspoken film making by left-leaning artists. It has hosted festivals and socialist protest groups on May Day in years gone by – *emek* in fact means 'labour', but the word is much more provocative in Turkish than 'labour' is in English. The Emek Partisi, for example, will never win an election here as the Labour Party has done in the UK, because *emek* is tied up in the Turkish consciousness with communism, an unacceptable concept to most people because it threatens the nationalist system Atatürk set up. Russian influence has always been a worry for Turkish governments, so they have clamped down hard on any whisper of socialism, and there is a distinct stigma attached to it; for many people it is synonymous with anarchy and terrorism. However, for many people who are of a vaguely leftist bent, communism is an attractive concept because it is so antithetical to the government they despise. Some of my friends are signed-up members of the Communist Party; they have no particular belief in communism as a concept, and certainly not as a practicable political system, but they want to formalise their dissatisfaction with what they call the 'fascist' mentality of the Turkish government. In Europe, communism is a bit of a joke. In Turkey, it is feared and loved because it actually has some relevance to the strength of people's convictions.

The Minister of the Interior who succeeded the homophobic Şahin is Muammer Güler, whose defence of the police brutality during the Emek protests in 2013 was that 'illegal individuals and organisations' had infiltrated the crowd of demonstrators. This excuse was copied verbatim after Taksim Square was cleared of protesters on 11 June 2013, and Egemen Bağış went even further, declaring that anyone who attempted to enter the square would be considered a terrorist.

The Turkish government is not keen on supporting contemporary arts, but nor is it keen on supporting more traditional aspects of Turkish culture. One example of this is camel wrestling, which the Turkish government finds rather embarrassing. The tradition stretches back thousands of years among Turkic tribes, but is now largely confined to the Aegean coastal area, and specifically to families of camel owners who are proud to train up the descendants of famous winners of bygone years. I was intrigued when a Turkish friend mentioned it, and headed down for the competition in Selçuk, near the ancient site of Ephesus.

Imagine the crowd at a British music festival, happy despite the rain, cheering, eating overpriced hotdogs, dancing tipsily to the music and thoroughly enjoying themselves. Now imagine this scene taking place near an ancient temple on the coast of Turkey: the air is thick with the smoke of seared camel sausage, Efes beer flows instead of Carling, some wandering gypsy minstrels have replaced Coldplay and everyone's attention is on the central arena, where two gaudily decorated camels are shuffling around in a mutual headlock. Over the roar of the supporters, the boom of the commentator's megaphone and the tinkle of camel bells, everyone is listening out for the scream of defeat which will surely come from one of the struggling combatants any moment now. The two are well matched. Puffs of spittle-foam fall from their lips over the crouching umpires, who are warily checking for illegal knee biting within the mêlée. Suddenly, one of the lurching beasts gets a knee on the other's neck and it's all over. Whistles blow. Fans whoop. The owner of the victor literally dances with delight, beaming happily into the lens of a national television camera hovering nearby.

The Aegean coast of Turkey is probably best known for the ancient sites of Ephesus, Troy and the seaside resort of Bodrum; this also happens to be the tour route of the annual Turkish camel wrestling competition, which snakes down the coastline every winter, attracting legions of camel fanciers but few Western tourists. I attended a day of wrestling mid-way through the tour, arriving the day before the big Selçuk competition in time for the obligatory pre-game beauty pageant. This contest is a traditional precursor to the main event, and is taken extremely seriously, with a panel of *X Factor*-style judges picked for their camel-related or academic backgrounds. The contestants are not beautiful. They are mighty wrestlers and do not display themselves to the best advantage at close quarters, in drizzly rain in a town square; however, their owners have spent a lot of time dressing them in glitzy banners and bells, and one old man in the crowd next to me notes that the animal who ends up winning first prize smells faintly of soap. Also, the arch of his neck is very fine.

So much for the peripheral ceremonies: the most beautiful camel wins a new bell, the owners have a booze-up before the big day, and the morning of the big match is upon us. Though a niche spectator sport, camel wrestling attracts a passionate fan base. These camels and their owners are serious celebrities, and old legends feature in black-and-white photographs displayed in ceremonial tents near the festivities. Currently several camels are household names, commanding vast sums from local municipalities for entering their competition because they raise the calibre of the event and the audience volume so significantly. The Rocky equivalent of recent years is Çılgın Özer ('Crazy Özer') – he is unbeatable, the darling of the carpet-betting punters, and has a magnificent, personalised trailer in which he arrives with great pomp and ceremony to each event, far outshining the plebeian contestants in their dusty open lorries. His estimated worth is two hundred thousand lira, or around £70,000.

The sport has always had a difficult relationship with the Turkish government. I attended the event with Sibel Samlı and Gizem Selçuk, two Turkish women who are in the process of making a documentary about the wrestling scene; in their search for funding, they have drawn a blank with the Department for Tourism, who are hesitant to back anything which might glorify a rather rough and supposedly barbaric traditional sport. In fact, the reputation for barbarism is unfair – the wrestling is far less violent than in the times when a female camel was parked alongside the arena to galvanise the male camels into furious, sexually charged battle. Now, the contestants are merely bored virgin males who would probably pick a fight if left to their own devices, as they would in the wild. Biting is forbidden, and the camels broken up if they succumb to temptation – most are well trained. The other controversial element of the sport is the fact that most camels are not bred in Turkey but are in fact smuggled over the border from Iran. This is nicely skated over now, but no one wants it getting into the public eye.

It would seem that cultural efforts both new and old are hampered by the government's attitude to what it sees as dangerous or embarrassing phenomena. I have to admit that I see the government's point when it comes to something like camel wrestling, because it is the kind of thing that plays into many Westerners' preconceptions about Turkish culture. Camel wrestling sounds archaic and weird, and might not necessarily be what you want to represent Turkey in the international arena. Spanish bullfighting is much crueller than Turkish camel wrestling but has managed to enjoy a glamorous reputation until quite recently, when the animal rights-sensitive conscience of the international community asserted itself. Turkey is always going to be more vulnerable to accusations of backwardness, and because of this Turks are more defensive of their practices than, say, Europeans. What could be more ridiculous or outdated than morris dancers with blackened faces stomping around a pagan pole, for example? And yet this tradition is treasured in England as dearly as the queen by many people, because it is old and therefore worthy of reverence. Camel wrestling is just as old, if not more so, but rather than being universally celebrated in Turkey it is treated like a quirky old cousin whom everyone wants to hurry up and die. Ironically, when I reminisce about my camel-wrestling experiences, foreigners are much more interested than Turks, who look askance. This is a classic example of interest in the Other; reciprocally, a Turk will be much more interested in morris dancing than a native English person.

'Orientalism' and 'occidentalism' refer to generalisations on Eastern and Western societies, respectively, and are no longer neutral terms. In 1978, Edward Said's *Orientalism* was published and gave the term a negative connotation; Said argued that most orientalist views simplified and patronised 'the Orient' (a patronising term in itself). The Orient, i.e. anything east of Europe, was seen as 'exotic' but also as backward, static and inferior to Western society. Likewise, occidentalist views simplify and often demonise Western society – many people in the Middle East associate 'the West' with American military aggression, pornography and exploitation, among other vices.

Both orientalist and occidentalist views are in force today, as they were a hundred years ago. In a way, wealthy, secular Turks are the biggest orientalists of all. They may not fetishise the exoticism of the Orient, but they definitely see themselves as belonging to Western society, and see that as superior to an oriental society. They aspire to Western art, or the lifestyles they see in American sitcoms. People living in Europe and America do not have the same level of exposure to life in Turkey but they read about Ottoman history and come to Turkey wanting to buy carpets, coffee pots and jewellery. Turks want to buy into a lifestyle, while Westerners want to come, see and acquire a souvenir of their exotic holiday. The average German or American tourist will have a vague idea of what they want from a souk, but they will be easily taken in by modern tat, especially if the word 'Ottoman' features on the packaging. The range of products aimed solely at foreigners is quite astonishing – pre-packaged baklava that no Turk would ever buy, tacky belly-dancing outfits and dubious 'love potions' from the Spice Bazaar. Souvenir shops in London fleece tourists, Turkish and otherwise, for mini plastic replicas of Big Ben and Beefeaters. Both classes of tourists are fair game.

Turkish belly dancers are a particularly good example of how Turks cater to Western taste. The dancers in seedy bars and upmarket bars alike favour a particularly raunchy style of outfit, with the long skirt traditional to the genre cut to the hip to reveal bare legs, spangly stilettos and plunging sequinned bras. This style of outfit was made popular in the early twentieth century by the misguided image that Hollywood had of the stereotypical 'Eastern Belle', or the exotic temptress vaguely associated with the world of the *Arabian Nights*. This style – featuring gauze veils and see-through layers – actually had more in common with Western burlesque and vaudeville dancers and certainly not much in common with Middle Eastern belles at the time, who were, for the most part, fully and opaquely clothed when in sight. The 'Eastern Belle' style of costume is, unsurprisingly, still popular in Turkey, and brings to mind the Ottoman author Ahmed Midhat Efendi's sarcastic description in 1889 of a

Turkish woman in the imagination of a Western man: 'Since her garments are intended to ornament rather than conceal her body, her legs dangling from the sofa are half naked and her belly and breasts are covered by fabrics as thin and transparent as a dream.' *Plus ça change* in the fantasy world of the *oryantalist*.

Nâzım Hikmet was a Turkish poet of the early twentieth century, a romantic communist who spent much of his life in prison for his political views and who was infuriated by the patronising views expressed by orientalists like the fez-wearing Frenchman Pierre Loti. Loti wrote in great detail about his visits to Morocco, Algeria and Turkey at the turn of the twentieth century and wrote a novel about three Turkish women escaping from their harem called *Les Désenchantées*. It has since been discovered that, during the course of his research for this novel, Loti was actually the subject of a hoax by three bored, wealthy Turkish women, who were probably in Hikmet's camp of wanting to ridicule misguided notions of the Orient. However, Loti was beloved by most Turks simply for being a celebrated Turkophile, and has been honoured with an eponymous school and café on a small hill in the Istanbul district of Eyüp. In his poem '*Piyer Loti*', a scathing Hikmet opens with a pastiche of the Western stereotype of 'the East', conjuring up images of mother-of-pearl slippers swinging off minaret spires, caravans of camels and belly-dancing sultans on silver trays. 'This is the European image of the Orient found in books printed a million times a minute. Not yesterday, nor today nor tomorrow has there been or will there ever be such an Orient.' The reality of the Orient, says Hikmet, is naked, starving prisoners dying on the bare ground, while the region serves as the breadbasket of the West.

This book is a form of orientalism, of course, in that it generalises and objectifies a Middle Eastern country. I am not Turkish enough to have the protection of my nationality when I make sweeping assertions about 'the Turks', but I am trying especially hard to understand this country, trying not to over- or under-gloss it. I certainly do not expect a café to be named after me.

These days, thanks to the internet and ease of travel, old-fashioned orientalist views are less prevalent than they used to be, but they do exist in both positive and negative guises. Tourists in Istanbul confess that they are surprised by the lack of souks and the presence of malls and skyscrapers, but are soon mollified by a trip to the Blue Mosque. Worried Londoners ask me whether Turkey is 'the next Iran', citing the rise of headscarves like a monstrous plague. The unknown can be both intriguing and threatening, depending on the scope of one's knowledge and insecurities; it always has been and it always will be. This is true not only of people living in different continents but within the same country, especially when that country is as huge and as diverse as Turkey.

11

Nations within Nations

The good old days of the Ottoman Empire were famous for ethnic and religious diversity long before the concept of multiculturalism came into Western vogue. Greeks, Armenians, Syriacs and Jews were all legally protected, self-governing minorities allowed to prosper under Ottoman rule during a time when minorities in Europe were persecuted. Ottoman society may have been organised along ethnic lines, with communities living and worshipping separately, but it was tolerant compared to global standards of the time, and as a result, the architecture and literature of Turkey have the stamp of myriad intellectual and cultural voices from the past. Having narrowly survived extinction in the early twentieth century at the hands of foreign powers, modern Turkey was forged in the fires of nationalism by a group of people whose ambition it was to create a state based upon a single national identity. Sub-national identities were seen as fault lines within society which could be exploited by foreign powers, and were treated accordingly as threats to the state's existence. As a result, Turkey is more famous today for the expulsion of Greek and Armenian populations and decades of strife with Kurdish terrorists than for being any kind of multicultural utopia. However, over the last decade, the position of minorities has evolved significantly as the AKP has tried to move beyond the desperately defensive paranoia of Turkish nationalism to promote Turkey's Islamist identity, in something approaching a return to the Ottoman mindset.

Minorities abound in Turkey, many of them living happy, integrated lives, content with their Turkish citizenship alongside their particular identities as Laz (from the Black Sea area), Circassian (the north Caucasus), Macedonian, Arab or otherwise. Talking to them, I felt I discovered the best legacy of the Ottoman Empire: a tolerant, eclectic community of individuals getting on with each other while retaining the heritage of their ancestors. Others, however, are not so happy, and for them the overt and insistent displays of Turkish nationalism must grate. The difference between the two groups is largely to do with how happy they are to remain as minorities who still identify themselves as Turkish: to be a Circassian Turk, for example, is fine, but to be simply a Kurd is not. Turkish nationalism is a supernationalism in the sense that it is happy to integrate sub-identities, but a direct challenge to Turkishness cannot be tolerated.

One of the few Turkish phrases I knew in my childhood was a jingoistic mantra with the rhythm of a football chant: *Türkiye, en iyi, başka millet yok* ('Turkey is the best, there is no other nation'). For a relatively young country, the uncompromising nature of its nationalism is not surprising, particularly when an individual of extraordinary influence (Atatürk) has forged the country out of unpromising circumstances and left an evergreen cult in his wake. When I first moved to Turkey I remember being struck by the number of flags flying from private houses, public buildings, boats and cars. Municipal parks boast hundreds of red and white flowers arranged in the form of a crescent and star, and portraits of Mustafa Kemal Atatürk grace key rings, car bonnets and mobile phone covers. For an English person, the equivalent would be a riot of BNP-inspired decoration, Union Jacks paired with portraits of Churchill flying proudly across Britannia, their numbers doubled on occasions like Guy Fawkes Night. For an American, the displays of national pride in Turkey are probably not so strange.

For Turks, patriotism is as natural as drawing breath, an instinctive emotion independent of political agenda. Political nationalism, while always present, is now at its lowest ebb in decades: the ruling AKP is popularly defined not by nationalism but by religion. By contrast, parties like the MHP (Nationalist Action Party) teeter on the edge of fascism, despite recent attempts to soften their image. Obsessed by the racial purity of 'true' Turks, the MHP was originally driven by an ambition to unite Turkic peoples from Istanbul to China in a pan-Turkic empire. In the seventies, its militia-style youth group, the 'Grey Wolves' (taken from Turkic mythology), were responsible for tracking and killing leftist intellectuals, including a number of Kurds. After the 1980 coup the party was banned, but today the MHP has thirteen per cent of the vote, bolstered no doubt by dissatisfied Turks reacting both to the religious nature of the AKP and to the outdated Kemalism of the main opposition party, the CHP (Republican People's Party).

The AKP's moderate Islamist approach, while diminishing the friction between ethnic minorities, has been seen to create new religious tensions which were less prominent before they came to power. The majority of Turks are Sunni

Muslims, and because of this, in the minds of many Turks, the two are synonymous. This means that non-Sunni Muslims are often seen as 'the other', most significantly the Alevis, who are the largest religious minority in Turkey. In May 2013 the government announced the name of the third Bosphorus Bridge – the Yavuz Sultan Selim Bridge, after an Alevi-slaughtering Ottoman Sultan, Selim the Grim. This drew furious protests from the Alevi community, who pointed out that there was no need to celebrate someone who had massacred tens of thousands of Alevis. Interestingly, the Ottomans considered 'heretic' (non-Sunni) Muslim minorities to be of lower rank than Christians, and Selim the Grim famously declared that 'the killing of one Alevi has as much heavenly reward as the killing of seventy Christians'. I am not suggesting the AKP share this sentiment, but it was shockingly tactless of them to honour the man who said it.

Many people are alarmed by the cliqueish nature of the ruling AKP, whose members belong to Sunni sects which are, to the trained eye, identifiable by the shape of their moustaches, among other things. In Turkey, moustache shape is extremely telling: a long Turkic horseshoe shape denotes a nationalist, while a bushy walrus moustache typically has a firebrand leftist owner. While very religious Muslim men grow moustache-less beards, the moderate Muslims currently in power tend to favour the neatly trimmed *badem*, 'almond' model. Some meticulously display the upper lip, like President Gül's and Prime Minister Erdoğan's. Others do not. I am not sufficiently knowledgeable about religious moustaches to explain the difference, but apparently it denotes their particular Sunni sect. Correspondingly, the way their wives arrange their headscarves is equally telling to those in the know.

Turkish patriotism may be varied and nuanced by political ideals but it is ever present and ever fervent, something that unites all Turks whatever their voting tendencies or moustache shape. Ever since the birth of the Turkish Republic, the issue of who has the right or, more importantly, the obligation to call himself or herself a Turk has taken on a life-or-death significance. As a consequence, racial minorities – or those who are not willing to call themselves Turks – have been marginalised and in some cases persecuted. This nationalism did not spring out of nowhere; it was a continuation of the survivalist mindset which drove the creation of the republic in 1923. Atatürk was Herculean in his achievements: he won a war of independence against European powers hungry for the remains of the Ottoman Empire, he kicked out an archaic Islamic sultan, built a modern republic from a shattered people and instilled this new republic with pride and vision. He could only achieve this by wielding strong notions of nationhood and the indivisibility of that nationhood, so that Turkey could survive and make something of itself. Turkey is very young, full of promise and the hubris which springs from insecurity.

Atatürk granted equal rights to religious minorities within Turkey and was a stalwart, single-minded secularist. He did not want religion to feature in the public sphere of modern Turkey, but he granted full freedom to private worship. However, he was a believer in the assimilation of ethnic minorities, which quite often coincide with religious minorities, like the Zaza Alevis, who were bombed by Atatürk's adopted daughter, the pilot Sabiha Gökçen (after whom Istanbul's second airport is named), in Dersim in 1937 after they resisted inclusion into the Turkish nation state. Minorities like the Greek or Armenian Christians were seen as incompatible with the popular idea of a modern Turk, being both ethnically and religiously different from the ideal prototype. They were largely removed from Turkey in the population exchanges which followed the War of Independence. These population exchanges involved the expulsion of Muslims from ex-Ottoman territories like Greece in exchange for the expulsion of Christians in Turkey. Only the Christian populations in Istanbul were exempted from these exchanges thanks to the Treaty of Lausanne in 1923.

In 1955, the hypersensitive and eternally unresolved issue of Who Owns Cyprus was inflamed by nationalist tensions on both Turkish and Greek sides, exacerbated by British anti-diplomacy, and quickly escalated into race riots in major Turkish cities. As a result of these riots, huge swathes of not only the Greek population but also the Armenian, Georgian and Jewish minority populations left the country (Armenians and Georgians are largely Orthodox Christians). It mattered more and more whether one called oneself a Turk, because that was seen to be fundamental to the existence of the country itself. In October 1927, four years after the establishment of the Republic, Atatürk gave a speech addressed to the Turkish Youth, warning them that 'in the future, too, there will be enemies at home and abroad who will wish to deprive you of [your existence]'. Like everything he said, this has never been forgotten, and the reference to enemies at home has been taken to mean anyone without due loyalty to the state –

politicians, poets and journalists included. Today, Turks who dare to criticise Turkey publicly are automatically traitors, the kind of enemies or 'malevolent people' Atatürk spoke of all those years ago. This kind of exclusive nationalism was responsible for scratching references to ethnic minorities from constitutional documents in the 1920s and forcing ethnic assimilation in the thirties. It was the product of an ideology that was started for constructive ends and twisted into something destructive – Atatürk's version of nationalism was a short-term fix. Something new is now needed, a more inclusive and tolerant form of patriotism which is not ethnicity-based, nor for that matter religion-based.

More often than not, the aggressive qualities of nationalism are more evident in diplomacy than in practice. The question of whether or not there was a genocide of Armenians by Ottoman powers between 1915 and 1917 has been endlessly discussed. In brief, Armenia and its supporters claim that 1.5 million Armenians were killed in an attempt to wipe out the entire Armenian population of the time; Turkey claims that three hundred thousand Armenians and similar numbers of Muslim Turks were killed in civil strife during this period but strongly rejects the term 'genocide', which implies a concerted effort to obliterate a racial demographic. Both sides demonise the other, after nearly a hundred years and a complete change of regime in Turkey. I see no merit in wielding either 'recognition' or 'denial' as political or academic weapons, as many have done. The death of these Armenians was a tragedy, and should not be treated as point-scoring fodder by anyone. Turks are masters in self-defence, because that is how they have rebuilt their nation, but paranoia is part and parcel of such a defensive attitude. They are worried about the possibilities of territorial reparations even at this stage – every inch of ground a Turkish solider has fought and shed blood over is considered sacred ground, and worth any amount of diplomatic wrangling necessary to defend it. It is impossible to overestimate the importance of the soldier–martyr in the Turkish psyche; it is even embedded in the flag, which is said to depict the reflection of a moon and crescent in a pool of Turkish warriors' blood.

The application of this extreme patriotism to a modern-day diplomatic problem may not be right, but some of the calls for recognition of a genocide are just as mulish. Significantly, many of the most strident calls come from the Armenian diaspora rather than from Armenians themselves, mainly because diasporas are often more fiercely patriotic than indigenous populations, and the Armenian diaspora in particular is disproportionately large. Expressions of solidarity come from the most unexpected of sources; in 2011 the American reality TV star Kim Kardashian, whose father is Armenian, petitioned President Obama to formally recognise a genocide (he did not oblige). The French-Armenian singer Charles Aznavour is another celebrity advocate for recognition. France already recognises a genocide but in February 2012 President Sarkozy went a step further by proposing a bill to punish the denial of genocide by up to a year in jail and a fine of €45,000. The bill did not pass but talk of it occasionally resurfaces under President Hollande.

There are close to half a million Armenians in France and Sarkozy's proposal, timed shortly before the general elections in 2012, was widely viewed as a vote-winning ploy. The bill was needlessly politically aggressive to Turkey and threatened free speech no matter what one's personal views on the issue. Its announcement had an immediate and dramatic effect on the relationship between France and Turkey: Ankara froze diplomatic relations with Paris and Prime Minister Erdoğan described the bill as racist and Islamophobic. He also accused France of hypocrisy, on the grounds that French troops committed a genocide when they massacred fifteen per cent of the Algerian population in the 1940s. Elaborating on this point, the municipality of Ankara decided to change the name of Paris Street, home of the French Embassy, to Algeria Street, and to erect a monument to the Algerian genocide near the embassy. Turkey has critics on home ground, too, and is similarly hard on them – if not more so. Orhan Pamuk, the Turkish author, spoke out against Turkish denial of a genocide in 2005, was charged with 'publicly insulting Turkey's national character' by a prosecutor in Istanbul and has been *persona non grata* in Turkey ever since. Cases like this put Turkey and France in a similar camp when it comes to free speech – both governments are insisting that 'what we say is true, is true, and no one is allowed to say it isn't'. It is a sad situation which just falls short of being risible because of the implications for free speech in general.

Official recognition of an Armenian genocide, while a controversial and emotional issue for many people, is on the whole more beloved by academics, politicians and the wider Armenian diaspora than by Armenians living in Turkey, at least the younger generations. Young Armenians are often more eager to integrate and identify themselves as Turks than their parents, and I have known several young Armenians who are respectful and conscious of their Armenian heritage without wanting to be defined by it. A young woman I once worked with only told me she was Armenian when I queried her name, Tanya, a few weeks after we had started working together. She also told me that her parents were eager for her to marry a good Armenian Catholic boy, although she was not particularly keen to. A half-Armenian boy from a totally different walk of life used to tell me how stupid he thought the genocide-denial wrangling was, but he strongly believed the border crossing between Armenia and Turkey should be opened, and trade resumed. His concerns were for the present and the future, not the past. In my experience, young Armenians are understandably more concerned with their own progress in life than with recognition for a past tragedy that consumes their parents or grandparents. They remind me of young Turkish Cypriots in Cyprus today, who want to identify themselves as Cypriots rather than *Turkish* Cypriots, and feel much more friendly towards Greek Cypriots than my mother's generation could ever feel. This is not necessarily a good sign; they might well be doing so because belonging to a minority is often an uncomfortable experience. Armenians have suffered decades of discrimination; perhaps young Armenians like those I talked to are just anxious to avoid that by distancing themselves from their minority identity. Even if that is true, I do think that anger over past events fades over time, unless there is an active and pertinent cause of some kind to keep that anger alive.

The Kurds of the south-east of Turkey have such a cause. The last thirty years of Turkish–Kurdish strife are being challenged today in the form of the Kurdish peace process (which is in tentative progress as I write), and it is to be hoped that this, along with other unresolved minority-related problems, will be successfully addressed in a less ferociously nationalistic age. In 1984, the emergence of the Kurdistan Workers' Party (PKK) posed the most serious threat that the Turkish nation-building project had ever faced. Since the founding of the republic, Kurds had been forced to assimilate, rebranded as 'Mountain Turks' and dismissed as backward peasants, but they had not formed an organised resistance. Ironically, it was as a result of the Turkish government's harsh treatment of Kurds as a problematic minority that Kurds formed such a strong concept of their own national identity. Before the PKK, there had been no organised Kurdish resistance to the Turkish government, and consequently no active fighting. There was the same nebulous prejudice towards them that existed towards many minorities, mainly because Kurds come from deprived areas in the south-east, but nothing comparable to the situation now. The Kurdish problem exploded in the 1980s, and a solution is long overdue.

'Kurdistan' is a politically problematic term in Turkey, but it is also a geographically problematic term because a country for Kurds does not currently exist. In the Ottoman period, Kurds lived in a province or *eyalet* called Kurdistan, which is now an area in south-east Turkey which encompasses the cities of Mardin and Diyarbakır. While many Kurds still live there, it is now only called 'Kurdistan' by Kurds or Kurdish sympathisers. After the collapse of the Ottoman Empire, Western Allies carved out borders for an independent Kurdish state in the Treaty of Sèvres, but this treaty was subsequently ignored by Atatürk's government. Instead, as a kind of compensation, Kurds were told to seize traditionally Armenian towns in Turkey like Van and were largely left to their own devices. Kurds did not have autonomy or land, but they were temporarily appeased. In 1970, 'Iraqi Kurdistan' in the north of Iraq was granted autonomy by the central government, and there is an unofficial province called Kurdistan in Iran, as well as many Kurds living in Syria. The ultimate aim of Kurdish nationalists today is to create a state encompassing all these communities, and the biggest obstacle to this has traditionally been Turkey, which up until now denied even the existence of a Kurdish minority.

The question of why the ruling party is initiating the Kurdish peace process has been much debated by their opponents. On a straightforward level, it is a great thing to be undertaking; no one wants to lose soldiers to guerrilla warfare, and the situation has already gone on far too long, costing tens of thousands of lives (of soldiers and civilians on both sides) and an estimated 766 billion lira to the Turkish government. The negotiations are good PR for the AKP, of course, but who cares, as long as they work? Some Turks accuse the AKP of *nouveau* Ottomanism because they portray themselves like sultans rebuilding an empire and magnanimously dealing with their subjects – in March 2013 Prime Minister Erdoğan controversially referred to the *eyalet* (province) system used by the Ottomans to manage their empire, specifically mentioning the *eyalet* of Kurdistan and causing considerable upset among Turkish nationalists. Other critics suspect the AKP of opening negotiations with Kurds because they want to be able to bargain with them to gain access to the petrol-rich areas in Northern Iraq

(Kurdistan); the AKP find it easier to negotiate with Kurds than previous governments because they are not defined by a nationalist, anti-Kurdish agenda. This is probably true, but it is irrelevant in the greater context. Peace is desperately needed now.

Kurds make up about twenty per cent of the Turkish population, a fifteen-million-strong minority. To give some idea of scale, there are an estimated fifty thousand Armenians living in Turkey. Many more millions of Kurds live in surrounding areas in Syria, Iraq and Iran, giving them a huge critical mass and the impetus for change. In Turkey there is an organised rights movement, which includes NGOs, artists and the BDP (Peace and Democracy Party), a relatively mainstream political party, as well as illegal organisations, the most famous of which is the PKK. Some groups are not directly associated with the Kurdish rights movement but involve the cause in their broadly leftist agenda, like the semi-illegal music group, Grup Yorum, which has been linked to illegal, far-leftist organisations such as the notorious anarchist group the Revolutionary People's Liberation Party. Grup Yorum's members regularly spend spells in prison, and their music is confiscated by police from the recording studio before it is due to be publicly released. I went to one of their concerts, and there were thousands of people there, young, old, Kurdish and otherwise, listening to three hours of music and poetry with a distinct freedom-fighting flavour. Other concerts have been shut down by police because the group explicitly talk about the Kurds' right to freedom, as well as other dangerous topics, but with the growth of social media and YouTube, their music is hugely popular and enjoyed in secret across the country. I shared a taxi to the concert in Istanbul with a Turkish friend who shushed me when I started to give the taxi driver more detailed directions to the concert venue. 'Just tell him to drop us by the mall,' whispered my friend in English. 'He might be a government informer.' I do not know whether this was over-cautious or not, but it shows how nervous Turks can be attending something as apparently innocuous as a music concert, when anything that might be construed as 'terrorism' is involved.

Countless articles, books and reports have been written about the Kurdish issue. I cannot begin to do justice here to an incredibly complicated situation, but as far as I can see, it is a terrible mess of contradictory demands, decades of hurt, and desperation on the Kurdish side. On the Turkish side, there is a whole gamut of reaction which ranges from fascist calls for the obliteration of the Kurdish race to acceptance that the Kurds should be allowed to speak Kurdish and call themselves Kurds. Practically all Turks fall short of wanting to give away Turkish soil to the Kurds. They are worried about making concessions because that could lead to all sorts of uncomfortable situations, like making reparations – perhaps in the form of land – not only to Kurds but to Armenians, as I've mentioned, or to Greeks. One can see their point. Considering all the minority elements that make up Turkish society, it is a potential slippery slope. However, concessions can be made – like granting the Kurds the right to speak their own language – without descending down this slope, and the PKK seem cautiously ready to accept these concessions.

There seems to be a problem with the word 'Turk': does it refer to an ethnicity or citizenship? If 'Turk' means someone living in Turkey, there should be no problem. However, many Kurds – even those who do not necessarily want an area of Kurdistan in current Turkish territory – object to the exclusive use of the word 'Turk' to define someone living in Turkey, not wanting to be lumped with the rest of the population when they have a perfectly good word for themselves. The institutionalised insistence on self-definition as a Turk creates problems from childhood onwards for everyone who might think otherwise, mainly because of the obligatory oaths of allegiance and the phrase which children utter in every Turkish school: *Ne mutlu Türküm diyene*, 'How happy is the one who can say "I'm a Turk".' This phrase is inscribed everywhere – public buildings, army bases and town squares, particularly in Kurdish areas where it is considered efficacious by authorities as a reminder of identity. The Turkish side of the Iraqi border (mainly populated by Kurds) is probably the most aggressively nationalistic area of Turkey; I have seen footage of school drills involving hundreds of children dressed in red and white doing military-style formations with Turkish flags in something approaching scenes from China. Most of all, expressions of Turkish sovereignty, typically quotations from Atatürk, are displayed everywhere in an obvious attempt to quash local Kurdish morale and ram home the idea of Turkish supremacy.

This is finally being challenged, often in an atmosphere of secrecy. In March 2013, the base of a statue of Atatürk in the predominantly Kurdish town of Batman was vandalised – or edited, depending on how you look at it – in the middle of the night. The *Ne mutlu* phrase was replaced with another famous quotation from Atatürk: 'Peace at home, peace in the world.'

Nationalists, of course, went crazy. The local authorities cringed and squirmed in their efforts to distance themselves from the crime. I think it was a wonderful thing to have happened, and as tactful a piece of graffiti as one could wish for. The new phrase is in keeping with the times and rejects the limitations of the 'How happy . . .' maxim while replacing it with something else Atatürk said, thus retaining respect for a national hero. The whole episode reminds me of Christians quoting different parts of the Bible to each other as a kind of moral point-scoring; sometimes material from the same source can be on the cusp of being contradictory while retaining integrity and competing in relevance. The original phrase on the statue could have been replaced with something violently separatist or anti-Atatürk, but it was in fact a very constructive change, reminding people of the current priority of the need for peace. The Kurdish gauntlet was not so much thrown as placed in a dignified and gentlemanly manner by someone who, understandably, had no wish to be thrown to the nationalist lions.

There have been suggestions from Kurds and Kurdish sympathisers that Turkey should be renamed 'the Republic of Turks and Kurds'. I think, firstly, that this will never happen, and secondly, it is impracticable – where would it stop? What about indigenous Armenian, Greek, Roma or Turkmen communities? 'The Republic of Turks and Various Minorities' is a nice thought but certainly not on the cards. Very few people in Turkey are ethnically one hundred per cent Turkish, or

Turkic (which is why, of course, the Turkish brand of nationalism is so extraordinary), but it is difficult to see how that could be reflected by rebranding Turkey. What is more important is to allow Kurds to call themselves so, without fear of prejudice, to speak Kurdish and to celebrate their culture freely, without construing these things as an attack on the Turkish state.

The Kurdish peace process initiated in March 2013 is the first attempt at dialogue with the PKK for around thirty years, and has been engineered by the AKP and the jailed head of the PKK, Abdullah Öcalan. 'Apo', as he is affectionately called by Kurds, has been held in solitary confinement on an island prison in the Sea of Marmara since 1999 but still wields great influence from his prison cell. At the Kurdish festival of Nowruz in March 2013, hundreds of thousands of Kurds gathered in Diyarbakır, the centre of the Kurdish region, to welcome his much anticipated call for peace. At the time of writing, there is a precarious ceasefire and PKK fighters are beginning to leave Turkish territory in small numbers, in return for unspecified concessions on behalf of the Turkish government. These concessions have not been made public, and many Kurds are deeply suspicious of what they will get in return for the laying down of arms. Is the constitution going to be changed? A lot of Turkish prejudice towards Kurds is ingrained, and cannot be changed by heartwarming speeches.

In June 2013, anti-government protests spread from Taksim, Istanbul, all over the country. In Western towns like Izmir, Ankara and Eskişehir, protesters were educated, mainly leftist people who had middle-class concerns like the preservation of Gezi Park or annoyingly restrictive anti-alcohol laws. However, the protests which sprang up in the Kurdish areas in the south-east were another matter entirely: they were aimed at the disproportionate number of gendarmeries and police stations in villages which have no water, schools or hospitals – an expression of Kurdish frustration with Turkish authorities. On 28 June 2013, nineteen-year-old Medeni Yıldırım was shot dead in Lice, southeast Turkey, when police opened fire on people protesting against the opening of a new gendarmerie. His death added to the toll of what were loosely called the 'Gezi protests', but it had a different significance from those killed in Western cities. The government immediately claimed that the unrest in the south-east was the result of an ongoing drugs war. They did not want anything to derail the peace process, which had started only a couple of months before, but it certainly seemed shaken – the Kurdish BDP did not hold back from criticising the government's vindictive backlash and its lack of recognition of the severity of the Lice incidents. Interestingly, not all Kurds felt the same; at the height of the protests, in the Kurdish town of Erbil, Northern Iraq, a group waving Turkish flags and pictures of Erdoğan staged a pro-AKP demonstration in front of the Turkish consulate, an unexpected counter-protest. They were worried about the Gezi protests derailing the peace process, and they were right to worry. However, the process now seems to be limping on.

I remember speaking to a Kurdish butcher in Istanbul who was scornful of all the fuss people were making about the tear gas and water cannon used by police around Taksim

Square. 'This is nothing,' he said. 'In Diyarbakır [his hometown] we get this sort of thing all the time. I was brought up on gas.'

I visited Diyarbakır a year before the protests and was struck by the tension in the air. There was an atmosphere of surveillance which made people both afraid and angry, and I felt a very similar atmosphere in Taksim following the evacuation of the square by police on 11 June 2013 – helicopters passing sporadically overhead, intimidating uniformed policemen hanging around on street corners and occasionally conferring with not-so-secret policemen wearing leather jackets and noisy walkie-talkies. It was unpleasant living in the atmosphere in Taksim. For people in Diyarbakır, this is normal life.

The reason for the surveillance and massive police presence in Diyarbakır is the PKK. Many Kurds have moved from remote Kurdish villages to Diyarbakır in the last twenty years, and some have family members hiding out in the mountains with the rebels – these migrants feel torn between their loyalties to freedom-fighting family members and their desire to live a trouble-free life in the city. The police presence in Kurdish cities is in many ways intrusive, but neither the current Turkish government nor any future government is ever going to leave the area free of gendarmerie while the PKK remain in Turkey.

Negotiations with the PKK are part of a bigger movement to improve Kurdish rights, which includes recent measures like allowing Kurdish to be taught in schools – completely unheard of until now. Kurdish children have been living with dual identities for decades: they speak Kurdish at home,

Turkish at school, and are punished by both parents and teachers if they mix them up. The hope is that this will no longer happen. Turkish will always be the primary language taught in Turkish schools, but if this Kurdish programme goes to plan, children will no longer feel like criminals for openly speaking the language their mothers have taught them. It is equally to be hoped that mothers will be easier on their children speaking Turkish if they are reassured that their Kurdish language is not in jeopardy. Other measures include the proposed legalisation, in October 2013, of the letters q, w and x, which had previously been illegal in Turkey as they appear in Kurdish but not Turkish words – an absurd but highly significant proposal.

The Kurdish issue dominates Turkey's minority PR at the moment, and it is easy to forget that there are many instances of minorities in Turkey living peaceful, happy lives. The concept of personal national identity fascinates and divides people looking in from the outside, but quite often the objects of their scrutiny are blissfully unaware of all the fuss. They are not necessarily racked with existential angst, or troubled by conflicting allegiances to a particular heritage or political power. The most uncomplicated notion of nationhood that I have encountered was embodied in a fellow passenger on a coach in south-east Turkey.

En route from Antep to Mardin, my boyfriend and I were the only non-locals on board a Tatlıses coach. As far as I could tell, most passengers were seasoned commuters either embarking on or returning from a visit to relatives, or doing local business. Most of them took no notice of the scenery and immersed themselves in one of the hundreds of films provided on the tiny TV screen set into the seat in front of them, courtesy of popular musician and coach-owning business mogul İbrahim Tatlıses. As we passed the Euphrates, an old lady dressed in black sitting behind me asked her neighbour whether this was the sea, and was assured it was not. This was clearly her first sighting of the enormous river, at a fairly advanced age, and I wondered if she might not be from the area. I asked her.

'I'm from Mardin, my dear,' came the proud response. Mardin is about two hours' drive from Antep; this was the lady's first trip away from her hometown, to visit her daughter, and the first time she had clapped eyes on such a large quantity of water. She had never seen the sea, and assumed this must be it. She was intensely curious about me, asking where I was from, eyes widening at the response. I was equally curious about her, especially when I heard her chatting to her fretting grandson in Arabic. 'Yes,' she said, in her accented Turkish. 'I speak Arabic at home. Kurdish I learned from my friends.'

'Are you Turkish or Arab?'

'*Yani*,' came the brilliant response – '*yani*' means 'you know' or 'I mean to say', and implies a kind of mutual understanding when used by itself. I doubt she had been asked this question before, and seemed to think it obvious that she was, of course, both. A Turk foremost, perhaps, but ethnically Arab and living so much on the cusp of what is technically the Middle East that it would be ludicrous to make some kind of distinction between her and her extended family living a few miles away just across the border (as I discovered). When we came to the subject of the trouble in

Syria – this was May 2012 – she looked terribly sad and could only say, 'May Allah save them. They are our brothers.' First and foremost, this lady was a Muslim, specifically a Sunni Muslim.

Mardin is an incredibly diverse city only a few kilometres away from Syria and Mesopotamia – most people are ethnically Arab, but a considerable proportion are Christian Syriacs, quite a few are Kurdish, and they all get on famously. A wonderfully seamless mixture of Turkish and Arabic is spoken on the street. This lady was an example of the unquestioning acceptance of this mix as a fact of life – she had no existential quandaries about who she was or with whom she belonged. National identity simply was not an issue for this multilingual, uneducated woman who instinctively prioritised a relationship with God over allegiance to a flag.

The Laz people are another interesting example of a happily integrated minority from a completely different area of Turkey. They are an ethnic, indigenous group who live along the Black Sea, and also across the border in Georgia. They have lived without much trouble in Turkey for centuries, converting from Christianity to Islam in the sixteenth century, under Ottoman rule. When Erdoğan controversially referred to the Ottoman *eyalet* (province) system in 2013, he mentioned not only Kurdistan but Lazistan, the Ottoman area in the Black Sea region which belonged to the Laz community. Like Kurdistan, Lazistan no longer formally exists but the community does. The difference between the two is that a significant number of Kurds want Kurdistan resurrected, while the Laz are happy to be left as they are, with no political aspirations to a state or even a province. They never keep their identity secret in mixed company, as some Kurds do, because they do not fear the prejudice that attends minorities with separatist ambitions.

It is open to debate how strict a minority the Laz are. There is a language, Lazca ('Laz-ish', or South Caucasian), which is distinct from Turkish and still spoken in some Black Sea communities, especially in the furthest eastern villages. There is also a small body of literature in Lazca, currently being collected, but mostly it is passed down orally through the generations. This happens less now that migration within Turkey leads to families marrying out of their immediate geographical circles – the Laz community, like many others, is becoming much less concentrated. While their ethnicity is vague, the popular concept of a 'Laz' is so celebrated that Turks apply to it anyone from the Black Sea, even though they only really live in pockets on the eastern side of the coast, mainly in the mountainous regions. So strong is the typified Laz personality and the scatty things they are meant to say and do that when Turks do something absent-minded they say *Lazlık yaptım* – 'I did a Laz-ism.'

When I travelled in the Black Sea region of Trabzon, I had a driver who mimicked the rather coarse Laz dialect for me, which is distinct from Lazca. He told me that he speaks it with his family, but wouldn't speak it to me because he said I wouldn't understand a word he was saying. In Turkey, the Laz are considered to have a hilarious accent and are the butt of many jokes, rather like the Irish are for Brits, but (as with Irish jokes) these are not intended maliciously. The jokes are especially innocuous because the Laz people have always happily existed within Turkey as an integrated and contented component of society.

The humour of the Laz people is celebrated as a kind of illogical logic, a harmless naïvety which brings bumbling Irish anti-heroes forcefully to mind (without their love of drinking). The local hero of the oral tradition is called Temel. In one Laz story, a man brings his watch to Temel, who is a watch repairer, and complains that it has stopped working. Temel scrutinises the watch, bangs it, opens it up and finds a dead ant inside. 'Look,' he says to his customer. 'Of course your watch has stopped – its mechanic is dead!'

The Anatolian equivalent of Temel is Nasreddin Hoca, a legendary holy man about whom there are hundreds of stories both in Turkey and in neighbouring countries like Iran. As a very small child I remember my grandmother telling me these stories, and my favourite one involved the Hoca's neighbour coming round to borrow his donkey. The Hoca tells him that his donkey has died and, just then, the donkey brays from the backyard. The neighbour chastises the Hoca for lying, to which the Hoca shakes his head reproachfully and says, 'My dear fellow, do you believe the word of a donkey over that of a Hoca?' Simple enough to appeal to a child, this kind of story celebrates the silliness of a roguish holy man and speaks volumes about the Turkish sense of humour.

The Black Sea region is in many ways the most beautiful part of Turkey. It is almost shockingly green, full of mountains running with ice-cold waterfalls of melted snow, hazelnut trees and fields of primroses. The people are also among the most hospitable in Turkey, which is saying something. I went for days without eating anywhere but in people's homes. In the mountains the people are self-sufficient, keeping cows for butter, cheese and yoghurt and hives for honey, growing hazelnuts, the famous black cabbage and apples. By the sea they have huge quantities of fresh fish, especially the Black Sea anchovy – *hamsi*. I ate like a queen.

Because there is very little work to be had in these mountainous regions, the men often leave to work in big cities like Istanbul, or abroad. One of the most surreal experiences I have had in Turkey was the moment when I was drinking tea with some American friends of mine in Pervare, a village high up in the mountains above Trabzon. We sat and chatted to the local men while a smiling man with one arm went around offering a tray laden with little glasses of golden tea from Rize, fifty kilometres to the east. One of the older men, dapper in a checked flat cap and little spectacles, started telling us about all the work he had done for big companies like Coca-Cola in countries as far afield as Kuwait. When he mentioned Thailand, my friend Abigale exclaimed that she, too, had lived there briefly and suddenly the two were exchanging greetings in Thai and counting up to twenty. This would have been fairly surprising in Istanbul, but here we were in the middle of nowhere, in a mountain village with no phone signal, let alone internet, among people who could not speak English, but could speak Thai and, it turned out, Arabic.

The Laz are very proud of their tough reputation, which they have earned by virtue of their hardy mountain-dwelling ways. I spoke to one professor at Trabzon University who tried to convince me that every single successful Turk in history has come from Black Sea stock, which reminded me of the way Turks in general claim that all successful people in the history of the world have Turkish heritage (Homer being a notable example), though they often make these claims with a self-mocking smile. This professor's argument was that when people from the Black Sea move to big cities like Istanbul, they do very well because they thrive in an easier environment, like athletes training at high altitude and then trouncing their competitors at sea level. Although I lifted an eyebrow at his claims, it must be admitted that a considerable number of Laz people throughout Turkish history have been very successful, particularly in politics – Erdoğan is from Rize, east of Trabzon, as is former Prime Minister Mesut Yılmaz, while Necmettin Erbakan, prime minister in the nineties, was from the town of Sinop on the Black Sea coast west of Trabzon. Most of the Laz people I have met in Istanbul are taxi drivers who always tell me how much they miss home, twenty years after they've left it. Very often, they are either hearty nationalists or supporters of Erdoğan, because of the Rize connection. Some of them, however, have surprisingly leftist views.

In the village of Pervare, my friends and I ate at the house of Emre Doğan, the head of the local branch of the Workers' Party – that is to say, he represented all and any socialists in this thousand-strong village. Emre was a quiet, very composed man who objected to me calling him *bey* (the equivalent to 'sir' which everyone uses in polite conversation in Turkey, especially on first meeting) – a nasty capitalist habit, apparently. He cooked for us, as he had no wife, and had an impressive library of books including the works of Plato. We talked a bit about *The Republic* and I soon realised there was a chasm of difference between our approaches to the text. What was to me an interesting work of philosophy was to him a work of enormous social and political significance – he read it as a Greek would have done, as something exciting and relevant. I have met many passionately ideological Turks, who care much more about government and justice as real terms than most of my PPE graduate friends, for all their abstract expertise. When you worry about the direction your country is going in, you can become both galvanised and radicalised, as I was to see very clearly during the Gezi protests.

Near Trabzon there are still a few villages where the last remaining descendants of Ottoman Greeks live. During the Ottoman Empire, Trabzon was an old trading hub controlled by Greeks. In one of these villages we met a couple in their seventies who invited us into their home. In the sitting room was a huge portrait of Atatürk in the form of a carpet hanging on the wall, and downstairs was a *mescit* (Muslim prayer room). In this utterly Turkish domestic setting, the old couple started speaking together in Greek, and listening to them was almost as surreal as hearing Thai spoken in Pervare. The fact that they spoke Greek was clearly the result of some kind of Greek heritage but they would never say that to us – the husband in particular was at pains to talk about his Turkish friends, and insisted that he and his wife were Turkish. I wondered if they had ever been marginalised because of their Greek ancestry. My guess was probably not, but the elderly gentleman was not sure where he stood with these strange foreign guests. His wife spoke heavily accented Turkish with us, and explained that she had grown up in an entirely Greek-speaking family and had learned Turk-ish from her daughter's schoolbooks. Her daughter, Meliz (probably a Turkification of the Greek Melissa) spoke a little Greek, too. After dinner, she allowed us to help put things away in the kitchen and laughingly explained to me that she wanted to be able to say to the neighbours: 'I made some Americans work for me!'

While you will always find a few Greeks and Turks who become incandescent with rage at the mere mention of the other, I have actually been pleasantly surprised by the lack of problems between these two ancient enemies. I have travelled in Greece, and met with nothing but friendliness. My Greek friends in Istanbul feel perfectly comfortable living here. I once talked to a restaurant owner on the Greek island of Kos who told me how he had learned some Turkish to chat to the Turkish fishermen who sold him fish, and how they agreed that any problems between the two countries lay with their respective politicians.

There is currently a similar atmosphere in Cyprus, which is even more surprising to me because my mother has always given me the impression that there is an animosity between Greeks and Turks there that will never die. A Turkish Cypri-ot who grew up in Lefkoşa (Greek Nicosia) and fled to Lon-don during the war in 1974, my mother has never forgotten how bad things were forty years ago. Now, young Turkish Cypriots are eager to identify themselves just as 'Cypriots' and get on perfectly well with their Greek neighbours. When I visited in late 2012, I sat at a bar in the middle of Lefkoşa, just north of the border which runs through the middle of town. There, I talked to a Greek Cypriot doctor who had popped over to join his Turkish Cypriot friend for a few beers, as easily as if he'd popped over Turnpike Lane via a small checkpoint. To my mother, this is the equivalent of water running backwards, and she finds the current ability of Turkish Cypriots to get on with Greek Cypriots and even to actively reject the patronage of the Turkish government (as many now do) deeply troubling. Rescued from Greek bombs and gunfire by Turkish soldiers at the height of the conflict, my mother feels that the current Grecophile attitude of Turkish Cypriots negates all that Turkey has done to protect North Cyprus, disrespects all the soldiers who lost their lives and forgets all the wrongs her extended family suffered. The way I see it, the world moves on, and young Turkish Cypriots are understandably keen to be regarded as part of an EU country (Cyprus was accepted into the EU, wrongly I believe, in 2004 at the insistence of Greece).

What is interesting is that, despite this feeling of debt my mother has to Turkey, and her sense of belonging, she is sensitive to the fact that mainland Turks have not traditionally regarded Turkish Cypriots as proper Turks. They are, like many others, a minority in a country composed of minorities. Before I moved to Istanbul she told me not to tell anyone I was Cypriot, because she thought I would not be taken seriously. Having not grown up in the region, I didn't understand her hang-ups and declared my heritage to anyone who asked. I have never got a bad reaction. Maybe this is because, to a Turk, I am more English than anything else, and so it is irrelevant where I claim to hail from. I also feel, however, that times have changed and people are both more educated and tolerant than they were in my mother's day, when she was made to feel very different when she turned up at Ankara University from Cyprus, at that time regarded as a kind of troublesome Outer Hebrides where people spoke in a boorish manner. Apart from anything else, there has been so much migration between the various corners of Turkey that many people don't live in their hometown any more, and indeed the most frequent question one Turk asks another is *Memleketiniz neresi?* (Where is your hometown?)

While social acceptance of minorities is getting better in Turkey, there are still institutionalised problems. Orthodox Christian communities in particular are upset by the double standards of the Turkish government's attitude to religion within the state – the Directorate of Religious Affairs currently funds mosques but not churches, for example. If you die a Muslim in Turkey, your family does not have to pay for your funeral because it is provided free of charge by the state via the directorate. By contrast, the families of religious Armenians and Greeks must pay for their funerals. In the last year, there have been calls by Greek Orthodox leaders for the directorate to allocate funds to non-Muslim populations as a requirement of equal citizenship.

Turkey is in practice a Muslim state but in theory it is secular, and to fund mosques but not churches seems wrong. The government seems to be getting more sensitive to criticism in this particular area; after the report of discrepancies in state funding of religious institutions, it announced that it would pay for churches' lighting bills. This may not seem like a dramatic development, but it does show that the government is willing to take on some constructive criticism, something that has not always been the case. The Kurdish peace process is another positive step, if we set our cynicism aside for the moment. Small steps are symbolic: last year, for the first time in Turkish history, a Greek footballer was signed to play for a Turkish team. He is adored admittedly more for his goal-scoring skills than for his nationality, but importantly the latter has not provoked resentment as it once would have done. By Turkish standards, this is progress.

The AKP government wants to show that it is improving minority rights, and in March 2013 the Culture Minister, Ömer Çelik, publicly invited Greek and Armenian Christians who had left Turkey to return, promising that the current government had learned to include them in society. While that might be an ambitious claim, it has been at least partially supported by Patriarch Bartholomew, the head of the Greek Orthodox community in Turkey, who has been open about the fact that the current government has been better than previous ones in improving minority rights, Greeks' and others'. He also says that there is still some way to go.

Will entirely peaceful and non-discriminatory co-existence between minorities in Turkey ever be attainable? Some say not; religious and cultural differences and resentment run too deep. I think it is attainable: the country is already naturally multicultural. Turks eat the same food as Greeks, Armenians, Arabs and Georgians, and share the same humour and superstitions, whether they know it or not. The last point is key, of course; I once got into an unexpectedly heated argument with a Turkish colleague who refused to countenance the idea that the Armenian dish *topik* was indeed Armenian rather than Turkish. While there are plenty of Turks like him, there are also, thankfully, plenty who not only admit the presence of minority cultures in Turkey but positively welcome their influence. From a minority perspective, the attitudes of individuals like the young half-Armenian boy I interviewed are very valuable. Tolerance and realism are needed on both sides; the boy never ignored the injustices done to past generations of his family, but he realised the need to progress in a rapidly developing country and get on with the many other minorities who make up its infinitely complex society.

12

Gezi Park: A New Chapter for Turkey

The Gezi protests of 2013 woke Turkey up. It was not a gentle awakening; it was a splash of cold water in the face for the public and the government alike. It woke me up to the latent political frustrations of the Turkish people, in the most unexpected and humbling way. Living in the midst of what felt like a revolution, it was difficult not to be affected by the emotions of tens of thousands of people demonstrating in the streets just outside. More tangibly, it was impossible not to be affected by the daily clouds of tear gas. Living through the Gezi protests was like teetering on the edge of a constant cliffhanger; no one knew what was going to happen next, and that was strangely thrilling. It was a period of intense uncertainty, but it made me much more certain about my feelings as a Turk because I was living through a dramatic period of change along with everyone else. It was a time of solidarity, when people communicated, collaborated and marched together for political change, with all the humour and courage and determination I should have expected from my years of observing Turks from the sidelines.

The movement had a strong communal mentality, a hive-like sense of purpose that kept it alive for much longer than anyone anticipated. People were killed and arrested, entirely peaceful demonstrations were suppressed, and still the protests continued. A month after the eruption of Gezi Park, the government estimated that 2.5 million people had demonstrated, and that number kept growing as summer passed.

The movement was an irrefutable, irrevocable step forward for democratic expression. Before the protests, I was convinced that Turks who disliked the government were hopelessly apathetic, unhappy but resigned to the current government for the foreseeable future. Friends and strangers discussed politics in restaurants and barber shops as though they were impassioned spectators of someone else's game; after their discussions, these fierce debaters went home to their individual concerns. Mainstream politics certainly did not present any significant opposition to the government. Everyone assumed that supporters of the AKP outnumbered their opponents, and the latter were too disparate and scattered to amount to anything much. June 2013 changed all that. While the protests may not have had dramatic results in the short term, Turkey's long-term political prognosis is now much more interesting than it would otherwise have been, because a previously silent opposition to the government has made itself heard, and discovered how loud its voice can be. The Gezi protest movement set the next stage in Turkey's development as a democracy.

I live two minutes' walk from Taksim Square and had often wandered through Gezi Park without giving it much thought. Coming from London and the glorious expanses of Hampstead Heath and Hyde Park, I had snobby views about its relatively garden-like size, which belied its name (*gezi* means 'sightseeing' or 'tour'). In May 2013, the park was due to be cleared as part of the controversial Taksim Square redevelopment project, and in an effort to stop this, about fifty environmentalists camped out in the park in the path of encroaching bulldozers. To my shame, I remember walking past these people on my way to the metro and thinking, 'You'll never save those trees. Nice try.'

That was the last day of Gezi Park's anonymity. At dawn the next day, 31 May 2013, police charged into the park, tearing down tents, spraying sleeping protesters in the face with pepper spray and beating anyone who resisted. Over the course of the next twenty-four hours, people returned to the park, in ever increasing numbers. What had begun as a small environmentalist protest exploded into a spontaneous popular movement which included people entirely unrelated to any tree-hugging agenda. Many people objected in principle to the government's plans to build over Taksim Square, traditionally an open space for political protest, and others objected to the police violence and went to lend support. Gezi proved to be the green light for previously unexpressed anger and served as something tangible to save, to fight for. It came to represent the many frustrations of many people.

The weeks following the initial Gezi occupation were filled with clashes between protesters and police. This period felt at times like stumbling onto the stage of *Les Misérables*, and at other times like living between the pages of *1984*. The first ten days were the most exciting and felt the most revolutionary, because there was hope in the air and what felt like victory. To everyone's astonishment, the police abandoned Taksim Square and the park, and there was a kind of unthreatening mob rule which was joyously anarchic. Joining the crowd felt like being a child again, running amok in a parentless house – deliciously liberating, but a little scary at the same time. The streets around Taksim were transformed: adrenaline-fuelled residents pulled paving stones up with their bare hands, building barricades on main roads to prevent police returning. Every night, they stood defiantly on these barricades with smudged faces and flags, shouting at the police who lurked further down the road like revolutionaries taunting royalist troops. Old ladies and children supported them by leaning out of their windows and banging pots and pans in an unholy frenzy of defiance. Young people, old people, leftists and Kemalists scrawled on walls and pavements with all the delight of children writing rude words on their teacher's blackboard: 'Government: resign!' 'Tayyip [Erdoğan] – run to your grandmother's side!' and my favourite: 'Nothing will ever be as it was before. Dry your tears' (a reference to the tear gas liberally used by riot police).

What caused this tirade of public outrage? The nominal cause was the government's attempt to destroy Gezi Park, but this was just the trigger. It was not even the controversial redevelopment plan of Taksim Square. It was the culmination of years of frustration given outlet by the opportunity to respond to a clear-cut instance of oppression. The first few images of the chaos went viral on social media and suddenly everyone was talking about it. The timing was perfect: it was the beginning of summer, just the wrong time to destroy a park, and hordes of Istanbullus came to the rescue of persecuted activists in the hub of the city. They were fed up with incessant urbanisation, high-handed government decisions and a leader who seemed increasingly out of touch and authoritarian. These concerns had been simmering for a while, impossible to confront directly, but suddenly there was a focal point which united disparate groups of people who would otherwise never have converged to share their criticisms of the government.

Gezi was, fittingly, a quintessential grassroots movement. No one expected it and no one could have predicted how it unfolded. In a few days, a mass of individuals with various concerns had achieved what the mainstream opposition parties had never managed in a decade: they had scared the government. They had massed from nowhere in their tens of thousands, and they were furious. Ordinary middle-class people, who could stay comfortable and safe in their homes if they wanted to, felt passionately enough about the movement to come back to an area they knew was far from safe, knowing they might end up in a prison cell or a hospital ward: not a decision to be taken lightly.

As I said, the protests were characterised by very Turkish traits of courage and determination. They were also full of stereotypes. In Taksim Square, the commune-like, carnival atmosphere was interspersed with typical Turkish opportunism. Amid the stands manned by public-spirited, smiling youths handing out food, water, books and anti-tear gas medicines to protesters, free of charge, there were the inevitable Turkish hawkers selling face masks, goggles, Turkish flags, Guy Fawkes masks and kebabs at considerable profit. For them, it was business as usual. The economy may have been looking bleak with a plunging stock market and depleted tourism, but the ubiquitous Turkish salesman was making a killing out of a protest movement which, ironically, had a significant anti-capitalism contingent.

Riot tourism emerged as a bizarre but totally logical by-product of the protests. One afternoon on my way home I came across a group of middle-aged American tourists staring wide-eyed at a wall of graffiti and taking photos of a barricade down the road. Their tour guide, a small man talking in authoritative tones, was translating the messages: 'This one says no to fascism. This one says something very rude about the police I cannot repeat. If you look to your right, you can see a three-metre-high barricade. It is made of carnage.'

At the beginning of the protests, I was often hit by tear gas, which is like being burned by invisible acid all over your skin, and in your eyes and lungs. At the beginning, it is frightening because it disorients you, but after a few nights it becomes a very painful inconvenience, necessitating strategic retreats. A week into the protests, I was wheezily beating such a retreat when an elderly lady standing on her doorstep stopped me and offered me some lemon cologne, just as she would have done had I been a guest in her home. Automatically, I cupped my hands and thanked her as she sprinkled it over them and wished me better. As I splashed the cologne on my face and breathed it in, the tear gas cleared from my nostrils. This was pure Turkish magic: a traditional gesture of hospitality transformed into makeshift first aid as tear gas billowed around and young men and women shouted for their rights.

On 11 June, police retook the square and a few days later the park, suddenly and violently. Protesters were shocked, and the joyful atmosphere which had characterised the first stage of protests dissipated as people scattered. Now came the *1984* phase, when people near Taksim Square were stopped and searched by police for the helmets they carried to protect themselves from flying tear-gas canisters, when secret police mingled with the crowd and protesters looked at each other askance, when law-abiding citizens shut down their Facebook and Twitter accounts in panic. This was the period of dawn raids, when police tracked protesters down in their homes and university dormitories, when media channels were shut down for showing footage of the protests, when government officials denounced anyone in Taksim as a 'terrorist'.

Any demonstration after this was stopped by police before it got within a kilometre of Taksim Square, so protesters refined their methods. In parks all over the country, people gathered in forums to discuss where to go next with their protest movement. Everyone was invited to speak in a scrupulously fair system which brought to mind the kind of perfect democracy invented by Athenians two and a half millennia ago. A specialised sign language emerged, so that the crowds could make their feelings heard without interrupting the speaker. This looked like a kind of semi-synchronised silent disco performance: a sea of shaking hands signified applause, crossed forearms meant 'I don't agree' and revolving hands or a thunder of stamping feet encouraged the speaker not to waffle. It was an extraordinary thing to watch, the antithesis of the lazy boos of bored backbenchers in parliament, and emblematic of the immediacy of these forums. This was direct representation, and even if it could never be replicated in government, it was a wonderful sign of the purity of people's intentions for a more honest and transparent democracy. Meanwhile, the protests continued, no longer every day, but an undercurrent of resistance to the government's reactions continued to make itself felt.

There were many moments of high drama during the protests, to put it mildly. There was the time a rubber bullet skimmed my friend's head as he sat in a café, the time I found another friend collapsed in a state of shock after a tear-gas attack, the time a policeman pointed a gun at me and told me not to move. Much worse, amateur footage showed police beating protesters viciously in side streets, away from news cameras, or throwing tear-gas canisters into the doorways of buildings where protesters had fled to supposed safety. Hundreds of thousands of people have seen the horrible moment when a policeman shot and killed Ethem Sarısülük in a sunny Ankara street, and many others watched Erdoğan's televised speech in which he hailed police as 'heroic' and 'restrained'.

What really stuck in my mind, however, were the unexpectedly beautiful moments of the protests. The day after police emptied Taksim Square without warning, a crowd of people gathered on the steps of Gezi Park towards midnight, and in place of the clamours and chants of previous days, the familiar notes of John Lennon's 'Imagine' emerged eerily from a grand piano that was almost obscured by a rapt, silent audience. It was indescribably moving to see hundreds of frightened people calmed by a lone pianist, their solidarity rebuilt as they formed an audience for this spontaneous performance. Far off in the crowd, a figure was hunched over the keyboard, wearing red in honour of the Turkish flag and a jaunty fedora. No one knew his name. He played all through the night, and the next night, and then the next, in pouring rain. On Saturday, Gezi Park was raided and his piano was seized by police, but he had cheered everyone in the interim.

By then, everyone knew that his name was Davide Martello and that he was an Italian-German musician who had come to Istanbul to support protesters with his 'piano of peace'. He had reminded them that the world was watching.

Less sensational but no less heroic was the man who, a few days later, stood and stared at the poster of Atatürk on the AKM building in Taksim Square for eight hours. All he did was stand there silently, but somehow he commanded attention. As time passed, he drew the attention of plain-clothes police, who became increasingly confused and irritated by his stance. He said nothing to their questions, passively allowing himself to be searched and hassled. As dusk fell, he was gradually joined by a crowd of around three hundred people who came and stood with him in solidarity. At around two in the morning these people were dispersed and ten of them were arrested for 'insisting on standing'. The protests were copied in other cities all over the country, and soon Erdem Gündüz was a national hero.

For weeks afterwards, there would always be a crowd of people standing in the square, facing Atatürk's portrait or Gezi Park. Some of them had put tape over their mouths to symbolise the restrictions on freedom of speech, others read copies of *1984*, and one girl went around giving people flowers. I stood there myself, and it was strangely relaxing. Standing still must be one of the most simple and powerful forms of protest. There is no need for noise, movement or anything that could possibly be construed as aggression: the protest movement had matured. And yet the line of police who stood facing these people looked very uncomfortable.

The image that reminds me most forcibly of the disparity

between police and protesters was that of red carnations pressed against advancing water-cannon tanks. Hundreds of people had gathered in Taksim Square on 22 June to commemorate the (then) four fatalities of the protests. They had no banners, because people had realised by then that any vaguely political element to the protests (like banners or chants) gave the government reason to denounce them. There was no political element to this crowd at all, but hundreds of people had gathered, so police had to act. People offered up their commemorative carnations, and still the water cannon kept on rolling. It seemed like the more determined people were to demonstrate peacefully, the more determined police were to stop them.

Eskişehir is a student town near Ankara which was rocked by protests long after foreign cameras got bored with Istanbul. One of my favorite pieces of footage showed an old lady in a headscarf giving food to young protesters in the town centre. The old lady in the video speaks in a voice cracked by age. She is frail and stooped, and is clearly concerned about the safety of these young people, and whether they're getting enough to eat. She reminded me very strongly of my Turkish grandmother, whose primary aim in life was to feed the young (mainly me). The young students respond to the old lady's kindness by thanking her in Allah's name and calling her 'mother'. One young woman takes her hand, kisses it and touches it to her forehead in an age-old gesture of respect.

To me, this was a beautiful symbol of the humanity which crosses generations in this country. It showed the way young Turks respect and cherish the customs of their elders while fighting for a more modern Turkey, and the straightforward kindness of an old lady who might not have understood what all the fuss was about, but worried for the safety of whoever might be taking part. Religious and secular Turks are not so very different. At times like this, it is obvious how mutual respect and compassion exists outside the perimeters of political ideologies and institutionalised religion.

When people were gassed in the streets of Taksim, they acted not as scared individuals but as a kind of responsible civil army. People handed out masks, water, lemons and lotions to help strangers deal with the gas. When there was a sense of panic and people started running, a general cry of *Yavaş, yavaş* ('Slowly, slowly') calmed everyone down. Football supporters wore the colours of rival teams and linked arms, cheering each other on. At seven every morning, protesters went around the streets clearing up the rubbish they had left the night before – discarded masks, bottles and broken paving stones. I saw two things during the protests that I had never seen in my two years in Turkey: friendly football fans, and people picking up rubbish.

During the Gezi protests the public took full responsibility for themselves and their actions in what felt like a war. People were traumatised, but they did not flinch. The uncertainty of not knowing what would happen next was, eventually, exhausting; messages from the government were incoherent, and no one trusted them anyway. The insistence of people to keep collaborating and caring for each other was humbling and much more impressive than the aggressive shouts of angry young men who taunted police on the 'front lines' of the resistance.

Some friends of mine seemed to have been waiting their

whole lives for the Gezi protest movement – liberal, secular leftists who do not identify with any of the mainstream political parties. One in particular, Gökhan, was in a frenzy of excitement at the beginning, barely sleeping, paying no heed to his job and hoping and praying that the protests would manage to bring some kind of pressure to bear on the government, as the opposition parties had failed to do throughout his lifetime. He lives nearly two hours away from Taksim Square in a distant suburb but would come without fail every night to protest, leaving at around 5 a.m., getting home for two hours' sleep and then off to work followed by yet another night of passionate resistance. It was an exhausting schedule, but my friend had never been happier or more energetic. He was one of those who said he would not leave Taksim Square until Erdoğan resigned. After the evacuation of the square and park and the government crackdown on those who had taken part in the protests, his hope and energy left him – he removed himself from social media and was conscious only of the danger of having been associated with the protests. It was very sad to watch.

Media censorship in Turkey usually takes the form of self-censorship by editors and media moguls who want to keep in with the government, and the Gezi protests brought this painfully to light. During the first couple of days of protest, CNN Türk broadcast nature documentaries, most famously a programme on penguins, instead of coverage of the protests. There were widespread calls for CNN to cut its Turkish division from the franchise, and penguin memes spread across social media like wildfire. The best was a stencil of a penguin wearing a gas mask that was replicated on walls around Taksim – an interesting instance of social media making a concrete mark on the protests.

Brave channels who decided to air footage of the protests were punished by the Radio and Television High Commission and the Supreme Council of Radio and Television. The latter fined several new channels, including Halk TV, for 'harming the physical, mental and moral development of children' by showing harrowing live footage of the police brutality in Taksim Square. The High Commission threatened to close down Hayat TV, another channel which had made the mistake of covering the protests too closely.

Sometimes it was individuals rather than regulatory bodies who took it upon themselves to mete out punishment. At the beginning of the protests, Erdoğan described Twitter as a dangerous bed of lies. A few weeks later, Melih Gökçek, the mayor of Ankara, strove to prove him right by directing a smear campaign over Twitter against a BBC journalist, Selin Girit, who had quoted a protester in one of her tweets. He used a hashtag meaning 'Don't be a spy for England, Selin Girit', and exhorted all his followers to retweet it. When the Twitter community responded by using the hashtag: 'Provokatör Melih Gökçek', he declared he would sue anyone who used it. He then announced plans to open a museum of vandalism, in which he would display smashed-up bus stops and chronicle the acts of hooliganism perpetrated by Gezi protesters. Apparently, this would be for the edification of the Turkish public, 'so that they know what can happen if they capture Ankara'.

There was a strong sense during the protests that, while protesters were to be punished for 'inciting public unrest' or damaging public property, people in authority and police officers were not accountable for what they might have said or done. The most notable instance of this was the policeman who killed Ethem Sarısülük, who was only identified and remanded after a public outcry, and was quickly released because he was deemed to have acted in self-defence, despite video evidence to the contrary.

There are many reasons why Turkish authorities are generally unwilling to admit to being at fault. The main reason is that they can get away with it. Another major factor is that, traditionally, they have always feared giving any grounds to groups who might be ready to depose them, namely the military. In Turkey, rather as in Egypt, the military has had the role of protecting the state against both internal and external threats, which has given them the licence to carry out coups against governments, as they did in 1960, 1971 and 1980. In 1997 they staged what became known as a 'post-modern coup' by issuing 'recommendations' which the government could follow or resign, and outlawed the ruling Islamist Welfare Party, of which Erdoğan was a member. In 1999 Erdoğan was sent to prison for reciting a poem which was regarded as an 'incitement to commit offence'. It included the lines: 'The mosques are our barracks, the domes our helmets, the minarets our bayonets and the faithful our soldiers.' Perhaps, in recent years, the overlapping images of mosques and barracks have made an impression on Erdoğan. In 2012 he announced plans to build an enormous mosque on Çamlıca hill in Istanbul, positioned so that it will be visible from any point in the city. In 2013, he ordered the rebuilding of an Ottoman barracks which had been the seat of an Islamic uprising against nationalists in 1909. This barracks was the proposed centrepiece for Taksim Square's redevelopment.

Erdoğan has been keen to show that the decades of military-backed nationalist control are now over, and that Islam can proudly return to public life in Turkey. He wants to say: 'We've won.' It hasn't been easy; Erdoğan has worked hard to limit the power of the military, both by changing the constitution and by prosecuting alleged ex-members of the shady, ultra-nationalist Ergenekon movement which had sought to bring down the AKP in the early 2000s, and had included many generals or ex-generals of the Turkish army. In 2010 he changed the constitution to bring the military and the judiciary under the control of the government by rushing through a constitutional amendment full of disparate reforms, to which the public could only vote yes or no in a general referendum. Because the bill was sugar-coated with vows to improve the environment and make public transport more accessible for people with disabilities, people voted 'yes' after a popular campaign by liberals who urged *Yetmez ama evet* ('Not enough but yes'). In 2011 Erdoğan appointed new heads of the armed forces and finally, after the Gezi protests, he oversaw a change in the wording of the military code so that now its duty is to protect the Republic of Turkey from *external* threats, but the protection of the republic from internal threats is no longer mentioned. Coups are now technically illegal, and probably impossible in practice given the change of crucial personnel; indeed, Erdoğan has boasted that Turkey is 'immune to coups'. Shortly after the Gezi protests, the Egyptian army staged a coup that overthrew President Morsi, a self-styled moderate Islamic leader not dissimilar to Erdoğan.

The AKP immediately, vociferously, denounced the coup. First came a statement from the AKP's spokesman, Hüseyin Çelik, calling Egypt 'backward' for staging a military coup. Next, Foreign Minister Davutoğlu demanded that Morsi be released from house arrest and reminded everyone: 'Leaders who come to power with open and transparent elections reflecting the will of the people can only be removed by elections, that is to say, the will of the nation.' This might as well as have been a statement directed to the Gezi protesters who were shouting: *'Tayyip, isitifa!'* ('Tayyip [Erdoğan], resign!').

The AKP's refusal to admit that democracy is comprised of anything other than ballot-box victories might be their undoing, because it makes them deaf and blind to other sources of criticism. Çelik claimed that foreign powers had 'mobilised the streets' in Egypt and staged the coup, which chimed perfectly with the government's insistence that the Gezi protests had been staged by an eclectic mix of terrorists, journalists, Jews and interest rate lobbyers. Çelik pointed out that the Egyptian military probably could not solve Egypt's economic problems – a reminder to Turks that their hard-won economic gains might be in jeopardy in the (unlikely) event of a Turkish coup. The potential for coups in Turkey was something that needed to be addressed, and while there was a vindictive air to the way the government neutered the military, it was a progressive rather than a regressive move. However, many weaknesses remain in the Turkish political system, in particular the hierarchical, top-down structure of political parties which means that unless you have a very strong leader all is lost. It is also extremely hard for new parties to gain any traction, which means that political opposition inevitably stagnates.

Mainstream opposition in Turkey is weak. The CHP (Republican People's Party) is outdated and disorganised, incapable of capitalising on these protests or anything else. Their policies are almost entirely reactionary, and they rarely bestir themselves beyond blanket criticism of AKP policies. The leader until 2010, Deniz Baykal, led the party for eighteen dreary years, and was only persuaded to leave after an alleged sex tape was leaked to the press. The current leader, Kemal Kılıçdaoğlu, seems like a nice man (his nickname is 'Gandhi' due to his alleged resemblance to the Indian leader) but has not taken the country by storm.

Erdoğan has no rivals, currently, because there is no new blood in Turkish politics. This is partly due to the ten per cent threshold which prevents any new political party from getting anywhere in elections. Even if a particular party candidate wins an overwhelming majority in their constituency, they will not win a seat in parliament unless their party has won over ten per cent of the votes nationwide. Anyone who voted for them effectively wasted their vote. This means that voters tend to support old dinosaurs like the CHP, even if they have no faith in these parties. Alternatively, they vote for independent candidates, who can legally win seats in parliament by winning over ten per cent of votes just in their constituency. The ten per cent nationwide threshold is, incidentally, by far the highest in Europe, and the subject of much debate. It was instigated after the military coup in 1980, so that the military could control the main parties in power and prevent opposition. It is a self-evidently unjust system, but unfortunately it never suits those in power to change it, so it has stayed like this for thirty years. During the protests, I heard a religious Turkish lady describe it as *haram* – a religious sin – which has come to mean anything unjust. Some parties have rather cleverly tried to buck the system by recruiting independent candidates; when these candidates win, they join the party to boost its profile and improve its chances for the next election. The Kurdish rights-promoting Peace and Democracy Party, for example, has done this to great effect.

Erdoğan is extremely ambitious, and has put his mind to winning over not only Turkey but much of the Middle East. In September 2011, his tour of liberated Middle Eastern countries – Egypt, Tunisia and Libya – was a tour de force of political ambition, characterised by the slamming of America and Israel combined with the portrayal of Turkey as the perfect example of a free Muslim democracy. His televised speech in Cairo was strikingly paternalistic: 'Management of people, management of science and management of money,' he said, grandly. 'If you do those three, you will accomplish your goal.'

Has he managed his own people? That is open to (discreet) debate. He has certainly taken pains to look as though he has. It is crucial to his plans to be in charge in some capacity, preferably as president, as Turkey turns one hundred in 2023. Here is how he might plan to do that: although there is no bar to the number of terms someone can serve as prime minister in the Turkish constitution, it is a rule within the AKP that no one can serve as a minister for more than three consecutive terms. Erdoğan, with characteristically grandiose magnanimity, has made a point of saying he will respect this rule. However, no one believes he has had his fill of power and the odds are decidedly against him bowing out in 2015 when his third term ends.

There will be direct presidential elections for the first time in Turkey in 2014, following amendments to the constitution carried through in the controversial 2010 referendum. Until now, Turkish presidents have been neutral by definition, but usually have an affiliation with the ruling party (or the military), and are not directly chosen by the public. They are, effectively, little more than ceremonial heads of state. In 2014, Turkish citizens will vote directly for their favourite candidate. Erdoğan has been pushing for a presidential system in Turkey, similar to the French system which gives more power to the president than the prime minister, rather than the other way round as is currently the case in Turkey. It looks like these changes won't go through, which must be annoying for Erdoğan. However, he can still serve as president for one term (rather than the two terms he would prefer as a French-style president) and then run again for prime minister, thus fulfilling his promise not to break the AKP rule of serving for no more than three *consecutive* terms. Most importantly, he would be in power in 2023.

During the protests, Erdoğan repeatedly and rather smugly called on Turks to 'express yourself at the ballot box'. This spectacularly missed the point made by protesters, who objected to the high-handed way he made decisions while in power. However, the call was made. Erdoğan was confident that he will win, and perhaps he will. Perhaps he won't, and if he doesn't, he will have no excuse to kick up a fuss.

The confidence of the AKP in their victories at the ballot box brings to mind Winston Churchill's criticism of unrestrained democracy, which he explained in a House of Commons debate in 1947: 'Democracy, I must explain . . . does not mean "We have got our majority, never mind how, and we have our lease of office for five years, so what are you going to do about it?" That is not democracy, that is only small party patter, which will not go down with the mass of the people of this country.' It seems that finally, in 2013, after coups and false hopes of transparent government in the twenty-first century, it has not gone down well with the people of Turkey either. Perhaps they can identify with what Lord Hailsham called in 1967 'an elective dictatorship', meaning a government elected on a simple majority acting without proper restraint on its power. You will notice that my references have been British. Gezi erupted without any open debate of this topic in their House of Commons equivalent, but the issue was, in essence, the driving force behind the protests.

Crushed in the middle of a huge crowd of angry, chanting protesters, it seemed at one point like the whole of Turkey wanted the government to resign. In the heat of the moment, it was easy to believe that a complete regime change was just around the corner, and that Turks were one hundred per cent united in their political ideals. Of course, this was not the case, and I had several sobering conversations with Turks who disapproved of the protests and were as supportive of Erdoğan as ever. It was disconcerting to go from the spitting rage of anti-Erdoğan demonstrators to the spitting rage of anti-protest Erdoğan supporters, and hear totally different sides of the same story.

Erdoğan is in many ways a victim of his own success. He is, or was, the most popular leader since Atatürk, and the longest continuously serving prime minister, but after a decade of increasingly authoritarian decisions many people think he has pushed it too far. During his leadership, Turks have become, broadly speaking, richer, better educated and more connected to the world through the spread of the internet. Young people are demanding more from their government; Erdoğan's achievements do not excuse his faults. Older Turks, on the other hand, have lower expectations. They have lived under previous, less successful prime ministers and they are painfully grateful for all Erdoğan has done for the economy and public services. Many Turks are so used to corrupt, power-hungry leaders that they don't even see the greed of those in power as a fault any more. Erdoğan is above average, because at least he gets things done.

While the Gezi protests were underway I had a conversation with Yahya, a traditional Istanbullu tailor in his fifties who is a stalwart supporter of the AKP. I asked him what he thought of the protesters' complaints that Erdoğan rules undemocratically. 'He is uncompromising, yes,' said the tailor. 'But I trust him. He is a good man.' Yahya then gave me an analogy to explain his conception of a good leader: when one goes abroad, one hands over power of attorney to a lawyer so that affairs can be dealt with in one's absence. It is the same with politics – we vote, we choose a leader, and we hand over the power of attorney for the next four years. This was a real eye-opener for me, explaining a great deal about the implicit trust many Turks have in their leader. When I asked the tailor about the rumours of Erdoğan handing out favours like building contracts to his friends, he replied steadily: 'We all bestow favours on friends, why shouldn't Erdoğan?'

Many Turks view corruption as an unproblematic fact of life. There are, of course, those who are not comfortable with the idea of politicians dishing out favours to their friends, but most do not question it. It is not even a matter of just being realistic, thinking that politicians get away with corrupt decisions because there is no accountability in Turkish government. It is worse than that – these Turks have lost sight of the moral problem with it, because it is so normal. Britain's 2009 MPs' expenses scandal would not even break as a story in the Turkish media, not because of censorship but because the public would not be remotely interested in what they all assume happens anyway. The leader of the main opposition, Kemal Kılıçdaoğlu, does not even consider using the government's alleged corruption as a vote-winning issue. I asked the tailor what he thought of Erdoğan's legendary wealth, and whether it seemed reasonable that a man employed by the state should have accumulated so much money. 'Oh yes,' said the tailor. 'He earned his billions. Don't you know a mayor is awarded ten per cent of the tenders he arranges for any successful municipal projects?' (Erdoğan was the mayor of Istanbul for two years before he moved on to bigger things. The ten per cent 'reward' of which the tailor spoke does not exist, to my knowledge, but it is perfectly obvious what the unofficial nature of this reward is.) This satisfied, unquestioning man was dismissive of the protesters' concerns of Erdoğan's authoritarian tendencies. 'Young people don't understand,' he reflected, sadly. 'They don't know how lucky they are.'

The chasm between those who have grown up during

Erdoğan's leadership and those who have not is huge – they have such different responses to his style of leadership, and whether or not he is entitled to his high-handed decision-making. Erdoğan has done a magnificent job of winning the hearts and minds of the traditional working classes and emerging middle classes of Turkey, but he has neglected a highly motivated, educated youth who are now speaking up. Previously, his strength lay in going unchallenged by apathetic opponents. That situation has been irrevocably changed in the wake of the Gezi protests.

On the evening of 8 June, Erdoğan met with Cemil Çiçek, the speaker of parliament, at Dolmabahçe Palace in Istanbul, to discuss the protests. Outside, a mighty, disembodied roar called for the prime minister's resignation. 'Everywhere is Taksim. Everywhere is resistance. Tayyip – resign!' Its source was a huge mass of Fenerbahçe football fans surging outside the palace on their way to Taksim Square, blowing whistles and banging drums like uniformed revolutionaries. Jostled by Fenerbahçe fans outside the palace, I wondered how Erdoğan felt at that point. It is hard to dismiss the voices of thousands of people demanding your resignation uncomfortably close at hand. The clamour certainly did not sound like it could have come from a negligible group of foreign agitators and marginal extremists, as he has always claimed. It must have hurt even more considering Erdoğan himself is a Fenerbahçe fan.

That roar of criticism did not chasten Erdoğan. It incensed him. He has often painted himself as a victim of anti-democracy, and his reaction to criticism is almost always anger – a very Turkish trait. He admitted that the protests were about him. His leadership was what, ironically, united all those against him. The protesters in Ankara, Istanbul, Eskişe-hir and Antakya were disparate and scattered. They didn't have a leader but they almost didn't need one because they had an anti-leader, a focus for their energies. *Tayyip, istifa!* ('Tayyip, resign!') was the most common chant in Taksim Square and in squares across Turkey. Tens of thousands of Turks were not protesting because of Gezi Park. They all had their various grievances, from Erdoğan's Syrian stance to his attempt to outlaw abortion to his restrictions on alcohol con-sumption, but they had one thing in common: resentment of their prime minister.

A question occurred to me after the initial excitement of Gezi died down: What would Atatürk say about these protests, and the direction the country is going in? Back in 1927 he warned the Turkish youth about 'the enemy at home' – did he mean the tear gas-wielding, democratically elected government or the banner-wielding, motley crew of protest-ers? I would like to believe that he would approve of the cour-ageous and determined struggle of those fighting, and indeed dying, for a better democracy. I asked a Turkish friend to get a second opinion. He laughed and said, 'If Atatürk were in government he would be cracking the whip like crazy. If he were a protester he would have staged a coup by now.' I would like to live in a Turkey where I could say something like that without fearing imprisonment, and at the same time be ac-knowledged as someone who is respectful but realistic about a national hero. When I look back at the founding of the re-public, it seems like Atatürk put together the broken pieces of the Ottoman Empire with superglue: modern Turkey was the result. Now the pieces are coming apart, but it is to be hoped that Gezi will have some part in putting it back together in a new shape more in keeping with the times.

Turkish citizens who criticise Turkey are often condemned as traitors, when in my experience they are usually the most genuine in their patriotism, because they see Turkey's faults and love it anyway. They do not criticise Turkey for the fun of it, or because they long for its demise. They are frustrated because there is so much good in this country, and yet so many faults imprisoning it in what sometimes feels like the Dark Ages. It is only by being honest and addressing problems that they can be solved, but this goes so against the grain of what any Turk thinks. Denial is a tragic flaw in the Turkish make-up.

When one thinks of how young the Republic of Turkey is, and how it behaves in both a domestic and international sphere, it is impossible not to draw comparisons with an insecure young man. This man is full of promise but prickly because, deep down, he is unsure of himself and his standing in the world. He is doing well financially, and that give him confidence – he is on the up, like a young man with his first pay cheque, determined to spend it as he wishes and not to listen to criticism. The Gezi protests were the equivalent of shouting criticism directly into the ear of this young man. He ignores it now, but perhaps it will make some mark on him a little down the line.

I am proud to be considered a Turk in any way, to any degree, however belatedly. I am now much more hopeful than I have ever been about a change in Turkey which will turn politics into less of an individual popularity contest, encourage people not to place unquestioning trust in the government and not to take high-handed decisions lying down. If these lessons are learned, Turkey will be on the way to real greatness, not the self-satisfaction which has too often passed for that.

During the Brazilian protests that coincided with the Gezi movement in 2013, the Brazilian president, Dilma Rousseff, said that the period had been the 'awakening' of the Brazilian people. No one in power said that about the Turkish protests, but they should have done. Luckily, many Turks have worked it out for themselves.

13

The Aftermath of Gezi

I finished writing this book towards the end of the Gezi Park protests in July 2013. At that point, my mood, and the mood of most people around me, was relatively hopeful: we did not expect an immediate political transformation, but we hoped that in a year or so the after-effects of millions of protesters calling for change would invigorate opposition parties, inspire a fresh challenger to the ruling AKP, perhaps even persuade the government to relax its increasing authoritarianism. We were wrong.

In the eighteen months that have passed since Gezi, the government has not only survived but capitalised on the protests, using an opportunity for reform as an opportunity to solidify its already unhealthy grip on power by launching a full-scale programme of revenge and suppression of any dissent. Doctors who treated injured Gezi protesters and lawyers who represented them in court have themselves been arrested, accused of 'aiding terrorism'; peaceful protest is now practically impossible, and art related to the Gezi protests censored. Internet use is carefully – and legally – monitored by the government, social media sites shut down at the command of former Prime Minister (now President) Erdoğan, and cartoonists can face up to nine years in jail for 'insulting' him.

More sinister than this fairly ham-fisted crackdown has

been the success with which Erdoğan and his ministers have managed to persuade much of the population that the Gezi protests were not heartfelt expressions of dissatisfaction by ordinary Turkish citizens but 'dark plots' cooked up by foreign agents jealous of Turkey's power. These loathsome enemies are now conveniently cited whenever the country is criticised by Western media outlets or diplomats, adding to Erdoğan's common appeal as Turkey's valiant protector in the face of global hostility.

After three consecutive terms in office, Prime Minister Erdoğan has 'done a Putin' and continued to lead the country as President Erdoğan, having fought off what he called a 'postmodern coup attempt' by his former ally, Islamic cleric Fethullah Gülen. This came in the form of a huge corruption scandal in December 2013 that implicated key members of the government, including himself. It seemed at the time to be a more serious threat to the AKP's credibility than the Gezi protests, but has since been dismissed as the machinations of a 'parallel state' composed of Gülen's followers. Sizeable AKP victories were won in the municipal elections of March 2014, which in the wake of the corruption scandal turned into a popularity test for Erdoğan and were plagued by allegations of vote rigging. While Erdoğan's popularity remains genuinely high, calls for recounts in municipalities with suspicious AKP victories (including the capital, Ankara) were carefully ignored, and it is clear that there is a back-up plan in case of any popularity blips. Overall, the ruling party's PR machine is humming nicely and the *Ak Parti* (which translates as 'White Party') is officially whiter than ever.

All this has happened as ever-worsening conflict unfolds on Turkey's doorstep in Syria and northern Iraq; nearly two million refugees have poured over the border, diplomatic relations with Western countries have become strained and the Kurdish peace process has been put into jeopardy. What is Turkey becoming? Yes, there has been a political awakening, but for many people living in Turkey the transformation it has undergone has become a kind of waking nightmare. Gezi was a crucial step in the country's long-term development as a democracy, undoubtedly, but those who participated are resigning themselves to hoping for a more distant outcome to the 2013 protests, a future point when their demands are not only heard but heeded.

Here are some striking images that have come out of the madness of the last eighteen months, images that can serve as bookmarks for an increasingly dark and confusing period: a mass of protesters wielding shoe boxes outside the state bank; a hologram of Erdoğan appearing unexpectedly at an election rally; an incarcerated Twitter bird emblem; voting officials sleeping with ballot boxes cradled in their arms; protesters with coal-smeared faces and mining hats; 25,000 riot police stationed around an empty Taksim Square; ISIS flags fluttering from cars in Istanbul suburbs; burning statues of Mustafa Kemal Atatürk; and, finally, a brand-new $615 million presidential palace in Ankara, the ultimate emblem of 'New Turkey', that much-trumpeted AKP vision of Turkey's true destiny.

Let's start with the shoe-box-wielding protesters, who emerged in arctic conditions on 18 December 2013 in Istanbul, Ankara and Izmir. The previous day had been full of exceptionally high political drama: police had arrested fifty-two high-profile figures closely linked to the government – including the general manager of a state bank (Halkbank), the sons of three AKP ministers, an Istanbul district mayor and the eighth richest man in Turkey – on the grounds of large-scale corruption. Later, news channels reported that prosecutors had asked parliament to lift the immunity of four ministers so they could also be investigated. Over the next few days, interested news followers were treated to images of shoe boxes and safes stuffed full of cash ($4.5 million was apparently found in the house of the Halkbank manager), as well as shots of the frenzied reactions of ministers fearing similar treatment. An atmosphere of panic emanated from government quarters, and undisguised glee from the opposition and much of the public. On the 19th, protesters gathered in Ankara to denounce the 'filth' of this corruption scandal, festooning the pavements of the parliamentary district of Kızılay with loo paper.

What was behind the slew of arrests? Over the previous months, Erdoğan had become embroiled in an ever more public falling-out with the shadowy Gülen movement, a moderate Islamic network run by the cleric Fethullah Gülen that was widely reputed to control much of the police and judiciary in Turkey (see Chapter 8). Erdoğan and Gülen used to be allies; no longer. In November 2013, Erdoğan announced he would shut down all private *dershane* (study centres), many of which are run very profitably by Gülen. This was a characteristically rash move, and Gülen – if indeed it was him – seemed to have responded with impressive alacrity and force, mobilising his followers in the police and media to air the AKP's dirty laundry in front of the world.

On the morning of 18 December, the deputy prime minister, Bülent Arınç, promised that nothing would be done to impede the investigation; however, by the end of that same day, twenty-nine police officers obliquely involved in the investigation, including the chiefs of the organised- and financial-crime units, were unceremoniously sacked and immediately replaced, as were two of the prosecutors in charge. According to government sources, the sacked prosecutors and police chiefs had 'abused their power'.

Incidentally, on the same day, and for a second consecutive year, Turkey was named by the Committee to Protect Journalists as having the largest number of imprisoned journalists in the world; a few hours later, one prominent journalist had been fired from a pro-government newspaper for saying that Erdoğan should resign – irony dished out with a heavy hand and without a trace of humour.

The eye of the storm, Prime Minister Erdoğan, launched an impassioned counter-attack on the afternoon of the 18th: he claimed that the arrests were part of a 'very dirty operation' cooked up by 'those who are jealous of Turkey's power', and were most likely related to the Gezi crooks who sought to bring down the might of Turkey with malicious rumours and double-dealing. The pro-government paper *Yeni Şafak* was even more alarmist, hinting darkly at Mossad plots and international conspiracies. Not since Gezi had Turks been so glued to their news screens, feverishly waiting on every tweet, every 'Flash!' update. In the days following the initial arrests, the sordid rumours continued: for example, that one minister received a 105-million-lira bribe from Reza Zarrab, an Iranian–Azeri gold-smuggling tycoon dogged by financial felony charges; and that the mayor of Fatih was allegedly bribed to allow dangerous and totally illegal construction at the mouth of the Marmaray tunnel, the new underwater link between Istanbul's European and Asian sides. Unofficial sources claimed scandalous evidence for a whole host of corruption charges: taped phone conversations between ministers and family members, photos of untoward meetings and never-ending hordes of cash hidden in shoe boxes and safes.

The government remained impressively scornful of charges both official and unofficial. The EU minister at the time, Egemen Bağış, said that he was 'relaxed' about the allegations (he was purged from the government a week later, on 25 December). The speaker of parliament flatly denied receiving any request to lift the immunity of four top cabinet ministers supposedly linked to the corruption case. With magnificent unconcern for public opinion, the government continued to sack key figures pursuing the investigation. In addition to the thirty-two police officers sacked and replaced since the arrests began, the Istanbul police chief himself was packed off on the 19th. Meanwhile, the three cabinet ministers' sons arrested on the 17th were reportedly moved from uncomfortable prison cells to the new police chief's personal quarters. The then Deputy Prime Minister Bekir Bozdağ delivered a heart-warming defence of the AKP as a 'big family' (which said it all) and declared he would write an official complaint about the 'violation of confidentiality' involved in the investigation – presumably the photos leaked to the press. Finally, the High Commission of Radio and Television issued a terse warning to journalists not to publish mere allegations.

Anger and hilarity characterised the public's reaction to these developments: in Izmir, for example, members of the Confederation of Public Sector Trade Unions placed shoe boxes in front of a central branch of Halkbank, the state bank supposedly involved in illegal transactions with Iran via its general manager, who may or may not have hidden millions of Turkish lira in shoe boxes in his house. When Erdoğan gave a speech in Manisa on 29 December, a local woman was arrested for waving an empty shoe box from her balcony in protest. Throughout the investigation (short-lived though it was) the opposition media had a field day, publishing photos of ministers on their mobile phones decorated with bribe-related speech bubbles and making puns on the names of the key figures involved.

But behind the jokes and wordplay, everyone was wondering how important these revelations would prove to be. Gezi seemed like a huge turning point at the time, but in reality most people who protested had lost hope by December, and the episode was quickly dismissed as a decadent middle-class strop by the state-supporting media. Would the same be true now? A corruption scandal on this scale could present a far greater threat to the government than Gezi.

As we were to see, the combination of mass purges of suspected Gülenists from the police and judiciary, the AKP's propaganda backlash, its blocking of online leaks related to the corruption claims and, finally, the constitutional changes made to control the judiciary succeeded in quashing what would have been a fatal blow to any Western government. To be fair to the AKP, they had a point – the taped phone recordings showed that the prime minister's offices had been bugged for years, and the infiltration of an opaque organisation into the police and judiciary was not an ideal situation. However, the way the AKP went about 'fixing' this problem succeeded only in extending the government's control over every possible bastion of law and order. The Gülenist 'postmodern coup', if that was what it was, backfired spectacularly.

On 25 December, a week after the first arrests were made, Muammer Akkaş, the main prosecutor in the corruption investigation, was removed from his post. The next day, he released a statement that should have been a cataclysmic embarrassment for the government, containing details of how suspects had been given time to destroy evidence and new search warrants ignored. Instead, the statement was quietly brushed aside. I quote briefly from it here:

> Today, I learned that the investigation dossier, which includes search, seizure and detention decisions, was taken from my authority without any justification being offered. From now on, the responsibility lies with the İstanbul chief public prosecutor and deputy chief public prosecutor. All my colleagues and the public should know that a public prosecutor prevented me from conducting the investigation.

A day after this statement, as more and more reports of stifled evidence and strategic police 'referrals' trickled down to the media, Gezi-like protests erupted in Ankara and Istanbul. Again, the familiar tanks, water cannon and rubber bullets were used, and again, the government described the protesters as spies and terrorists. Erdoğan cleverly created continuity by linking Gezi and the current protests, saying: 'Those who tried to bring us down with the Gezi protests did not succeed; they won't succeed this time, either.' His target voters lapped this up, rather chuffed at the thought that Turkey is great enough to engender such dramatic displays of jealousy, and emboldened by the prime minister's promise that the plotters wouldn't succeed. Erdoğan had played the part of a brave, beleaguered leader who weathered the storm six months earlier, and he would weather it yet again – the ultimate comic-book hero. Unfortunately, conspiracy theories are so common in Turkey that many ordinary people cannot see the wood for the trees – whom to believe, those who talk of obscene levels of corruption, hoarded gold and dodgy tenders, or those who talk of foreign spies, plots and 'dirty operations'?

Erdoğan made some bold claims during his vengeful backlash against the corruption allegations, so libellous and outrageous by European standards that the very fact that he got away with them speaks volumes about his level of support. Speaking in the province of Sakarya on 27 December, he said that 'the CHP & MHP [the main and junior opposition parties] are contractors for foreign powers'. Turning his attention to the Supreme Council of Judges and Prosecutors, who overturned a government decree intended to block the investigation the previous week, he said: 'Who will judge the [Supreme Council]? Do you know who will do it? The people. I would like to judge them, if I had adequate authority.' He also said that Turkey was entering its own civil war, and complained that the separation of powers in the country was holding the government back from achieving what it wanted to achieve: 'Bureaucracy blocks our path, or we face the judiciary unexpectedly.'

So, what was the outcome of all this, as a fraught December rolled into the new year? With the quashing of the investigation and a blanket media ban on anything connected to the allegations, the instigators of the corruption claims – most probably supporters of Fethullah Gülen, though he strenuously denied any involvement whatsoever – took to more underhand methods. Material purporting to relate to official corruption started appearing on YouTube and circulating on social media. Most of the supposed evidence – which took the form of taped telephone conversations (allegedly) featuring AKP ministers, their sons and the mysterious tycoon Reza Zarrab – came from a handful of accounts that were periodically blocked by Twitter in Turkey, but soon resurfaced.

As these leaks coincided with the run-up to municipal elections in March, drastic measures were taken by the AKP, and the election campaign was taken in hand by Erdoğan himself, who construed the elections as a personal vote of confidence, and who appeared daily at rallies. His most dramatic appearance was in the form of a ten-foot hologram at an election rally in Izmir at the end of January, and his message was a call to arms: 'We are going to elections in the shadow of attacks prepared by treasonous networks. I urge all my mayoral candidates not to lose a moment.'

As election day drew nearer, the taped telephone conversations became more prolific, and more serious – one of them seemed to be a recording of Erdoğan telling his son to 'zero' vast amounts of cash in his house. In another, he shouts at the editor of *Milliyet* (a major national newspaper) and reduces him to tears, complaining about his coverage of an opposition leader's speech. Most of these tapes Erdoğan dismissed as 'dubbed montages', and he produced sound technicians to discredit their authenticity (other technicians delivered resounding certificates of authenticity). However, he obliquely admitted to the *Milliyet* conversation, claiming that 'advising the media is the job of the prime minister'.

While the Gezi protests had shown that the government, and Erdoğan in particular, enjoyed fairly unquestioning support from millions of Turks, I could not quite believe that these leaks were not causing it more damage. I didn't appreciate the strength of these pro-Erdoğan feelings. For some time after the phone tapes started circulating on the internet, I thought: 'People must not have heard them. The tapes are not on the news – it must be that. Otherwise there would be a nationwide outcry.' So I went with laptop in hand to my local tailor, a devout and intelligent man in his fifties called Yahya, who is a staunch supporter of the AKP. I knew he had not heard the tapes. Our conversation went as follows:

– I've got the tapes here – do you want to listen to them?
– I'm not really interested.
– But you could decide for yourself whether they sound fake or not.
– I know they're fake.
– Really? How?
– That man in America makes them all up!
– Do you mean Fethullah Gülen?

– Yes, but I won't say his name any more. Not after what he has done.

– OK, but just listen to the tapes and see for yourself.

– Why? Even if I heard these conversations with my own ears, I wouldn't believe them. *Even if I saw him stealing with my own eyes, I wouldn't believe it.*

This last sentence floored me. How do you argue with a man who trusts his prime minister more than he trusts the evidence of his own eyes and ears? If news channels were permitted to play these tapes (which they're not), if nothing but these tapes played from morning till night on every news channel in the land, Yahya the tailor would remain unmoved.

His assistant, Mehmet Ali, shed further light on the matter when he entertained the hypothesis that the corruption claims *might* be true. 'Even if they are true, he will be called to account in the afterlife. It is not for us to judge him, but Allah.'

This kind of view reflects the status of Erdoğan as a demigod in Turkey, a man who remains above mortal laws, a man whose overt religiosity convinces his followers that he has God on his side. For me, this was a profoundly depressing realisation, and it has made me reassess the future of the country and wonder how long it will be until road-building and personal charisma are not lifelong tickets to power. For the moment, however, they are. While accusations of corruption and authoritarianism may have tainted Erdoğan's image abroad, and reinforced the opinions of those Turks who dislike him, for many in Turkey he remains above reproach.

Nonetheless, the online leaks were not allowed to circulate freely for long. On 5 February, a controversial law regulating internet use was signed into law by the then president, Abdullah Gül, allowing any site to be closed down by the authorities without needing the permission of a judge, and – worse – forcing internet providers to store users' details and browsing history for two years, and to make these details available to the government on request. Censorship and surveillance were, henceforth, legal and merely waiting to be put into effect.

On 21 March, nine days before the municipal elections, Turkish Twitter users woke to find access to the site blocked by the Telecommunications Board. Or was it? Three hours after access was blocked, in the small hours of the 21st, Melih Gökçek, the mayor of Ankara, tweeted a smiley face. Five hours later, Bülent Arınç, the deputy prime minister, was tweeting about his upcoming rally. And, most surprisingly of all, Abdullah Gül broke a month-long Twitter absence to denounce the ban. Far from being silenced, tweets from Turkish accounts rose significantly over the weekend, making a mockery of attempts to block the site's users.

Officially, the ban was a response to Twitter's refusal to comply with Turkish court orders requesting the removal of 'unspecified illegal material' (undoubtedly the taped conversations). 'We will root out Twitter,' Erdoğan declared at a rally in Bursa, hours before the site was blocked. 'I don't care what the international community says. Everyone will witness the power of Turkey.'

Instead, everyone witnessed the impressive technological prowess of millions of Turkish Twitter users who managed to avoid the block. They also witnessed the fact that Erdoğan was willing to risk international condemnation by placing Turkey in the same camp as North Korea, China and Iran insofar as internet freedom is concerned. As soon as the block hit home, social media exploded as Turks swiftly changed their internet-provider settings to sidestep the ban.

The authorities retaliated by blocking the most popular IP addresses, only for their Twitter-using adversaries to find new alternatives. Watching this was like watching a grandfather taking on his grandson at a computer game – an inevitably pathetic battle of unequal expertise and agility. It was not so much a question of age but of energy and outlook: Turkish Twitter users are typically news-hungry individuals seeking to find out more about their environment, who are comfortable in a forum of opinion and discourse. They innovate and adapt as a matter of course. The AKP, on the other hand, hardly used social media before the Gezi protests last June. Then, at last, they realised the importance of Facebook and Twitter in reaching out to a population of 75 million, and are now far ahead of any other political party in terms of online reach (another example of the dinosaur-like quality of opposition parties such as the CHP).

The Twitter block came and went (it was revoked on 3 April after the Supreme Court ruled that it breached laws protecting freedom of expression, a cheering reminder that some checks and balances are still in working order), but on 27 March, three days before the elections, YouTube was banned. This was an attempt to stop the circulation of a newly leaked tape which appeared to show the then foreign minister, Ahmet Davutoğlu (now the prime minister), discussing the possibility of provoking war in Syria with the head of the intelligence services and a high-ranking general; the authenticity of the tape has never been officially denied, but its circulation was denounced as 'traitorous'. There was a reaction similar to the Twitter block from the YouTube-loving, social-media-using community, and the ban was officially revoked a couple of days later, but access wasn't restored until June.

The municipal elections themselves were fraught with speculation – many people really believed the bad PR generated by the corruption arrests and the tapes could result in opposition victories, particularly in Ankara, where the Twitter-mad AKP mayor, Melih Gökçek, who had held his seat for twenty years, was in the habit of fighting off criticism by suing his tweeting detractors en masse (in September 2014, he said he had sued 'around three thousand people'). A few hours after the ballot boxes closed on 30 March, Gökçek claimed yet another victory, with ninety-five per cent of the votes counted. The news then emerged that hundreds of thousands of CHP votes had not been counted or had been transferred to other parties – it seemed that the numbers entered into the electoral computer system did not tally with the physical ballot papers.

Soon afterwards, bags filled with ballots were found binned in the vicinity of the polling centres (mainly schools), and after photographs had circulated on social media over a thousand volunteers went to track them down and guard the remaining ballots until morning. Cheering images of people wrapped in blankets, asleep, with their arms around sacks of ballots, circulated illicitly on Twitter. Further confusion was caused by a widespread blackout in municipalities across the country in the early hours of the morning – the energy minister responded to outrage and claims that further electoral foul play had been conducted under cover of darkness by saying a cat had got into a power substation and tampered with the electricity flow.

Two days after this fiasco, the CHP lodged a complaint with the Supreme Electoral Council (YSK) and hundreds of people started protesting outside the council's headquarters in Ankara, despite heavy police intervention. Gökçek, the self-proclaimed victor, vacillated between accusing the CHP and Gülenists of planning provocations and claiming that, if there had been a 'mistake' with the vote-counting, the blame lay not with him but with the YSK. The YSK repeatedly refused the CHP's requests to recount the votes in Ankara, despite granting new votes to municipalities where CHP wins were being challenged by AKP candidates. In Ağrı, eastern Turkey, the pro-Kurdish Peace and Democracy Party (BDP) and AKP indulged in a game of retaliatory recount requests, fourteen in total; the BDP finally won a repeat election in June.

Even after these controversies, the AKP's victories in polls across the nation suggested that Erdoğan's conservative Anatolian base was still firmly behind him after the hurricane of potentially damaging PR caused by the corruption claims. Conversely, the opposition parties – the CHP and MHP – had failed to take advantage of a golden opportunity, as they had after Gezi. There was, however, a glimmer of good news to emerge from the elections: significant wins in the south-east for the BDP, a party which shares each of its mayoral posts between a male and a female candidate and believes in decentralisation of power. Whatever the pros or cons of this party, it was nice to see someone presenting a genuine alternative to the AKP.

May Day, traditionally a day for labour union marches in Taksim Square, was effectively cancelled in 2014, the square closed off and 39,000 riot police stationed around it to guard against any Gezi-like incidents occurring; despite this, around forty people were hospitalised and two hundred detained. The legacy of Gezi was palpable, and resurfaced again two weeks later, under tragic circumstances.

On 13 May 2014, an explosion in a coal mine in Soma, near Izmir on the Aegean coast, killed 301 people in total, devastating the local community and resulting in a period of mourning for weeks afterwards across the country. What looked at first like a tragic accident began to reveal more sinister roots in negligence, some of which seemed to be traceable to the government's privatisation deal with the company responsible for running the mine. The government's attempts to deal with the fingers of blame were appallingly insensitive, and Erdoğan managed to botch his commiseration visit the day after the blast spectacularly. A crowd of angry mourners mobbed his convoy as it drove slowly through the streets, and boos and jeers threatened to drown him out as he addressed the families of those who died in the blast. When he attempted – briefly – to walk among the crowds, their hostile reaction forced his anxious bodyguards to hustle him into a nearby supermarket, where he became embroiled in a scuffle. This was a far cry from the welcoming flowers, smiles and cheers that the prime minister was used to receiving on official visits.

Erdoğan badly misjudged the Soma disaster by delivering a speech bristling with self-defence. Telling the relatives of dead and dying miners that 'these types of incidents are ordinary things' was his way of deflecting any kind of responsibility for the blast, after reports circulated that the government had ignored safety concerns about the privately owned Soma mine, which had been raised just two weeks before the blast by opposition MPs. To ram home his point, Erdoğan delivered a lesson in mining disasters throughout European history, recounting a long list, including a British disaster in 1862. The anger in Soma was echoed in cities across Turkey as thousands of people with coal-smeared faces took to the streets, carrying placards that read: 'Soma was not an accident, it was a massacre.' They called for the resignation of the energy minister, Taner Yıldız, and of Erdoğan himself.

There was anger at the generally blasé attitude to worker safety that prevails nationwide, and a strong sense that this blast in particular could have been prevented. Twitter yet again proved itself to be Erdoğan's bête noire by facilitating the spread of several damning photographs relating to the government's response to Soma, pre- and post-blast. One of these showed an opposition minister speaking in parliament on 29 April, brandishing a miner's hard hat and warning of poor conditions in the mine, as two AKP ministers chat among themselves in the background. Another photograph, taken during Erdoğan's visit, showed his adviser, Yusuf Yerkel, enthusiastically kicking a protester in Soma as he lay on the ground, already overpowered by a couple of gendarmes. The protests that raged across the country had a raw anger that was missing from those arising out of the corruption scandal. People were sickened by the scale of the disaster but also by signs of serious negligence. 'Prime Minister, resign!' shouted the crowds. 'Soma was a massacre, not an accident!' The day after the blast, during a protest in Istanbul I saw a young woman with a coal-smeared face quietly holding a placard that read: 'So it seems coal isn't free.' Here was a cynical message that got to the heart of the protesters' anger.

Erdoğan's government has made itself extremely popular over its twelve years in power by declaring itself the champion of the masses and giving out subsidies to poor families all over the country. These subsidies include bread, macaroni and coal, and they are often bestowed in the run-up to elections. So far, so socialist, at least superficially. At the same time, however, the AKP has thrown itself into accelerating the programme of privatisation in Turkey that began in 1984. While government spokesmen boast of the billions of lira generated by these sales, the AKP's critics accuse it of selling assets cheaply and strategically to sole bidders, and failing to check up on workers' safety standards post-sale. A statement from the four main Turkish unions shortly after the blast accused the government of complicit guilt, for 'even privatising the safety supervision in the workplace'.

The Soma mine was privatised in 2005, and Soma Holding now pays royalties to the government in the form of fifteen per cent of its coal production. Technically the mine still belongs to the state, which guarantees that it will buy all coal produced at the site, giving every incentive to the mining company to ramp up production while cutting costs (in January 2014, the Turkish Court of Accounts announced that Soma Holding had sold more than 750,000 tons of 'stone' or unusable coal to the state). In an interview in 2012, the owner of Soma Holding, Alp Gürkan, boasted that he had reduced the cost of extracting coal from £77 per tonne to £14 via extreme cost-cutting measures. Miners who worked at the site also said that the company employed cheap technical specialists who were not union members, and failed to replace old, outdated equipment, which became particularly dangerous given the furious rate of production. When asked why the mine did not have a refuge chamber, Gürkan replied that it was not required by law.

All this adds up to the powerful impression that the government does not legislate on safety measures and the mine owners do not bother to meet them because this is mutually beneficial. Only two weeks before the blast, on 29 April, the AKP majority rejected the opposition's parliamentary proposal to look into safety standards at this particular mine, saying that it was perfectly satisfactory and that 'God willing, nothing will happen – not even a nose bleed.' The energy minister, Taner Yıldız, had visited the Soma mine nine months earlier and had branded it 'an example to all mines in Turkey'. Despite Erdoğan's claims that the Soma disaster was on a par with almost any other mining accident in the world since 1862, the rate of mining deaths in Turkey is shocking – seven lives per million tonnes of coal, compared to China's four. In terms of general workplace safety, Turkey is the third worst in the world.

Only five months after Soma, on 27 October, eighteen miners were trapped in a coal mine in Ermenek in southern

Turkey that had been flooded, again due to negligence by the mine owners. (There were reports that the miners' families had written 124 unheeded letters of complaint before the 'accident'.) This time, the government acted promptly by arresting the owners and technicians working at the mine; lessons had been learned, but not the important ones.

On Saturday 31 May 2014, people gathered in the streets near Gezi Park, Istanbul, as they had done exactly one year before. This time their mood was very different, however – bitter and fatalistic, with little of the exhilarated energy that characterised the protests twelve months earlier. This year, Gezi Park was cordoned off hours in advance. Civil policemen holding batons patrolled street corners, sinister backup for the thousands of riot police and their water cannon trucks stationed around Taksim Square. Only the most determined and politicised of protesters headed out to the unequal battle with their gas masks and hard hats, leaving mainstream Gezi veterans to watch events unfold on their TV or via Twitter at home. The government had learned from its mistakes.

In the midst of the post-Gezi crackdown in 2013, the AKP presented a new law to target what sounded suspiciously like thought crime. On 6 October 2013, four months after the protests started, a law was proposed which aimed to give police the power to lock up anyone who they suspect *might* be about to partake in a public protest. These would-be protesters would be detained for up to twenty-four hours, without the need for permission from a court or judge, to ensure that nothing on the scale of Gezi could ever happen again. It was a rather creative stroke of legislation. Under the proposed law, any potential protester would be effectively guilty until proven innocent – of what? Free assembly is still a right in Turkey, at least on paper, if not in practice. Although the law has yet to be put through parliament (it is probably on hold until serious protest starts to brew again), sadly – absurdly – it might well pass with an AKP majority.

The obvious but crucial point to be made about 2014's 'Geziversary' protests is that they happened at all: people were – and are – still angry. There is still plenty to protest about in Turkey, arguably much more than pre-May 2013. Yes, Gezi Park has been saved, but the Gezi protest movement has moved far beyond that now, and 'Gezi' has become short-hand for 'fighting back'. The reason so many people rushed to support the original group of protesting environmentalists back in May 2013 was the violence of the police suppression, and that is still part of what people are protesting about, in a horribly predictable vicious circle. Images of people beaten, gassed and detained in cities across Turkey circulate with sickening regularity on social media, and they are certainly not confined to those protesting about the status of a small but iconic urban park. The images are shocking, but the shock is – sadly – dulled now by the knowledge that this has become the norm, and will probably stay that way for some time. It is difficult to imagine anything on the scale of the public's two-week occupation of Gezi Park happening again under this government's watch, which looks increasingly secure.

The events of May 2013 caught the government off guard. Since then, there has been plenty of practice for the police force described by the then prime minister, Erdoğan, as 'hero-ic' to become adept at stopping any significant protest from gathering momentum. That knowledge is at the core of many people's anger towards the government, and at the same time the reason that they cannot fully express it. During the original Gezi movement, people were so determined to protest peacefully, so united, it was impossible not to be moved. One year later, the event that stuck in my mind was someone throwing a glass bottle at police from an unseen window on high. The bottle smashed and police quickly pointed their guns at the crowd, who backed off. Here was explosive anger and cowed fear, a horrible indication of how peaceful protest is becoming increasingly desperate.

Over the last eighteen months, one of the most worrying developments has been the polarising language used by government and pro-government media to describe journalists. The most widely circulated clip of the Geziversary protests was of CNN journalist Ivan Watson being forcibly detained mid-broadcast by a policeman who refused to accept his press card as proof of his journalistic credentials. The ridiculous spoof-like quality of the clip caused much merriment, especially when pro-government paper *Takvim* claimed that Watson was responsible for provoking the protests, calling him '*Gezi zekalı*' (a pun on '*geri zekalı*', meaning 'retarded'). Even Erdoğan singled him out as a 'creep' and an 'agent' who was caught 'red-handed' causing trouble.

(Watson entered into the spirit of events by changing his description on Twitter to '*siyenenci*' – or *CNN-ci*, purveyor of CNN-ism – and this moniker had later relevance during the Hong Kong protests of September 2014. Watson had moved from Istanbul to Hong Kong a couple of months before, so was on hand to cover the so-called 'Umbrella Revolution'. This was far too suspicious to go unremarked by *Takvim*,

which declared with evident satisfaction that '*Gezi zekalı
Ivan*' was starting protests again, apparently addicted to a life
of political hooliganism.)

By the summer of 2014, Foreign Minister Ahmet
Davutoğlu's tired policy of 'zero problems with neighbours'
was visibly struggling with the escalation of the Syrian war
on the border, the rise of the self-proclaimed Islamic State of
Iraq and al-Sham (ISIS) and, more specifically, the capture of
forty-nine staff from the Turkish consulate in Mosul, Iraq, by
ISIS militants in June. Since 2011, the Syrian civil war has
infiltrated Turkey in terms of the masses of refugees pouring through its borders (around 1.5 million by the end of
2014) and rebel fighters using Turkish border towns as bases.
The government's oft-stated priority in Syria has been the removal of Bashar al-Assad, a priority that has received little
support from Western powers more concerned by the threat
posed by ISIS. Unofficially, it has been claimed by NGO
workers, journalists and off-the-record diplomats that the
Turkish authorities have long given considerable and indis-
criminate help to the rebels (including members of ISIS)
fighting the Assad regime, allowing passage to fighters, arms
and aid across the border, and even treating injured rebel
fighters for free in hospitals on the Turkish–Syrian border.

This policy of aiding rebel forces backfired when ISIS
came onto the radar in June, seizing the consular staff in Mosul and capturing American and British journalists and aid
workers for gruesomely publicised beheadings. The international spotlight turned onto the passage of Western jihadists
through Turkey into Syria to join the ISIS cause, and Turkey
was roundly criticised for giving them free rein. (The Turkish

authorities were also accused of doing little to stop the widespread recruitment by ISIS of wayward young men on its home turf, something that was particularly prevalent in poor suburbs of Istanbul and Ankara with drug problems and low employment, areas where ISIS flags can occasionally be seen fluttering from cars.) Turkey responded that the Western powers should do more to stop jihadists at their own borders by introducing exit passport control (as already exists in Turkey). When, on 20 September, the Turkish consular staff were released by ISIS in a rumoured prisoner exchange, diplomatic relations with the West became even more strained after it emerged that some of the ISIS prisoners released by Turkey were European-passport holders wanted in their home countries on terrorism charges.

Turkey's problems escalated in the aftermath of Eid al-Adha in September 2014, when the small Kurdish town of Kobane on Syria's border with Turkey came under attack by the forces of ISIS. The town was defended – just about – by militia from the Kurdish Democratic Union Party (PYD), but within days several black flags fluttered grimly from the rooftops, proclaiming ISIS's partial victory. Watchers of Western media were appalled by images of Turkish tanks lined up a couple of kilometres away, overseeing the streams of refugees pouring over the border – old women and men, young families, terrified, clutching blankets and bulging plastic bags. Herded by Turkish soldiers, they stood on Turkish soil and watched as plumes of smoke rose from the devastated town they had just left.

Meanwhile, in Istanbul, and in towns all over Turkey, there was immense anger among the 15 million-strong Kurdish

community at Turkey's apparent callousness, at the reluct-
ance of President Erdoğan's government to allow Kurdish
fighters at the border to relieve the siege (contrary to common Western belief, the PYD had never asked for nor expected direct Turkish intervention). Young men took to the
streets, burning cars and government buildings, convinced
that Turkey was deliberately allowing Kurds to die on its
doorstep. Some even ripped down statues and burned busts
of Turkey's founder, Mustafa Kemal Atatürk, horrifying patriotic Turks who regard his figure as sacred and remember
all too well the attacks in the 1990s by the PKK and the
deaths of Turkish soldiers. In the first week of protests, more
than thirty people died, and in six predominantly Kurdish
provinces in the south-east of the country martial law was en-
forced with curfews and tank patrols, a horrible re-enactment
of scenes from the Kurdish–Turkish conflict's bloody past.

While everyone concedes that Turkey has displayed impressive generosity to victims of the Syrian civil war thus far,
this no longer seems enough. In the first week of fighting in
Kobane, Turkey took around 150,000 refugees, far outstrip-
ping the total number of Syrian refugees accepted by EU
countries in the last three years of the conflict. Overall, Turkey
is hosting around 1.5 million Syrian refugees, and the financial
strain has become unbearable – so much so that the Turkish
government has started awarding work permits to Syrians
(hitherto called 'guests' and not allowed to work), despite opposition from those who are already worried about high un-
employment in some areas of Turkey. There does not seem to
be a limit to Turkey's willingness to take on Syrian refugees,
something that has not gone unremarked by Western states.

However, Kobane was different: it touched a nerve of nationalist distrust between Turks and Kurds which, until recently, had lain relatively dormant, lulled by the last two years of peace talks between the AKP and Abdullah Öcalan, the jailed leader of the PKK. Much of the goodwill caused by those talks seemed to evaporate in the immediate wake of the Kobane protests; nonetheless, at the time of writing the peace process is still officially ongoing, with the backing of Öcalan himself. What the protests showed was that the Kurds felt extremely strongly that they had been callously and deliberately abandoned by the Turks, when they could have been helped by the opening of a humanitarian corridor. On 31 October, the Turkish border authorities did start letting through Peshmerga fighters (the armed forces of Iraqi Kurdistan), a decision due less to international pressure than to a good relationship between the Turkish government and Kurdish prime minister Nechirvan Barzani, and perhaps a realisation that not letting fighters through was causing more problems than the alternative. Still, many Turks are extremely unhappy that armed Kurds are passing through Turkish soil, just as many Kurds will never forgive the Turkish army for standing by when Kobane was first attacked. To them, the geopolitical and historical arguments explaining Turkey's stance make no difference, and they never will.

Meanwhile, amid war, kidnappings and diplomatic tensions with the West, Erdoğan managed to win the presidential election on 10 August 2014 with 51.8 per cent of the vote, beating a joint CHP and MHP candidate, former diplomat and religious scholar Ekmeleddin İhsanoğlu (whose candidacy was announced by a flustered opposition coalition less than two months earlier), and the young, compelling candidate of the HDP (the People's Democratic Party, a branch of the Kurdish-rights-promoting BDP), Selahattin Demirtaş. While there had been some hope, after the corruption scandal and Soma disaster, that Erdoğan's brand was sufficiently tarnished to allow an opportunity for someone – anyone – to unite more than 50 per cent of the population in opposition, as the elections drew nearer and enormous posters with Erdoğan's face emblazoned upon them spread like a mighty rash over buildings across the country, while TV stations showed almost uninterrupted footage of him, that hope died. When it came to the crunch, İhsanoğlu was not charismatic enough to steal any of Erdoğan's limelight, and Demirtaş could never realistically have won. Erdoğan's campaign focused on a 'New Turkey' – a grand vision of an AKP-led future, the logic of its twelve-year-old 'newness' lost amid the huge capitalised slogans and pomp of the electoral campaign.

Just three months after his victory, Erdoğan posed solemnly for photographs in a newly built, illegal presidential palace in Ankara. At four times the size of Versailles and thirty times the size of the White House, the $615 million building (which Erdoğan has named the Ak Saray or 'White Palace') is a monument to controversy-immune ambition and self-regard. It was conveniently completed in time for Erdoğan's appointment as president (as was the new $195 million presidential jet, which arrived the day after he took office), and was built entirely with taxpayers' money. The palace is equipped with the latest cyber-defence systems, no doubt reinforced with extra care after the corruption scandal. Erdoğan ignored several court cases forbidding construction of the palace on protected land, saying: 'Let them demolish it if they have enough power to do so. They ordered a stay of execution but they won't be able to stop it. I will open it and I will use it.'

And so he has.

Gargantuan palace. Disregard for law. Increasing indifference to foreign opinion, and – more serious – hostility towards those who don't support him on home ground. Many Turks are understandably worried by Erdoğan's box-ticking of classic dictator-like traits, but many others are not even aware of the boxes that are being ticked. They are excited by the much-heralded 'New Turkey' Erdoğan keeps talking about, and comforted by a strong leader in troubled times.

Is this a brave new era or a continuation of the old? Erdoğan has embarked on a presidency which, if all goes to plan, will grant him as much power as he has enjoyed over the last eleven years as prime minister. He will continue to control the ruling AKP in all but name, having personally chosen his successor, Ahmet Davutoğlu, Turkey's former foreign minister, like a sultan choosing a suitably loyal vizier. On 27 August 2014, MPs from the AKP 'voted' for Davutoğlu, the only candidate for the role of head of the party, while Abdullah Gül, Turkey's overshadowed president for the past seven years, was shuffled off stage like a redundant great-uncle. Two days later, a new cabinet was announced – no big surprises, bar a last-minute announcement that Yiğit Bulut, a controversial ex-journalist who believes assassins are trying to murder Erdoğan via telekinesis, was to be the new president's chief economic adviser (a step up from his 2013 post of 'senior adviser').

After this game of political musical chairs, we were left with the status quo: Erdoğan, stern of face and booming of voice, taking key decisions and shaping party policy, while Davutoğlu, the smiling stooge, continues to sidestep delicate matters such as the threat of ISIS on Turkey's borders. Party members toe the line, as before, grand construction projects continue, as before, opposition parties grumble uselessly, as before. Yet this is 'New Turkey', apparently. We are on the brink of something big, at least in the imagination of the AKP: a prosperous future for a proudly Islamic Turkey that leads its neighbours and refuses to bow to the West. To achieve this, Erdoğan will apparently have to remain firmly at the helm.

The aim of the AKP in the 2015 general election is to get a large enough majority to pass a constitutional change that will grant full executive powers to the president. Erdoğan will be in power for at least the next five years, and very likely more. So keen is he on uninterrupted power that when he won the presidential election on 10 August, the results were not published in the official gazette, which would have necessitated his stepping down as prime minister before his inauguration as president on the 28th. This also, incidentally, meant he retained his immunity from prosecution for the intervening seventeen days.

Erdoğan is the face and guts of 'New Turkey', a Turkey which is actively stepping away from the broadly secular republic shaped by Mustafa Kemal Atatürk from the debris of the Ottoman Empire in 1923. Two days before becoming Turkey's new prime minister, Davutoğlu laid out his plan to repair the 'damage' of the last ninety years – in other words, Atatürk's republic. While insisting that this did not mean a return to an Islamic Ottoman state, Davutoğlu's statement echoed many made by Erdoğan, who has made a point of celebrating Ottoman history and culture, recently presiding over the reintroduction of Ottoman Turkish (taught in Arabic script) to the high school curriculum, eighty-five years after Atatürk purged Arabic words from the Turkish language, Latinised the script and made its teaching compulsory in schools across the country.

Erdoğan aslo has a great penchant for Ottoman sultans, calling his new mosque in Çamlıca, Istanbul, a *'selatin'* or 'sultan's' mosque and pointing ahead to important upcoming Ottoman anniversaries in Turkey's historical calendar. Some of these are less obvious than others, and commemorate not just the Ottomans but even earlier ancestors – Muslim warriors from the steppes.

In December 2012, Erdoğan urged Turkish youth to look forward to 2071, the thousand-year anniversary of the Battle of Manzikert, when the Byzantines were defeated by the Seljuk Turks. This is, according to the new president, when 'Turkey will reach the level of our Ottoman and Seljuk ancestors' – *Inşallah*, he is not envisaging a return to old-fashioned cavalry charges near the borders of modern Armenia. Erdoğan will not be alive then, but he understands very well that a lofty vision of the future is vital for keeping up momentum and cementing support for the continuation of the AKP and, of course, for himself.

The closer and more obvious anniversary will be October 2023, the centenary of the founding of the Republic of Turkey – now only eight years away, and an event of huge importance for most Turks. Erdoğan has given every indication that he will be firmly in charge at this point, marking the celebration of the 'New Turkey' being sold to the public by the

AKP's hard-working marketing team. Meanwhile, the debris of protests and 'coup attempts' has been swept quietly away, the four ex-ministers accused of corruption in the 17 December probe have been officially exonerated and Gezi protesters remain behind bars.

Grand plans, limitless ambition and ever-increasing self-confidence. Turkish cynics see neither New Turkey nor Old Turkey: they see, for the foreseeable future, Erdoğan's Turkey. It need not be so. Turkey is a fast-moving, unpredictable place and its future belongs to the young generations who will shape it beyond the Ottoman-centric AKP or the Kemalist old-guard opposition. It will take time, but it will happen – this Gezi child has hope.

Acknowledgements

I would like to thank all the Turks who have unwittingly helped me write this book, and whom I haven't always been able to name. I thank Alex Reddaway, Tim Hoare, Bulut Girgin and Andrew Boord for their invaluable advice, and my parents and sisters for their support. I am also very grateful to the following people: Sir David Reddaway, Aziz Akgül, Roger Scruton, my agent Georgina Capel and editor Walter Donohue. To all my friends and most of all to Alex.

Index

Index

Index

Index

Index

Erdogan's attempt to limit power of 288

military coups 287, 288
  (1980) 290

millionaires 143

minorities 242–73
  Armenians 247–52
  ethnic assimilation 246–7, 248
  improvement in rights of 272
  instances of peaceful integration 261–4
  Laz people 263–7
  marginalisation of 246
  see also Kurds

MIPCOM 140–1

Montreux Convention 194

monuments, faux-grandiose 195–6

Morsi, President 288–9

mosques, funding of 271

moustache shape 245

moustache transplant surgery 151

Muhteşem Yüzyıl (Magnificent Century) 122, 135, 136

Müren, Zeki 110–11

music 183

Muslim Association 29

national identity 261

national university placement exam 177–8

nationalism 186, 243–4, 248

Nationalist Action Party *see* MHP

natural disasters: attitude to 213–14

nazar (evil eye charm) 12

NBC Universal 141

Ne mutlu Türküm diyene phrase 256

Nicholas I, Tsar 223

Nishizawa, Ryue 230

Noor (Light) 124–5

Obama, President 53

Öcalan, Abdullah 145, 258, 326

occidentalism 238

Olüdeniz 210

One Love music festival 31–2

opposition parties 290

Orient Express 223

orientalism 238–41

Ottoman Empire 16, 18, 222, 223, 242, 268, 330

Ottoman Greeks 268–9

Palestine 123

Pamuk, Orhan 17, 184, 250

patriarchy 81

patriotism 244, 246

pavyon scene 116–19

Peace and Democracy Party *see* BDP

Pervare 266, 267

Pilsen, Efes 158

PKK (Kurdistan Workers' Party) 89, 252, 325, 326 254, 258, 260

Plato: *The Republic* 267–8

police 11–12
  clash with protesters during Gezi Park protests 276–7, 279, 283
  deployment of at football matches 38–9
  and protests 37

political parties 289–90

political system 289–91

population exchanges 247

prayer 12

presidential elections (2014) 292, 326–7

Primo Moda 78

private study centres see *dershane*

property scams 210–12

prostitution 107–9, 117

protests: and police 37
  suppression of 232–3, 234
  see also Gezi Park protests

race riots 247

Radio and Television High Commission 286

Index